1992 Edition

CHILDREN'S BOOKS:

Awards & Prizes

Includes Prizes and Awards
for Young Adult Books

*Compiled & Edited by
the Children's Book Council*

The Children's Book Council, Inc.
568 Broadway, New York, NY 10012

Book design by Carol Goldenberg
Cover illustration on paperback edition by Chris Conover

Copyright © 1969, 1971, 1973, 1975, 1977, 1979, 1981, 1986, 1992
by The Children's Book Council, Inc.
568 Broadway, New York, NY 10012
ISBN hardcover edition 0-933633-01-7
ISBN paperback edition 0-933633-02-5
ISSN 0069-3472
Manufactured in the United States of America

This edition of *Children's Books: Awards & Prizes* is dedicated to the late John Donovan, whose profound commitment to children's literature and international literacy efforts helped make this a better world.

Contents ❧

PART II
United States Awards Selected by Young Readers

PART III

Australian, Canadian, New Zealand, and United Kingdom (UK) Awards

AUSTRALIA

CANADA

PART IV

Selected International and Multinational Awards

PART V

PART VI

Introduction ❧

Children's Books: Awards & Prizes (Including Award Programs for Young Adult Books), hereafter called *Awards & Prizes,* began as a series of information sheets about prizewinning children's books. It was issued annually, mainly at the request of librarians and others who sought an accessible short document on this subject that could be distributed to staff and patrons.

Gradually there was a call for more information about more awards, until it was clear that nothing other than a regular publication about award-winning children's books would satisfy the information needs of generations who have come to value children's books as a major resource in publishing, librarianship, teaching, and bookselling. You will note that *Awards & Prizes* has appeared in nine editions since 1969. Each new volume has increased in both sophistication and usefulness.

Our readers have told us that their needs are for information about winning titles in prize programs that are currently in existence, and that are likely to interest them either as readers or as persons answering reference questions of others. Their needs encouraged the Council to break out "United States Awards Selected by Young Readers" as a separate section in the 1986 edition of this work, and to add "Publications and Lists for Selecting U.S. Children's and Young Adult Books" to this edition.

Some observations

It is impossible to work on each edition of *Awards & Prizes* without noting that prizegiving in children's books is subject to a lot of changes from year to year. The two oldest prizes listed here are the Newbery and Caldecott Medals of the American Library Association. They occupy a unique position in this field, and for this reason we include Honor Books, as well as the winners, in listing those two awards. You will note that some other award programs have a long list of winners, too. It is a mark of health that our literature can honor so many titles and in prize programs that continue year after year. Some suggest that there are too many awards; it is a subject often discussed in children's book circles, especially when a new award is plotted.

It has been observable to publishers, at least, that the children's literatures of both Canada and Australia are now major forces in the field, and not just in the English language. Whether or not this fact can be correlated with prize-giving in those countries is not certain, but CBC is fascinated that while we listed eight Canadian programs in the 1986 edition of this work, the new edition lists nineteen; and while we listed two Australian awards in 1986, in 1992 we list fourteen. These increases are impressive by any measure. In all, we include 191 awards in the new edition; we had 125 awards in the last one. There were twenty-eight statewide child-selected awards in 1986; forty-one in 1992.

In the United States there is a small trend for state and regional groups to give awards; very few of them previously engaged in this work, which is being taken up by regional bookseller associations, and also by statewide Centers for the Book affiliated with the Library of Congress. In both instances, children's books are part of a program that customarily includes fiction and nonfiction, all of which may have regional authors or themes. These types of programs are not new; their sponsorships are new.

With the exception of the International Board on Books for Young People (IBBY) Hans Christian Andersen Awards program, which is the world's most prestigious in children's literature, the international and multinational awards listed in *Awards & Prizes* are few and specialized in nature. Most North Americans are unfamiliar with them. Information about them may whet your appetite for more, and the cultures they represent.

Many thanks

A volume like this one does not exist without the help of the award sponsors whose work we list in it, often difficult to locate and seldom easy to assemble. We are grateful for their help. Special gratitude to the volunteers associated with this work.

We would be remiss in not acknowledging the special help and criticism of earlier editions of this book by author and children's book promoter *extraordinaire* Sue Alexander. The staff at Book Trust in London—especially Anne Sarrag during her watch—was helpful to us on this edition. When people want to sing the praises of an Australian, the sound of *Waltzing Matilda* can usually be heard off in the background; somehow *Waltzing Alf Mappin* doesn't have the same ring to it; we could not have expanded into Australia so extensively without the assistance of Alf Mappin, the eminently capable editor and publisher of *Magpies*.

John Donovan
New York City
April, 1992

PART I 🕭

*United States Awards
Selected by Adults*

Jane Addams Book Award ❧

Given annually in the fall since 1953 by the Women's International
League for Peace and Freedom and the Jane Addams Peace
Association (777 United Nations Plaza, New York, NY 10017) to
the children's book of the year that has "themes stressing peace,
social justice, world community and the equality of the sexes and
all races." (Certificate)

1953
PEOPLE ARE IMPORTANT by Eva Knox Evans *(Golden)*

1954
STICK-IN-THE-MUD by Jean Ketchum *(Scott)*

1955
RAINBOW ROUND THE WORLD by Elizabeth Yates *(Bobbs)*

1956
STORY OF THE NEGRO by Arna Bontemps *(Knopf)*

1957
BLUE MYSTERY by Margot Benary-Isbert *(HBJ)*

1958
THE PERILOUS ROAD by William O. Steele *(HBJ)*

1959
No Award

1960
CHAMPIONS OF PEACE by Edith Patterson Meyer *(Little,
Brown)*

1961
WHAT THEN, RAMAN? by Shirley L. Arora *(Follett)*

1962
THE ROAD TO AGRA by Aimee Sommerfelt *(Criterion)*

1963
THE MONKEY AND THE WILD, WILD WIND by Ryerson
Johnson *(Abelard)*

1964
PROFILES IN COURAGE by John F. Kennedy *(Harper)*

1965
MEETING WITH A STRANGER by Duane Bradley *(Lippincott)*

1966
BERRIES GOODMAN by Emily Cheney Neville *(Harper)*

1967
QUEENIE PEAVY by Robert Burch *(Viking)*

1968
THE LITTLE FISHES by Erik Christian Haugaard *(Houghton)*
1969
THE ENDLESS STEPPE by Esther Hautzig *(Crowell)*
1970
THE CAY by Theodore Taylor *(Doubleday)* Note: The author of
the 1970 Award returned the Certificate to the donors in 1975.
See *Top of the News* (American Library Association, 50 E.
Huron St., Chicago, IL 60611), April 1975, pp. 284-8.
1971
JANE ADDAMS: PIONEER OF SOCIAL JUSTICE by Cornelia
Meigs *(Little, Brown)*
1972
THE TAMARACK TREE by Betty Underwood *(Houghton)*
1973
THE RIDDLE OF RACISM by S. Carl Hirsch *(Viking)*
1974
NILDA by Nicholasa Mohr *(Harper)*
1975
THE PRINCESS AND THE ADMIRAL by Charlotte Pomerantz
(Addison)
1976
PAUL ROBESON by Eloise Greenfield *(Crowell)*
1977
NEVER TO FORGET: THE JEWS OF THE HOLOCAUST by
Milton Meltzer *(Harper)*
1978
CHILD OF THE OWL by Laurence Yep *(Harper)*
1979
MANY SMOKES, MANY MOONS by Jamake Highwater
(Lippincott)
1980
THE ROAD FROM HOME: THE STORY OF AN
ARMENIAN GIRL by David Kherdian *(Greenwillow)*
1981
FIRST WOMAN IN CONGRESS: JEANNETTE RANKIN by
Florence White *(Messner)*
1982
A SPIRIT TO RIDE THE WHIRLWIND by Athena Lord
(Macmillan)
1983
HIROSHIMA NO PIKA by Toshi Maruki *(Lothrop)*
1984
RAIN OF FIRE by Marion Dane Bauer *(Clarion)*
1985
THE SHORT LIFE OF SOPHIE SCHOLL by Hermann Vinke
(Harper)

1986
AIN'T GONNA STUDY WAR NO MORE: THE STORY OF
AMERICA'S PEACE SEEKERS by Milton Meltzer *(Harper)*

1987
NOBODY WANTS A NUCLEAR WAR by Judith Vigna
(Whitman)

1988
WAITING FOR THE RAIN by Sheila Gordon *(Orchard)*

1989 (Joint winners)
ANTHONY BURNS: THE DEFEAT AND TRIUMPH OF A
FUGITIVE SLAVE by Virginia Hamilton *(Knopf)*
LOOKING OUT by Victoria Boutis *(Four Winds)*

1990
A LONG HARD JOURNEY: THE STORY OF THE
PULLMAN PORTER by Patricia and Frederick McKissack
(Walker)

1991
THE BIG BOOK FOR PEACE edited by Ann Durell and
Marilyn Sachs *(Dutton)*

American Institute of Physics 🐾
CHILDREN'S SCIENCE-WRITING AWARD

Works eligible for this award are books (and also articles and
booklets) written in English or translated into English, dealing
primarily with physics and astronomy, and directed at children
from preschool ages up to fifteen years of age. The sponsor is the
American Institute of Physics (335 East 45th St., New York, NY
10017). The award's purpose is to "recognize and stimulate
distinguished writing and illustration that improves childrens'
understanding and appreciation of physics and astronomy."
($3,000 to winner(s), a Windsor Chair, and testimonial;
publisher also receives testimonial)

1988
SPLASH! ALL ABOUT BATHS by Susan Kovacs Buxbaum and
Rita Golden Gelman, ill. by Maryann Cocca-Leffler *(Little,
Brown)*

1989
MICROMYSTERIES: STORIES OF SCIENTIFIC DETECTION
by Gail Kay Haines *(Putnam)*

1990
THE WAY THINGS WORK by David Macaulay *(Houghton)*

1991
AIRBORNE: THE SEARCH FOR THE SECRET OF FLIGHT
by Richard Maurer *(Simon & Schuster)*
1992
ALMOST THE REAL THING by Gloria Skurzynski *(Bradbury)*

Avon/Flare Young Adult Novel Competition 🍂

A biennial award for a 125-200 page manuscript by a writer between the ages of 13 and 18: "We not only want fiction about teens written for teens, but written by teens as well." The competition is sponsored by Books for Young Readers, Avon Books (1350 Avenue of the Americas, New York, NY 10019). ($2,500 publishing contract)

1983
DRAGON FALL by Lee J. Hindle *(Avon)*
1985
BUCK by Tamela Larimer *(Avon)*
1987
AT THE EDGE by Michael Behrens *(Avon)*
1989
FLUTE SONG MAGIC by Andrea Shettle *(Avon)*
1991
FACE-OFF by Stacy Drumtra *(Avon)*

Mildred L. Batchelder Award 🍂

Established in 1966, this annual award honors the former Executive Director of the Association for Library Service to Children (ALSC), a division of the American Library Association (ALA). Announced during ALA's annual Midwinter Conference, a citation is awarded to an American publisher for a children's book (any trade book for children from pre-nursery through eighth grade) considered to be the most outstanding of those books originally published in a foreign language in a foreign country, and subsequently published in the United States. As of 1979 the award has been given to a publisher for a book published in the preceding year. Before 1979, the award had been given to a book published two years previously. The award is made annually unless the award committee is of the opinion no book of that particular year is worthy of the award. As of the 1991 award, the selection committee may also designate Honor Book publishers. Donated and administered by Association for Library Service to Children of ALA (50 E. Huron St., Chicago, IL 60611). (Citation)

1968
THE LITTLE MAN by Erich Kästner, translated from German by James Kirkup *(Knopf)*

1969
DON'T TAKE TEDDY by Babbis Friis-Baastad, translated from Norwegian by Lise Sømme McKinnon *(Scribner)*

1970
WILDCAT UNDER GLASS by Alki Zei, translated from Greek by Edward Fenton *(Holt)*

1971
IN THE LAND OF UR, THE DISCOVERY OF ANCIENT MESOPOTAMIA by Hans Baumann, translated from German by Stella Humphries *(Pantheon)*

1972
FRIEDRICH by Hans Peter Richter, translated from German by Edite Kroll *(Holt)*

1973
PULGA by S. R. Van Iterson, translated from Dutch by Alexander and Alison Gode *(Morrow)*

1974
PETROS' WAR by Alki Zei, translated from Greek by Edward Fenton *(Dutton)*

1975
AN OLD TALE CARVED OUT OF STONE by A. Linevski, translated from Russian by Maria Polushkin *(Crown)*

1976
THE CAT AND MOUSE WHO SHARED A HOUSE by Ruth Hürlimann, translated from German by Anthea Bell *(Walck)*

1977
THE LEOPARD by Cecil Bødker, translated from Danish by Gunnar Poulsen *(Atheneum)*

1978
No Award

1979
KONRAD by Christine Nöstlinger, translated from German by Anthea Bell *(Watts)* (Published 1977)
RABBIT ISLAND by Jörg Steiner, translated from German by Ann Conrad Lammers *(HBJ)* (Published 1978)

1980
THE SOUND OF THE DRAGON'S FEET by Alki Zei,
translated from Greek by Edward Fenton *(Dutton)*
1981
THE WINTER WHEN TIME WAS FROZEN by Els Pelgrom,
translated from Dutch by Maryka and Raphael Rudnik *(Morrow)*
1982
THE BATTLE HORSE by Harry Kullman, translated from
Swedish by George Blecher and Lone Thygesen Blecher
(Bradbury)
1983
HIROSHIMA NO PIKA by Toshi Maruki, translated from
Japanese through Kurita-Bando Literary Agency *(Lothrop)*
1984
RONIA, THE ROBBER'S DAUGHTER by Astrid Lindgren,
translated from Swedish by Patricia Crampton *(Viking)*
1985
THE ISLAND ON BIRD STREET by Uri Orlev, translated from
Hebrew by Hillel Halkin *(Houghton)*
1986
ROSE BLANCHE by Christophe Gallaz and Robert Innocenti,
translated from Italian by Martha Coventry and Richard Craglia
(Creative Education)
1987
NO HERO FOR THE KAISER by Rudolf Frank, translated
from German by Patricia Crampton *(Lothrop)*
1988
IF YOU DIDN'T HAVE ME by Ulf Nilsson, translated from
Swedish by Lone Thygesen Blecher and George Blecher
(McElderry)
1989
CRUTCHES by Peter Härtling, translated from German by
Elizabeth D. Crawford *(Lothrop)*
1990
BUSTER'S WORLD by Bjarne Reuter, translated from Danish by
Anthea Bell *(Dutton)*
1991
A HAND FULL OF STARS by Rafik Schami, translated from
German by Rika Lesser *(Dutton)*
1992
THE MAN FROM THE OTHER SIDE by Uri Orlev, translated
from Hebrew by Hillel Halkin *(Houghton)*

Bay Area Book Reviewers Association Awards ಶ

This San Francisco Bay Area awards program is designed to honor outstanding contributions to books and literature by writers living and working in the Bay Area. The award for children's literature—the only category we list—was added in the fourth year of the program, which is administered by the *San Francisco Chronicle* (901 Mission St., San Francisco, CA 94119). (Citation)

1985
LIKE JAKE AND ME by Mavis Jukes *(Knopf)*

1986
THE HAPPIEST ENDING by Yoshiko Uchida *(McElderry)*

1987
FISH FRIDAY by Gayle Pearson *(Atheneum)*

1988
FRAN ELLEN'S HOUSE by Marilyn Sachs *(Dutton)*

1989
A GIRL FROM YAMHILL: A MEMOIR by Beverly Cleary *(Morrow)*

1990
BERCHICK: MY MOTHER'S HORSE by Esther Blanc *(Volcano)*

1991
STARGONE JOHN by Ellen Kindt McKenzie *(Holt)*

John and Patricia Beatty Award ಶ

"The purpose of this annual award is to encourage the writing of quality children's books highlighting California, its culture, heritage and/or future." The late John and Patricia Beatty wrote eleven novels together; separately, Patricia Beatty wrote many other young peoples' books, some with California settings. She was also a recipient of the Scott O'Dell Award for Historical Fiction. She established the endowment for the Beatty Award in 1987. The administrator is the California Library Association (717 K St., Suite 300, Sacramento, CA 95814). One important standard for selecting the winner is that "the California setting must be depicted authentically and must serve as an integral focus for the book." (Plaque and $500)

1989
CHANG'S PAPER PONY by Eleanor Coerr *(Harper)*
1990
THE GREAT AMERICAN GOLD RUSH by Rhoda Blumberg
(Bradbury)
1991
BASEBALL IN APRIL by Gary Soto *(HBJ)*

Boston Globe—Horn Book Awards ❧

Awarded annually in the fall since 1967 by *The Boston Globe* and *The Horn Book Magazine* (14 Beacon St., Boston, MA 02108). Through 1975, two awards were given—for outstanding text and for outstanding illustration; in 1976 the award categories were changed to and currently are Outstanding Fiction or Poetry, Outstanding Nonfiction and Outstanding Illustration. ($500 to the winner in each category)

1967
Text: THE LITTLE FISHES by Erik Christian Haugaard
(Houghton)
Illustration: LONDON BRIDGE IS FALLING DOWN! ill. by
Peter Spier *(Doubleday)*
1968
Text: THE SPRING RIDER by John Lawson *(Crowell)*
Illustration: TIKKI TIKKI TEMBO by Arlene Mosel, ill. by
Blair Lent *(Holt)*
1969
Text: A WIZARD OF EARTHSEA by Ursula K. Le Guin
(Parnassus/Houghton)
Illustration: THE ADVENTURES OF PADDY PORK by
John S. Goodall *(HBJ)*
1970
Text: THE INTRUDER by John Rowe Townsend *(Lippincott)*
Illustration: HI, CAT! by Ezra Jack Keats *(Macmillan)*
1971
Text: A ROOM MADE OF WINDOWS by Eleanor Cameron
(Atlantic-Little, Brown)
Illustration: IF I BUILT A VILLAGE by Kazue Mizumura
(Crowell)
1972
Text: TRISTAN AND ISEULT by Rosemary Sutcliff *(Dutton)*
Illustration: MR. GUMPY'S OUTING by John Burningham
(Holt)

1973
Text: THE DARK IS RISING by Susan Cooper *(McElderry)*
Illustration: KING STORK by Trina Schart Hyman *(Little, Brown)*

1974
Text: M. C. HIGGINS, THE GREAT by Virginia Hamilton *(Macmillan)*
Illustration: JAMBO MEANS HELLO by Muriel Feelings, ill. by Tom Feelings *(Dial)*

1975
Text: TRANSPORT 7-41-R by T. Degens *(Viking)*
Illustration: ANNO'S ALPHABET by Mitsumasa Anno *(Crowell)*

1976
Fiction: UNLEAVING by Jill Paton Walsh *(Farrar)*
Nonfiction: VOYAGING TO CATHAY: AMERICANS IN THE CHINA TRADE by Alfred Tamarin and Shirley Glubok *(Viking)*
Illustration: THIRTEEN by Remy Charlip and Jerry Joyner *(Four Winds)*

1977
Fiction: CHILD OF THE OWL by Laurence Yep *(Harper)*
Nonfiction: CHANCE, LUCK AND DESTINY by Peter Dickinson *(Atlantic-Little, Brown)*
Illustration: GRANFA' GRIG HAD A PIG AND OTHER RHYMES WITHOUT REASON FROM MOTHER GOOSE by Wallace Tripp *(Little, Brown)*

1978
Fiction: THE WESTING GAME by Ellen Raskin *(Dutton)*
Nonfiction: MISCHLING, SECOND DEGREE: MY CHILDHOOD IN NAZI GERMANY by Ilse Koehn *(Greenwillow)*
Illustration: ANNO'S JOURNEY by Mitsumasa Anno *(Philomel)*

1979
Fiction: HUMBUG MOUNTAIN by Sid Fleischman *(Atlantic-Little, Brown)*
Nonfiction: THE ROAD FROM HOME: THE STORY OF AN ARMENIAN GIRL by David Kherdian *(Greenwillow)*
Illustration: THE SNOWMAN by Raymond Briggs *(Random)*

1980
Fiction: CONRAD'S WAR by Andrew Davies *(Crown)*
Nonfiction: BUILDING: THE FIGHT AGAINST GRAVITY by Mario Salvadori *(McElderry)*
Illustration: THE GARDEN OF ABDUL GASAZI by Chris Van Allsburg *(Houghton)*

1981
Fiction: THE LEAVING by Lynn Hall *(Scribner)*
Nonfiction: THE WEAVER'S GIFT by Karthryn Lasky *(Warne)*

Illustration: OUTSIDE OVER THERE by Maurice Sendak *(Harper)*

1982

Fiction: PLAYING BEATIE BOW by Ruth Park *(Atheneum)*
Nonfiction: UPON THE HEAD OF THE GOAT:
A CHILDHOOD IN HUNGARY 1939—1944 by Aranka Siegal *(Farrar)*
Illustration: A VISIT TO WILLIAM BLAKE'S INN: POEMS FOR INNOCENT AND EXPERIENCED TRAVELERS by Nancy Willard, ill. by Alice and Martin Provensen *(HBJ)*

1983

Fiction: SWEET WHISPERS, BROTHER RUSH by Virginia Hamilton *(Philomel)*
Nonfiction: BEHIND BARBED WIRE: THE IMPRISONMENT OF JAPANESE AMERICANS DURING WORLD WAR II by Daniel S. Davis *(Dutton)*
Illustration: A CHAIR FOR MY MOTHER by Vera B. Williams *(Greenwillow)*

1984

Fiction: A LITTLE FEAR by Patricia Wrightson *(McElderry)*
Nonfiction: THE DOUBLE LIFE OF POCAHONTAS by Jean Fritz *(Putnam)*
Illustration: JONAH AND THE GREAT FISH retold and ill. by Warwick Hutton *(McElderry)*

1985

Fiction: THE MOVES MAKE THE MAN by Bruce Brooks *(Harper)*
Nonfiction: COMMODORE PERRY IN THE LAND OF THE SHOGUN by Rhoda Blumberg *(Lothrop)*
Illustration: MAMA DON'T ALLOW by Thacher Hurd *(Harper)*
Special Award: 1, 2, 3 by Tana Hoban *(Greenwillow)*

1986

Fiction: IN SUMMER LIGHT by Zibby Oneal *(Viking)*
Nonfiction: AUKS, ROCKS AND THE ODD DINOSAUR: INSIDE STORIES FROM THE SMITHSONIAN'S MUSEUM OF NATURAL HISTORY by Peggy Thomson *(Crowell)*
Illustration: THE PAPER CRANE by Molly Bang *(Greenwillow)*

1987

Fiction: RABBLE STARKEY by Lois Lowry *(Houghton)*
Nonfiction: PILGRIMS OF PLIMOTH by Marcia Sewall *(Atheneum)*
Illustration: MUFARO'S BEAUTIFUL DAUGHTERS by John Steptoe *(Lothrop)*

1988

Fiction: THE FRIENDSHIP by Mildred Taylor *(Dial)*
Nonfiction: ANTHONY BURNS: THE DEFEAT AND TRIUMPH OF A FUGITIVE SLAVE by Virginia Hamilton *(Knopf)*

Illustration: THE BOY OF THE THREE-YEAR NAP by Dianne Snyder, ill. by Allen Say *(Houghton)*

1989
Fiction: THE VILLAGE BY THE SEA by Paula Fox *(Orchard)*
Nonfiction: THE WAY THINGS WORK by David Macaulay *(Houghton)*
Illustration: SHY CHARLES by Rosemary Wells *(Dial)*

1990
Fiction: MANIAC MAGEE by Jerry Spinelli *(Little, Brown)*
Nonfiction: THE GREAT LITTLE MADISON by Jean Fritz *(Putnam)*
Illustration: LON PO PO translated and ill. by Ed Young *(Philomel)*
Special Award: VALENTINE AND ORSON by Nancy Ekholm Burkert *(Farrar)*

1991
Fiction: THE TRUE CONFESSIONS OF CHARLOTTE DOYLE by Avi *(Orchard)*
Nonfiction: APPALACHIA: THE VOICES OF SLEEPING BIRDS by Cynthia Rylant, ill. by Barry Moser *(HBJ)*
Illustration: THE TALE OF THE MANDARIN DUCKS by Katherine Paterson, ill. by Leo and Diane Dillon *(Lodestar)*

Randolph Caldecott Medal 🕮

Donated by the Frederic G. Melcher family, the Caldecott Medal, named in honor of the nineteenth-century illustrator, has been awarded annually since 1938, under the supervision of the Association for Library Service to Children of the American Library Association (50 E. Huron St., Chicago, IL 60611), to the illustrator of the most distinguished picture book for children published in the U.S. during the preceding year. Announced in January, the award is limited to residents or citizens of the U.S. (Medal)

1938
ANIMALS OF THE BIBLE by Helen Dean Fish, ill. by Dorothy P. Lathrop *(Lippincott)*
HONOR BOOKS
FOUR AND TWENTY BLACKBIRDS by Helen Dean Fish, ill. by Robert Lawson *(Stokes)*
SEVEN SIMEONS by Boris Artzybasheff *(Viking)*

1939
MEI LI by Thomas Handforth *(Doubleday)*
HONOR BOOKS
ANDY AND THE LION by James Daugherty *(Viking)*

BARKIS by Clare Newberry *(Harper)*
THE FOREST POOL by Laura Adams Armer *(Longmans)*
SNOW WHITE AND THE SEVEN DWARFS by Wanda Gág *(Coward)*
WEE GILLIS by Munro Leaf, ill. by Robert Lawson *(Viking)*

1940
ABRAHAM LINCOLN by Ingri and Edgar Parin d'Aulaire *(Doubleday)*
HONOR BOOKS
THE AGELESS STORY by Lauren Ford *(Dodd)*
COCK-A-DOODLE DOO by Berta and Elmer Hader *(Macmillan)*
MADELINE by Ludwig Bemelmans *(Viking)*

1941
THEY WERE STRONG AND GOOD by Robert Lawson *(Viking)*
HONOR BOOK
APRIL'S KITTENS by Claire Newberry *(Harper)*

1942
MAKE WAY FOR DUCKLINGS by Robert McCloskey *(Viking)*
HONOR BOOKS
AN AMERICAN ABC by Maud and Miska Petersham *(Macmillan)*
IN MY MOTHER'S HOUSE by Ann Nolan Clark, ill. by Velino Herrera *(Viking)*
NOTHING AT ALL by Wanda Gág *(Coward)*
PADDLE-TO-THE-SEA by Holling C. Holling *(Houghton)*

1943
THE LITTLE HOUSE by Virginia Lee Burton *(Houghton)*
HONOR BOOKS
DASH AND DART by Mary and Conrad Buff *(Viking)*
MARSHMALLOW by Clare Newberry *(Harper)*

1944
MANY MOONS by James Thurber, ill. by Louis Slobodkin *(HBJ)*
HONOR BOOKS
A CHILD'S GOOD NIGHT BOOK by Margaret Wise Brown, ill. by Jean Charlot *(Scott)*
GOOD LUCK HORSE by Chin-Yi Chan, ill. by Plao Chan *(Whittlesey)*
THE MIGHTY HUNTER by Berta and Elmer Hader *(Macmillan)*
PIERRE PIGEON by Lee Kingman, ill. by Arnold E. Bare *(Houghton)*
SMALL RAIN: VERSES FROM THE BIBLE selected by Jessie Orton Jones, ill. by Elizabeth Orton Jones *(Viking)*

1945
PRAYER FOR A CHILD by Rachel Field, ill. by Elizabeth Orton Jones *(Macmillan)*

HONOR BOOKS
THE CHRISTMAS ANNA ANGEL by Ruth Sawyer, ill. by Kate Seredy *(Viking)*
IN THE FOREST by Marie Hall Ets *(Viking)*
MOTHER GOOSE ill. by Tasha Tudor *(Walck)*
YONIE WONDERNOSE by Marguerite de Angeli *(Doubleday)*

1946
THE ROOSTER CROWS (traditional Mother Goose) ill. by Maud and Miska Petersham *(Macmillan)*
HONOR BOOKS
LITTLE LOST LAMB by Golden MacDonald, ill. by Leonard Weisgard *(Doubleday)*
MY MOTHER IS THE MOST BEAUTIFUL WOMAN IN THE WORLD by Becky Reyher, ill. by Ruth C. Gannett *(Lothrop)*
SING MOTHER GOOSE by Opal Wheeler, ill. by Marjorie Torrey *(Dutton)*
YOU CAN WRITE CHINESE by Kurt Wiese *(Viking)*

1947
THE LITTLE ISLAND by Golden MacDonald, ill. by Leonard Weisgard *(Doubleday)*
HONOR BOOKS
BOATS ON THE RIVER by Marjorie Flack, ill. by Jay Hyde Barnum *(Viking)*
PEDRO, THE ANGEL OF OLVERA STREET by Leo Politi *(Scribner)*
RAIN DROP SPLASH by Alvin Tresselt, ill. by Leonard Weisgard *(Lothrop)*
SING IN PRAISE: A COLLECTION OF THE BEST LOVED HYMNS by Opal Wheeler, ill. by Marjorie Torrey *(Dutton)*
TIMOTHY TURTLE by Al Graham, ill. by Tony Palazzo *(Welch)*

1948
WHITE SNOW, BRIGHT SNOW by Alvin Tresselt, ill. by Roger Duvoisin *(Lothrop)*
HONOR BOOKS
BAMBINO THE CLOWN by George Schreiber *(Viking)*
McELLIGOT'S POOL by Dr. Seuss *(Random)*
ROGER AND THE FOX by Lavinia Davis, ill. by Hildegard Woodward *(Doubleday)*
SONG OF ROBIN HOOD edited by Anne Malcolmson, ill. by Virginia Lee Burton *(Houghton)*
STONE SOUP by Marcia Brown *(Scribner)*

1949
THE BIG SNOW by Berta and Elmer Hader *(Macmillan)*
HONOR BOOKS
ALL AROUND THE TOWN by Phyllis McGinley, ill. by Helen Stone *(Lippincott)*
BLUEBERRIES FOR SAL by Robert McCloskey *(Viking)*
FISH IN THE AIR by Kurt Wiese *(Viking)*

JUANITA by Leo Politi *(Scribner)*
1950
SONG OF THE SWALLOWS by Leo Politi *(Scribner)*
HONOR BOOKS
AMERICA'S ETHAN ALLEN by Stewart Holbrook, ill. by Lynd
Ward *(Houghton)*
BARTHOLOMEW AND THE OOBLECK by Dr. Seuss
(Random)
THE HAPPY DAY by Ruth Krauss, ill. by Marc Simont
(Harper)
HENRY FISHERMAN by Marcia Brown *(Scribner)*
THE WILD BIRTHDAY CAKE by Lavinia Davis, ill. by
Hildegard Woodward *(Doubleday)*
1951
THE EGG TREE by Katherine Milhous *(Scribner)*
HONOR BOOKS
DICK WHITTINGTON AND HIS CAT by Marcia Brown
(Scribner)
IF I RAN THE ZOO by Dr. Seuss *(Random)*
THE MOST WONDERFUL DOLL IN THE WORLD by Phyllis
McGinley, ill. by Helen Stone *(Lippincott)*
T-BONE, THE BABY SITTER by Clare Newberry *(Harper)*
THE TWO REDS by Will, ill. by Nicolas *(HBJ)*
1952
FINDERS KEEPERS by Will, ill. by Nicolas *(HBJ)*
HONOR BOOKS
ALL FALLING DOWN by Gene Zion, ill. by Margaret Bloy
Graham *(Harper)*
BEAR PARTY by William Pène du Bois *(Viking)*
FEATHER MOUNTAIN by Elizabeth Olds *(Houghton)*
MR. T. W. ANTHONY WOO by Marie Hall Ets *(Viking)*
SKIPPER JOHN'S COOK by Marcia Brown *(Scribner)*
1953
THE BIGGEST BEAR by Lynd Ward *(Houghton)*
HONOR BOOKS
APE IN A CAPE by Fritz Eichenberg *(HBJ)*
FIVE LITTLE MONKEYS by Juliet Kepes *(Houghton)*
ONE MORNING IN MAINE by Robert McCloskey *(Viking)*
PUSS IN BOOTS by Charles Perrault, ill. by Marcia Brown
(Scribner)
THE STORM BOOK by Charlotte Zolotow, ill. by Margaret
Bloy Graham *(Harper)*
1954
MADELINE'S RESCUE by Ludwig Bemelmans *(Viking)*
HONOR BOOKS
A VERY SPECIAL HOUSE by Ruth Krauss, ill. by Maurice
Sendak *(Harper)*
GREEN EYES by A. Birnbaum *(Capitol)*

JOURNEY CAKE, HO! by Ruth Sawyer, ill. by Robert
McCloskey *(Viking)*
THE STEADFAST TIN SOLDIER by Hans Christian Andersen,
ill. by Marcia Brown *(Scribner)*
WHEN WILL THE WORLD BE MINE? by Miriam Schlein, ill.
by Jean Charlot *(Scott)*

1955
CINDERELLA, OR THE LITTLE GLASS SLIPPER by Charles
Perrault, ill. by Marcia Brown *(Scribner)*
HONOR BOOKS
BOOK OF NURSERY AND MOTHER GOOSE RHYMES ill.
by Marguerite de Angeli *(Doubleday)*
THE THANKSGIVING STORY by Alice Dalgliesh, ill. by Helen
Sewell *(Scribner)*
WHEEL ON THE CHIMNEY by Margaret Wise Brown, ill. by
Tibor Gergely *(Lippincott)*

1956
FROG WENT A-COURTIN' retold by John Langstaff, ill. by
Feodor Rojankovsky *(HBJ)*
HONOR BOOKS
CROW BOY by Taro Yashima *(Viking)*
PLAY WITH ME by Marie Hall Ets *(Viking)*

1957
A TREE IS NICE by Janice May Udry, ill. by Marc Simont
(Harper)
HONOR BOOKS
ANATOLE by Eve Titus, ill. by Paul Galdone *(McGraw-Hill)*
GILLESPIE AND THE GUARDS by Benjamin Elkin, ill. by
James Daugherty *(Viking)*
LION by William Pène du Bois *(Viking)*
MR. PENNY'S RACE HORSE by Marie Hall Ets *(Viking)*
1 IS ONE by Tasha Tudor *(Walck)*

1958
TIME OF WONDER by Robert McCloskey *(Viking)*
HONOR BOOKS
ANATOLE AND THE CAT by Eve Titus, ill. by Paul Galdone
(McGraw-Hill)
FLY HIGH, FLY LOW by Don Freeman *(Viking)*

1959
CHANTICLEER AND THE FOX adapted from Chaucer, ill. by
Barbara Cooney *(Crowell)*
HONOR BOOKS
THE HOUSE THAT JACK BUILT by Antonio Frasconi *(HBJ)*
UMBRELLA by Taro Yashima *(Viking)*
WHAT DO YOU SAY, DEAR? by Sesyle Joslin, ill. by Maurice
Sendak *(Scott)*

1960
NINE DAYS TO CHRISTMAS by Marie Hall Ets and Aurora Labastida, ill. by Marie Hall Ets *(Viking)*
HONOR BOOKS
HOUSES FROM THE SEA by Alice E. Goudey, ill. by Adrienne Adams *(Scribner)*
THE MOON JUMPERS by Janice May Udry, ill. by Maurice Sendak *(Harper)*

1961
BABOUSHKA AND THE THREE KINGS by Ruth Robbins, ill. by Nicholas Sidjakov *(Parnassus)*
HONOR BOOK
INCH BY INCH by Leo Lionni *(Astor-Honor)*

1962
ONCE A MOUSE... by Marcia Brown *(Scribner)*
HONOR BOOKS
THE DAY WE SAW THE SUN COME UP by Alice E. Goudey, ill. by Adrienne Adams *(Scribner)*
THE FOX WENT OUT ON A CHILLY NIGHT ill. by Peter Spier *(Doubleday)*
LITTLE BEAR'S VISIT by Else Holmelund Minarik, ill. by Maurice Sendak *(Harper)*

1963
THE SNOWY DAY by Ezra Jack Keats *(Viking)*
HONOR BOOKS
MR. RABBIT AND THE LOVELY PRESENT by Charlotte Zolotow, ill. by Maurice Sendak *(Harper)*
THE SUN IS A GOLDEN EARRING by Natalia M. Belting, ill. by Bernarda Bryson *(Holt)*

1964
WHERE THE WILD THINGS ARE by Maurice Sendak *(Harper)*
HONOR BOOKS
ALL IN THE MORNING EARLY by Sorche Nic Leodhas, ill. by Evaline Ness *(Holt)*
MOTHER GOOSE AND NURSERY RHYMES ill. by Philip Reed *(Atheneum)*
SWIMMY by Leo Lionni *(Pantheon)*

1965
MAY I BRING A FRIEND? by Beatrice Schenk de Regniers, ill. by Beni Montresor *(Atheneum)*
HONOR BOOKS
A POCKETFUL OF CRICKET by Rebecca Caudill, ill. by Evaline Ness *(Holt)*
RAIN MAKES APPLESAUCE by Julian Scheer, ill. by Marvin Bileck *(Holiday House)*
THE WAVE by Margaret Hodges, ill. by Blair Lent *(Houghton)*

1966

ALWAYS ROOM FOR ONE MORE by Sorche Nic Leodhas, ill. by Nonny Hogrogian *(Holt)*

HONOR BOOKS

HIDE AND SEEK FOG by Alvin Tresselt, ill. by Roger Duvoisin *(Lothrop)*

JUST ME by Marie Hall Ets *(Viking)*

TOM TIT TOT by Evaline Ness *(Scribner)*

1967

SAM, BANGS & MOONSHINE by Evaline Ness *(Holt)*

HONOR BOOK

ONE WIDE RIVER TO CROSS by Barbara Emberley, ill. by Ed Emberley *(Prentice-Hall)*

1968

DRUMMER HOFF by Barbara Emberley, ill. by Ed Emberley *(Prentice-Hall)*

HONOR BOOKS

THE EMPEROR AND THE KITE by Jane Yolen, ill. by Ed Young *(World)*

FREDERICK by Leo Lionni *(Pantheon)*

SEASHORE STORY by Taro Yashima *(Viking)*

1969

THE FOOL OF THE WORLD AND THE FLYING SHIP retold by Arthur Ransome, ill. by Uri Shulevitz *(Farrar)*

HONOR BOOK

WHY THE SUN AND THE MOON LIVE IN THE SKY by Elphinstone Dayrell, ill. by Blair Lent *(Houghton)*

1970

SYLVESTER AND THE MAGIC PEBBLE by William Steig *(Windmill/Simon & Schuster)*

HONOR BOOKS

ALEXANDER AND THE WIND-UP MOUSE by Leo Lionni *(Pantheon)*

GOGGLES by Ezra Jack Keats *(Macmillan)*

THE JUDGE by Harve Zemach, ill. by Margot Zemach *(Farrar)*

POP CORN & MA GOODNESS by Edna Mitchell Preston, ill. by Robert Andrew Parker *(Viking)*

THY FRIEND, OBADIAH by Brinton Turkle *(Viking)*

1971

A STORY—A STORY by Gail E. Haley *(Atheneum)*

HONOR BOOKS

THE ANGRY MOON by William Sleator, ill. by Blair Lent *(Atlantic-Little, Brown)*

FROG AND TOAD ARE FRIENDS by Arnold Lobel *(Harper)*

IN THE NIGHT KITCHEN by Maurice Sendak *(Harper)*

1972

ONE FINE DAY by Nonny Hogrogian *(Macmillan)*

HONOR BOOKS

HILDILID'S NIGHT by Cheli Durán Ryan, ill. by Arnold Lobel *(Macmillan)*

IF ALL THE SEAS WERE ONE SEA by Janina Domanska *(Macmillan)*

MOJA MEANS ONE by Muriel Feelings, ill. by Tom Feelings *(Dial)*

1973

THE FUNNY LITTLE WOMAN retold by Arlene Mosel, ill. by Blair Lent *(Dutton)*
36

HONOR BOOKS

ANANSI THE SPIDER adapted and ill. by Gerald McDermott *(Holt)*

HOSIE'S ALPHABET by Hosea, Tobias and Lisa Baskin, ill. by Leonard Baskin *(Viking)*

SNOW-WHITE AND THE SEVEN DWARFS ill. by Nancy Eckholm Burkert *(Farrar)*

WHEN CLAY SINGS by Byrd Baylor, ill. by Tom Bahti *(Scribner)*

1974

DUFFY AND THE DEVIL retold by Harve Zemach, ill. by Margot Zemach *(Farrar)*

HONOR BOOKS

CATHEDRAL by David Macaulay *(Houghton)*

THREE JOVIAL HUNTSMEN by Susan Jeffers *(Bradbury)*

1975

ARROW TO THE SUN by Gerald McDermott *(Viking)*

HONOR BOOK

JAMBO MEANS HELLO by Muriel Feelings, ill. by Tom Feelings *(Dial)*

1976

WHY MOSQUITOES BUZZ IN PEOPLE'S EARS retold by Verna Aardema, ill. by Leo and Diane Dillon *(Dial)*

HONOR BOOKS

THE DESERT IS THEIRS by Byrd Baylor, ill. by Peter Parnall *(Scribner)*

STREGA NONA retold and ill. by Tomie de Paola *(Prentice)*

1977

ASHANTI TO ZULU: AFRICAN TRADITIONS by Margaret Musgrove, ill. by Leo and Diane Dillon *(Dial)*

HONOR BOOKS

THE AMAZING BONE by William Steig *(Farrar)*

THE CONTEST retold and ill. by Nonny Hogrogian *(Greenwillow)*

FISH FOR SUPPER by M.B. Goffstein *(Dial)*

THE GOLEM by Beverly Brodsky McDermott *(Lippincott)*

HAWK, I'M YOUR BROTHER by Byrd Baylor, ill. by Peter Parnall *(Scribner)*

1978
NOAH'S ARK ill. by Peter Spier *(Doubleday)*
HONOR BOOKS
CASTLE by David Macaulay *(Houghton)*
IT COULD ALWAYS BE WORSE retold and ill. by Margot
Zemach *(Farrar)*

1979
THE GIRL WHO LOVED WILD HORSES by Paul Goble *(Bradbury)*
HONOR BOOKS
FREIGHT TRAIN by Donald Crews *(Greenwillow)*
THE WAY TO START A DAY by Byrd Baylor, ill. by Peter
Parnall *(Scribner)*

1980
OX-CART MAN by Donald Hall, ill. by Barbara Cooney
(Viking)
HONOR BOOKS
BEN'S TRUMPET by Rachel Isadora *(Greenwillow)*
THE GARDEN OF ABDUL GASAZI by Chris Van Allsburg
(Houghton)
THE TREASURE by Uri Shulevitz *(Farrar)*

1981
FABLES by Arnold Lobel *(Harper)*
HONOR BOOKS
THE BREMEN-TOWN MUSICIANS retold and ill. by Ilse
Plume *(Doubleday)*
THE GREY LADY AND THE STRAWBERRY SNATCHER by
Molly Bang *(Four Winds)*
MICE TWICE by Joseph Low *(McElderry)*
TRUCK by Donald Crews *(Greenwillow)*

1982
JUMANJI by Chris Van Allsburg *(Houghton)*
HONOR BOOKS
ON MARKET STREET words by Arnold Lobel, ill. by Anita
Lobel *(Greenwillow)*
OUTSIDE OVER THERE by Maurice Sendak *(Harper)*
A VISIT TO WILLIAM BLAKE'S INN: POEMS FOR
INNOCENT AND EXPERIENCED TRAVELERS by Nancy
Willard, ill. by Alice and Martin Provensen *(HBJ)*
WHERE THE BUFFALOES BEGIN by Olaf Baker, ill. by
Stephen Gammell *(Warne)*

1983
SHADOW by Blaise Cendrars, ill. by Marcia Brown *(Scribner)*
HONOR BOOKS
A CHAIR FOR MY MOTHER by Vera B. Williams
(Greenwillow)
WHEN I WAS YOUNG IN THE MOUNTAINS by Cynthia
Rylant, ill. by Diane Goode *(Dutton)*

1984

THE GLORIOUS FLIGHT: ACROSS THE CHANNEL WITH LOUIS BLÉRIOT by Alice and Martin Provensen *(Viking)*

HONOR BOOKS

LITTLE RED RIDING HOOD retold and ill. by Trina Schart Hyman *(Holiday House)*

TEN, NINE, EIGHT by Molly Bang *(Greenwillow)*

1985

SAINT GEORGE AND THE DRAGON rctold by Margaret Hodges, ill. by Trina Schart Hyman *(Little, Brown)*

HONOR BOOKS

HANSEL AND GRETEL retold by Rika Lesser, ill. by Paul O. Zelinsky *(Dodd)*

HAVE YOU SEEN MY DUCKLING? by Nancy Tafuri *(Greenwillow)*

THE STORY OF JUMPING MOUSE retold and ill. by John Steptoe *(Lothrop)*

1986

THE POLAR EXPRESS by Chris Van Allsburg *(Houghton)*

HONOR BOOKS

KING BIDGOOD'S IN THE BATHTUB by Audrey Wood, ill. by Don Wood *(HBJ)*

THE RELATIVES CAME by Cynthia Rylant, ill. by Stephen Gammell *(Bradbury)*

1987

HEY, AL by Arthur Yorinks, ill. by Richard Egielski *(Farrar)*

HONOR BOOKS

ALPHABATICS by Suse MacDonald *(Bradbury)*

RUMPELSTILTSKIN by Paul O. Zelinsky *(Dutton)*

THE VILLAGE OF ROUND AND SQUARE HOUSES by Ann Grifalconi *(Little, Brown)*

1988

OWL MOON by Jane Yolen, ill. by John Schoenherr *(Philomel)*

HONOR BOOK

MUFARO'S BEAUTIFUL DAUGHTERS: AN AFRICAN TALE by John Steptoe *(Lothrop)*

1989

SONG AND DANCE MAN by Karen Ackerman, ill. by Stephen Gammell *(Knopf)*

HONOR BOOKS

THE BOY OF THE THREE-YEAR NAP by Dianne Snyder, ill. by Allen Say *(Houghton)*

FREE FALL by David Wiesner *(Lothrop)*

GOLDILOCKS AND THE THREE BEARS by James Marshall *(Dial)*

MIRANDY AND BROTHER WIND by Patricia C. McKissack, ill. by Jerry Pinkney *(Knopf)*

1990
LON PO PO: A RED-RIDING HOOD STORY FROM CHINA
translated and ill. by Ed Young *(Philomel)*
HONOR BOOKS
BILL PEET: AN AUTOBIOGRAPHY by Bill Peet *(Houghton)*
COLOR ZOO by Lois Ehlert *(Lippincott)*
HERSHEL AND THE HANUKKAH GOBLINS by Eric Kimmel,
ill. by Trina Schart Hyman *(Holiday House)*
THE TALKING EGGS by Robert D. San Souci, ill. by Jerry
Pinkney *(Dial)*
1991
BLACK AND WHITE by David Macaulay *(Houghton)*
HONOR BOOKS
"MORE MORE MORE," SAID THE BABY: 3 LOVE STORIES
by Vera B. Williams *(Greenwillow)*
PUSS IN BOOTS by Charles Perrault, translated by Malcolm
Arthur, ill. by Fred Marcellino *(Farrar)*
1992
TUESDAY by David Wiesner *(Clarion)*
HONOR BOOK
TAR BEACH by Faith Ringgold *(Crown)*

California Children's Book, Video, and Software Awards 🖤

This awards program is designed to recognize excellence in
children's media and to provide "parents with a reader-friendly
children's entertainment resource." It is sponsored by a
consortium of California parenting magazines, including *L.A.
Parent, Parenting* (Santa Ana), *San Diego Parent, Bay Area
Parent, San Francisco Peninsula Parent,* and *Parents' Press*
(Berkeley). (Wingate Enterprises, 443 E. Irving Dr., Burbank, CA
91504). We list the book awards. (Honored titles featured in
end-of-year issues of magazines)

1990
Baby/Toddler
FOLLOW ME! by Nancy Tafuri *(Greenwillow)*
HO FOR A HAT by William Jay Smith, ill. by Lynn Munsinger
(Joy Street/Little, Brown)
I WENT WALKING by Sue Williams, ill. by Julie Vivas *(HBJ)*
"MY FIRST LOOK AT" series *(Random)*
Picture Book
AIDA told by Leontyne Price, ill. by Leo and Diane Dillon *(HBJ)*
GUESS WHAT? by Mem Fox, ill. by Vivienne Goodman
(Gulliver/HBJ)

THE TUNNEL by Anthony Browne *(Knopf)*
THE VERY QUIET CRICKET by Eric Carle *(Philomel)*
Nonfiction
THE BIG BOOK FOR PEACE edited by Ann Durell and
Marilyn Sachs *(Dutton)*
"EYEWITNESS JUNIORS" series *(Knopf)*
FAMILIES: A CELEBRATION OF DIVERSITY,
COMMITMENT, AND LOVE by Aylette Jenness *(Houghton)*
SPRING FLEECE: A DAY OF SHEEPSHEARING by Catherine
Paladino *(Joy Street/Little, Brown)*
1991
Baby/Toddler
COLOR FARM by Lois Ehlert *(Lippincott)*
"FINGER MAGIC BOOKS" series *(Schneider)*
HATCH, EGG, HATCH! by Shen Roddie *(Little, Brown)*
TEN LITTLE RABBITS by Virginia Grossman, ill. by Sylvia
Long *(Chronicle)*
Picture Book
BORREGUITA AND THE COYOTE by Verna Aardema, ill. by
Petra Mathers *(Knopf)*
MAMA, DO YOU LOVE ME? by Barbara M. Joose, ill. by
Barbara Lavalle *(Chronicle)*
THE SALAMANDER ROOM by Anne Mazer, ill. by Steve
Johnson *(Knopf)*
TAR BEACH by Faith Ringgold *(Crown)*
Early Elementary
BROTHER EAGLE, SISTER SKY: A MESSAGE FROM CHIEF
SEATTLE by Susan Jeffers *(Dial)*
FLY AWAY HOME by Eve Bunting, ill. by Ronald Himler
(Clarion)
THE JOLLY CHRISTMAS POSTMAN by Janet and Allan
Ahlberg *(Little, Brown)*
TO RIDE A BUTTERFLY edited by Nancy Larrick and Wendy
Lamb *(Bantam/Doubleday/Dell)*
Nonfiction
THE BUCK STOPS HERE by Alice Provensen *(HarperCollins)*
CHILDREN OF PROMISE: AFRICAN-AMERICAN
LITERATURE AND ART FOR YOUNG PEOPLE edited
by Charles Sullivan *(Abrams)*
THE RANDOM HOUSE CHILDREN'S ENCYCLOPEDIA
(Random)
A YOUNG PAINTER: THE LIFE AND PAINTINGS OF
WANG YANI—CHINA'S EXTRAORDINARY YOUNG
ARTIST by Zheng Zhensun and Alice Low *(Scholastic)*

Catholic Book Awards ⅋
CHILDREN'S AND YOUTH BOOK CATEGORIES

The Catholic Press Association of the United States and Canada, a professional trade association for publishers of Catholic newspapers, magazines, books, and other media, sponsors an annual awards program that includes books. For three years children's books were a part of the program. The last edition of *Children's Books: Awards & Prizes* listed the awards for 1984 and 1985; the final year in which children's books were a part of the program is included here for the record. (Certificate)

1984
Children
THE STORY OF BROTHER FRANCIS by Lene Mayer-Skumanz *(Ave Maria)*
Youth
NO STRANGERS TO VIOLENCE, NO STRANGERS TO LOVE by Boniface Hanley *(Ave Maria)*
1985
Children
STRINGS AND THINGS: POEMS AND OTHER MESSAGES FOR CHILDREN by Christy Kenneally *(Paulist)*
Youth
MOTHER TERESA OF CALCUTTA by David Michelinie and Roy M. Gasnick *(Franciscan Communications Office/Marvel Comics/Paulist)*
1986
Children
BACK-BACK AND THE LIMA BEAR by Thomas L. Weck *(Winston-Derek)*
Youth
HANG TOUGHF by Matthew Lancaster *(Paulist)*

Child Study Children's Book Committee at Bank Street College Award ⅋

Given each year by The Child Study Children's Book Committee (Bank Street College of Education, 610 West 112th St., New York, NY 10025) to honor a book for children or young people that deals realistically and in a positive way with problems in their world. In the listing below, the year cited is the year of the book's publication. (This award was once known as the Child Study Association/Wel-Met Children's Book Award.) (Scroll and honorarium)

1943
KEYSTONE KIDS by John R. Tunis *(HBJ)*
1944
THE HOUSE by Marjorie Allee *(Houghton)*
1945
THE MOVED-OUTERS by Florence Crannell Means *(Houghton)*
1946
HEART OF DANGER by Howard Pease *(Doubleday)*
1947
JUDY'S JOURNEY by Lois Lenski *(Lippincott)*
1948
THE BIG WAVE by Pearl Buck *(John Day)*
1949
PAUL TIBER: FORESTER by Maria Gleit *(Scribner)*
1950
THE UNITED NATIONS AND YOUTH by Eleanor Roosevelt and Helen Ferris *(Doubleday)*
1951
No Award
1952
JAREB by Miriam Powell *(Crowell)*
TWENTY AND TEN by Claire Huchet Bishop *(Viking)*
1953
IN A MIRROR by Mary Stolz *(Harper)*
1954
HIGH ROAD HOME by William Corbin *(Coward)*
THE ORDEAL OF THE YOUNG HUNTER by Jonreed Lauritzen *((Little, Brown)*
1955
CROW BOY by Taro Yashima *(Viking)*
PLAIN GIRL by Virginia Sorensen *(HBJ)*
1956
THE HOUSE OF SIXTY FATHERS by Meindert DeJong *(Harper)*
1957
SHADOW ACROSS THE CAMPUS by Helen R. Sattley *(Dodd)*
1958
SOUTH TOWN by Lorenz Graham *(Follett)*
1959
JENNIFER by Zoa Sherburne *(Morrow)*

1960
JANINE by Robin McKown *(Messner)*

1961
THE GIRL FROM PUERTO RICO by Hila Colman *(Morrow)*
THE ROAD TO AGRA by Aimee Sommerfelt *(Criterion)*

1962
THE TROUBLE WITH TERRY by Joan M. Lexau *(Dial)*

1963
THE PEACEABLE KINGDOM by Betty Schechter *(Houghton)*
THE ROCK AND THE WILLOW by Mildred Lee *(Lothrop)*

1964
THE HIGH PASTURE by Ruth Harnden *(Houghton)*

1965
THE EMPTY SCHOOLHOUSE by Natalie Savage Carlson
(Harper)

1966
QUEENIE PEAVY by Robert Burch *(Viking)*
Special Citation: CURIOUS GEORGE GOES TO THE
HOSPITAL by Margaret and H. A. Rey *(Houghton)*

1967
THE CONTENDER by Robert Lipsyte *(Harper)*

1968
WHAT IT'S ALL ABOUT by Vadim Frolov *(Doubleday)*
Special Citation: WHERE IS DADDY? THE STORY OF A
DIVORCE by Beth Goff *(Beacon)*

1969
THE EMPTY MOAT by Margaretha Shemin *(Coward)*

1970
MIGRANT GIRL by Carli Laklan *(McGraw-Hill)*
ROCK STAR by James Lincoln Collier *(Four Winds)*

1971
JOHN HENRY McCOY by Lillie D. Chaffin *(Macmillan)*
Special Citation: THE PAIR OF SHOES by Aline Glasgow *(Dial)*

1972
A SOUND OF CHARIOTS by Mollie Hunter *(Harper)*

1973
A TASTE OF BLACKBERRIES by Doris Buchanan Smith
(Crowell)

1974
LUKE WAS THERE by Eleanor Clymer *(Holt)*

1975
THE GARDEN IS DOING FINE by Carol Farley *(Atheneum)*

1976
SOMEBODY ELSE'S CHILD by Roberta Silman *(Warne)*

1977
THE PINBALLS by Betsy Byars *(Harper)*
1978
THE DEVIL IN VIENNA by Doris Orgel *(Dial)*
1979
THE WHIPMAN IS WATCHING by T. A. Dyer *(Houghton)*
1980
A BOAT TO NOWHERE by Maureen Crane Wartski
(Westminster)
1981
A SPIRIT TO RIDE THE WHIRLWIND by Athena Lord
(Macmillan)
1982
HOMESICK: MY OWN STORY by Jean Fritz *(Putnam)*
1983
THE SIGN OF THE BEAVER by Elizabeth George Speare
(Houghton)
THE SOLOMON SYSTEM by Phyllis Reynolds Naylor
(Atheneum)
1984
ONE-EYED CAT by Paula Fox *(Bradbury)*
1985
WITH WESTIE AND THE TIN MAN by C. S. Adler
(Macmillan)
Special Citation: AIN'T GONNA STUDY WAR NO MORE:
THE STORY OF AMERICA'S PEACE SEEKERS by Milton
Meltzer *(Harper)*
1986
JOURNEY TO JO'BURG: A SOUTH AFRICAN STORY by
Beverley Naidoo *(Lippincott)*
1987
RABBLE STARKEY by Lois Lowry *(Houghton)*
1988
DECEMBER STILLNESS by Mary Downing Hahn *(Clarion)*
THE MOST BEAUTIFUL PLACE IN THE WORLD by Ann
Cameron *(Knopf)*
1989
SHADES OF GRAY by Carolyn Reeder *(Macmillan)*
1990
SECRET CITY, U. S. A. by Felice Holman *(Scribner)*

Children's Book Council Honors Program ❧

Irregularly, and customarily at conferences sponsored by the Children's Book Council (568 Broadway, New York, NY 10012), the Council Honors Program salutes individuals for sustained contributions to children. The first program cited three people: J. Larry Brown for Child Advocacy, Fred Rogers ('Mister Rogers') for Communications, and the author noted below for Books and Literature. The second program cited two authors "for a body of work that has examined significant social issues in outstanding books for young readers." The listing below includes honorees for literature only. (Citation)

1985   Beverly Cleary

1988   Milton Meltzer
        Mildred D. Taylor

Christopher Awards ❧
CHILDREN'S BOOK CATEGORY

Established in 1949, the award is given by The Christophers (12 E. 48th St., New York, NY 10017) to works "of professional excellence that affirm the highest values of the human spirit." Awards are given to books, motion pictures and television specials. Books for young people were first honored as of the 1970 program. (Bronze medallion that incorporates the Christopher motto, "It is better to light one candle than to curse the darkness.")

1970
Ages 4-8
ALEXANDER AND THE WIND-UP MOUSE by Leo Lionni *(Pantheon)*
Ages 8-12
TUCKER'S COUNTRYSIDE by George Selden *(Farrar)*
Teen-age
BROTHER, CAN YOU SPARE A DIME? by Milton Meltzer *(Knopf)*
ESCAPE FROM NOWHERE by Jeannette Eyerly *(Lippincott)*
1971
Ages 4-8
THE ERIE CANAL by Peter Spier *(Doubleday)*

Ages 8-12
A MOMENT OF SILENCE by Pierre Janssen *(Atheneum)*
THE CHANGELING by Zilpha Keatley Snyder *(Atheneum)*
Teen-age
THE GUARDIANS by John Christopher *(Macmillan)*
SEA AND EARTH: THE LIFE OF RACHEL CARSON by
Philip Sterling *(Crowell)*
All Ages
UNICEF BOOK OF CHILDREN'S LEGENDS, UNICEF BOOK
OF CHILDREN'S POEMS, UNICEF BOOK OF CHILDREN'S
PRAYERS and UNICEF BOOK OF CHILDREN'S SONGS by
William I. Kaufman *(Stackpole)*

1972
Ages 4-8
EMMET OTTER'S JUG-BAND CHRISTMAS by Russell Hoban
(Parents)
ON THE DAY PETER STUYVESANT SAILED INTO TOWN
by Arnold Lobel *(Harper)*
Ages 8-12
ANNIE AND THE OLD ONE by Miska Miles *(Atlantic-Little,
Brown)*
POCAHONTAS AND THE STRANGERS by Clyde Robert
Bulla *(Crowell)*
Teen-age
THE HEADLESS CUPID by Zilpha Keatley Snyder *(Atheneum)*
THE RIGHTS OF THE PEOPLE – THE MAJOR DECISIONS
OF THE WARREN COURT by Elaine and Walter Goodman
(Farrar)

1973
Ages 4-8
THE ADVENTURES OF OBADIAH by Brinton Turkle *(Viking)*
Ages 8-12
THE BOOK OF GIANT STORIES by David L. Harrison
(McGraw-Hill)
TRACKING THE UNEARTHLY CREATURES OF MARSH
AND POND by Howard G. Smith *(Abingdon)*
Teen-age
FREAKY FRIDAY by Mary Rodgers *(Harper)*
VANISHING WINGS by Griffing Bancroft *(Watts)*
Young Adult
THIS STAR SHALL ABIDE by Sylvia Louise Engdahl
(Atheneum)
All Ages
DOMINIC by William Steig *(Farrar)*

1974
Pre-School
IT'S RAINING SAID JOHN TWAINING by N.M. Bodecker
(McElderry)

Ages 4-8
I'LL PROTECT YOU FROM THE BEASTS by Martha
Alexander *(Dial)*
GORILLA, GORILLA by Carol Fenner *(Random)*
Ages 8-12
THE WOLF by Michael Fox *(Coward)*
Ages 12 up
GUESTS IN THE PROMISED LAND by Kristin Hunter
(Scribner)
THE RIGHT TO KNOW—CENSORSHIP IN AMERICA by
Robert A. Liston *(Watts)*
1975
Pre-school
DAWN by Uri Shulevitz *(Farrar)*
Ages 4-8
MY GRANDSON LEW by Charlotte Zolotow *(Harper)*
Ages 8-12
FIRST SNOW by Helen Coutant *(Knopf)*
SAVE THE MUSTANGS by Ann E. Weiss *(Messner)*
Ages 12 up
A BILLION FOR BORIS by Mary Rodgers *(Harper)*
1976
Picture book
ANNO'S ALPHABET by Mitsumasa Anno *(Crowell)*
Ages 7-11
HOW THE WITCH GOT ALF by Cora Annett *(Watts)*
Ages 9-12
TUCK EVERLASTING by Natalie Babbitt *(Farrar)*
Ages 12 up
BERT BREEN'S BARN by Walter D. Edmonds *(Little, Brown)*
Nonfiction
PYRAMID by David Macaulay *(Houghton)*
1977
Picture book
WILLY BEAR by Mildred Kantrowitz *(Parents)*
Ages 6-8
FROG AND TOAD ALL YEAR by Arnold Lobel *(Harper)*
Ages 9-12
THE CHAMPION OF MERRIMACK COUNTY by Roger W.
Drury *(Little, Brown)*
Ages 9 up
HURRY, HURRY, MARY DEAR! AND OTHER NONSENSE
POEMS by N.M. Bodecker *(McElderry)*
Ages 12 up
DEAR BILL, REMEMBER ME? AND OTHER STORIES by
Norma Fox Mazer *(Delacorte)*
1978
Picture book
NOAH'S ARK by Peter Spier *(Doubleday)*

Ages 6-9
THE SEEING STICK by Jane Yolen *(Crowell)*
Ages 12 up
COME TO THE EDGE by Julia Cunningham *(Pantheon)*
WHERE'S YOUR HEAD? PSYCHOLOGY FOR TEENAGERS
by Dale Carlson *(Atheneum)*
All Ages
THE WHEEL OF KING ASOKA by Ashok Davar *(Follett)*

1979
Picture book
PANDA CAKE by Rosalie Seidler *(Parents)*
Ages 7-9
CHESTER CHIPMUNK'S THANKSGIVING by Barbara
Williams *(Dutton)*
Ages 9-12
THE GREAT GILLY HOPKINS by Katherine Paterson *(Crowell)*
Young Adult
GENTLEHANDS by M.E. Kerr *(Harper)*

1980
Ages 5-8
FREDERICK'S ALLIGATOR by Esther Allen Peterson *(Crown)*
Ages 9-12
WHAT HAPPENED IN HAMELIN by Gloria Skurzynski *(Four
Winds)*
Ages 12 up
ALL TOGETHER NOW by Sue Ellen Bridgers *(Knopf)*
All Ages
THE NEW YORK KID'S BOOK edited by Catherine Edmonds
et al. *(Doubleday)*

1981
Picture book
PEOPLE by Peter Spier *(Doubleday)*
Ages 8-12
ALL TIMES, ALL PEOPLE: A WORLD HISTORY OF
SLAVERY by Milton Meltzer *(Harper)*
SON FOR A DAY by Corrine Gerson *(Atheneum)*
Ages 12 up
ENCOUNTER BY EASTON by Avi *(Pantheon)*
THE HARDEST LESSON: PERSONAL ACCOUNTS OF A
SCHOOL DESEGREGATION CRISIS by Pamela Bullard and
Judith Stoia *(Little, Brown)*

1982
Picture book
MY MOM TRAVELS A LOT by Caroline Feller Bauer, ill. by
Nancy Winslow Parker *(Warne)*
Ages 6-9
EVEN IF I DID SOMETHING AWFUL by Barbara Shook
Hazen *(Atheneum)*

Ages 10-14
A GIFT OF MIRRORVAX by Malcolm Macloud *(Atheneum)*
Young Adult
THE ISLANDERS by John Rowe Townsend *(Lippincott)*

1983
Ages 4-7
WE CAN'T SLEEP by James Stevenson *(Greenwillow)*
Ages 8-12
HOMESICK: MY OWN STORY by Jean Fritz *(Putnam)*
Ages 12 up
A FORMAL FEELING by Zibby Oneal *(Viking)*
All Ages
DRAWING FROM NATURE by Jim Arnosky *(Lothrop)*

1984
Picture book
POSY by Charlotte Pomerantz *(Greenwillow)*
Ages 8-10
DEAR MR. HENSHAW by Beverly Cleary *(Morrow)*
Ages 10-12
THE SIGN OF THE BEAVER by Elizabeth George Speare
(Houghton)
Ages 12 up
THE NUCLEAR ARMS RACE—CAN WE SURVIVE IT? by
Ann E. Weiss *(Houghton)*

1985
Picture book
PICNIC by Emily Arnold McCully *(Harper)*
Ages 6-8
HOW MY PARENTS LEARNED TO EAT by Ina R. Friedman,
ill. by Allen Say *(Houghton)*
Ages 8-10
SECRETS OF A SMALL BROTHER by Richard J. Margolis
(Macmillan)
Ages 10 up
ONE-EYED CAT by Paula Fox *(Bradbury)*
All Ages
IMAGINE THAT!!! EXPLORING MAKE BELIEVE by Joyce
Strauss *(Human Sciences)*

1986
Ages 4-8
THE PATCHWORK QUILT by Valerie Flournoy, ill. by Jerry
Pinkney *(Dial)*
Ages 8-10
SARAH, PLAIN AND TALL by Patricia MacLachlan *(Harper)*
Ages 8 up
PROMISE NOT TO TELL by Carolyn Polese, ill. by Jennifer
Barrett *(Human Sciences)*

Ages 10-12
UNDERDOG by Marilyn Sachs *(Doubleday)*
Young Adult
THE MOUNT RUSHMORE STORY by Judith St. George
(Putnam)

1987
Ages 4-6
DUNCAN AND DOLORES by Barbara Samuels *(Bradbury)*
Ages 6-8
THE PURPLE COAT by Amy Hest, ill. by Amy Schwartz *(Four Winds)*
Ages 8-12
BORROWED SUMMER by Marion Walker Doren *(Harper)*
Young Adult
CLASS DISMISSED II by Mel Glenn *(Clarion)*

1988
Picture Book
HECKEDY PEG by Audrey Wood, ill. by Don Wood *(HBJ)*
Ages 6-8
HUMPHREY'S BEAR by Jan Wahl, ill. by William Joyce *(Holt)*
Ages 9-12
THE GOLD CADILLAC by Mildred D. Taylor *(Dial)*
Ages 12 up
INTO A STRANGE LAND: UNACCOMPANIED REFUGEE
YOUTH IN AMERICA by Brent Ashabranner and Melissa
Ashabranner *(Dodd)*

1989
Ages 5-7
THE GOOD-BYE BOOK by Judith Viorst, ill. by Kay
Chorao *(Macmillan)*
Ages 7-10
FAMILY FARM by Thomas Locker *(Dial)*
Ages 10-14
LIES, DECEPTION AND TRUTH by Ann E. Weiss *(Houghton)*
Young Adult
LOOKING THE TIGER IN THE EYE: CONFRONTING THE
NUCLEAR THREAT by Carl B. Feldbaum and Ronald J. Bee
(Harper)

1990
Ages 4-7
KEEPING A CHRISTMAS SECRET by Phyllis Reynolds Naylor,
ill. by Lena Shiffman *(Atheneum)*
Ages 8-11
WILLIAM AND GRANDPA by Alice Schertle, ill. by Lydia
Dabcovich *(Lothrop)*
Ages 10-12
CAN THE WHALES BE SAVED? by Philip Whitfield *(Viking)*

Young Adult
SO MUCH TO TELL YOU... by John Marsden *(Joy Street/ Little, Brown)*

1991
Ages 9-12
MISSISSIPPI BRIDGE by Mildred D. Taylor, ill. by Max Ginsburg *(Dial)*
All Ages
PAUL REVERE'S RIDE by Henry Wadsworth Longfellow, ill. by Ted Rand *(Dutton)*

1992
Ages 4-6
SOMEBODY LOVES YOU, MR. HATCH by Eileen Spinelli, ill. by Paul Yalowitz *(Bradbury)*
Ages 6-8
STEPHEN'S FEAST by Jean Richardson, ill. by Alice Englander *(Little, Brown)*
Ages 8-10
THE GOLD COIN by Alma Flor Ada, translated by Bernice Randall, ill. by Neil Waldman *(Atheneum)*
Ages 10 up
THE STAR FISHER by Laurence Yep *(Morrow)*
All ages
WHERE DOES GOD LIVE? QUESTIONS AND ANSWERS FOR PARENTS AND CHILDREN by Marc Gellman and Thomas Hartman, ill. by William Zdinak *(Triumph)*

Colorado Book Authors Competition

Sponsored jointly by the Colorado Authors' League and the Colorado Center for the Book (201 East Colfax, Suite 309, Denver, CO 80203), this awards program honors books written by Colorado residents in four categories, including Children's Books, the category we list. (Honored at Annual Governor's Reception)

1991
SAND DUNE PONY by Franklin Folsom *(Roberts Rinehart)*

Commonwealth Club of California Book Awards ❧
CHILDREN'S BOOK CATEGORIES

This annual awards program honors books "with exceptional literary merit" in several categories. As of the program for books published in 1990, there have been two children's book categories: fiction or nonfiction for children up to 10, and also for children ages 11-16. Authors must have been legal residents of California at the time the manuscript was submitted for publication. In the listing below, the year cited is the year of a book's publication. The sponsor is Commonwealth Club of California (595 Market St., San Francisco, CA 94105). (For children's books, silver medals)

1939
BRIGHT HERITAGE by Mary Virginia Powers *(Longmans)*

1940
BLUE WILLOW by Doris Gates *(Viking)*

1942
LONG ADVENTURE: THE STORY OF WINSTON CHURCHILL by Hildegarde Hawthorne *(Appleton)*

1943
SPURS FOR ANTONIA by Katherine Wigmore Eyre *(Oxford)*

1944
THUNDERBOLT HOUSE by Howard Pease *(Doubleday)*

1945
THE SINGING CAVE by Margaret Leighton *(Houghton)*

1946
TOWARDS OREGON by E.H. Staffelbach *(Macrae)*

1947
SANCHO OF THE LONG, LONG HORNS by Allen R. Bosworth *(Doubleday)*

1948
SEABIRD by Holling C. Holling *(Houghton)*

1949
AT THE PALACE GATES by Helen Rand Parrish *(Viking)*

1950
TOMAS AND THE RED HEADED ANGEL by Marion Garthwaite *(Messner)*

1951
SANDRA AND THE RIGHT PRINCE by Mildred N. Anderson *(Oxford)*

1952
WAPITI THE ELK by Rutherford Montgomery *(Little, Brown)*

1953
ROARING RIVER by Bill Brown *(Coward)*

1954
EPICS OF EVEREST by Leonard Wibberley *(Farrar)*

1955
WESTWARD THE EAGLE by Frederick A. Lane *(Holt)*

1956
SPOOK THE MUSTANG by Harlan Thompson *(Doubleday)*

1957
DAVID AND THE PHOENIX by Edward Ormondroyd *(Follett)*

1958
FIRST SCIENTIST OF ALASKA: WILLIAM HEALY DALL by Edward A. Herron *(Messner)*

1959
THIS IS THE DESERT by Phillip H. Ault *(Dodd)*

1960
HAWAII, THE ALOHA STATE by Helen Bauer *(Doubleday)*

1961
THE GRAY SEA RAIDERS by Gordon D. Shirreffs *(Chilton)*

1962
FIRST WOMAN AMBULANCE SURGEON: EMILY BARRINGER by Iris Noble *(Messner)*

1963
THE KEYS AND THE CANDLE by Maryhale Woolsey *(Abingdon)*

1964
THE SPELL IS CAST by Eleanor Cameron *(Atlantic-Little, Brown)*

1965
CAMPION TOWERS by John and Patricia Beatty *(Macmillan)*

1966
CHANCY AND THE GRAND RASCAL by Sid Fleischman *(Atlantic-Little, Brown)*

1967
SILENT SHIP, SILENT SEA by Robb White *(Doubleday)*

1968
QUEST FOR FREEDOM by Paul Rink *(Messner)*

1969
THE CAY by Theodore Taylor *(Doubleday)*

1970
JONAH AND THE GREAT FISH by Clyde Robert Bulla *(Crowell)*

1971
ANNIE AND THE OLD ONE by Miska Miles *(Atlantic-Little, Brown)*
1972
SAMURAI OF GOLD HILL by Yoshiko Uchida *(Scribner)*
1973
No Award
1974
THE PAPER PARTY by Don Freeman *(Viking)*
1975
COYOTES, LAST ANIMALS ON EARTH? by Harold E. Thomas *(Lothrop)*
1976
THE BOY WHO SANG THE BIRDS by John Weston *(Scribner)*
1977
A SHEPHERD WATCHES, A SHEPHERD SINGS by Louis Irigaray and Theodore Taylor *(Doubleday)*
1978
NORTH OF DANGER by Dale Fife *(Dutton)*
1979
THE FOOL AND THE DANCING BEAR by Pamela Stearns *(Atlantic-Little, Brown)*
1980
FLIGHT OF THE SPARROW by Julia Cunningham *(Pantheon)*
THE HALF-A-MOON INN by Paul Fleischman *(Harper)*
1981
A JAR OF DREAMS by Yoshiko Uchida *(McElderry)*
1982
JAKE AND HONEYBUNCH GO TO HEAVEN by Margot Zemach *(Farrar)*
1983
DEAR MR. HENSHAW by Beverly Cleary *(Morrow)*
1984
MONKEY PUZZLE AND OTHER POEMS by Myra Cohn Livingston *(McElderry)*
1985
THE WILLOW MAIDEN by Meghan Collins *(Dial)*
1986
THE SECRET OF THE MOUNTAIN by Esther Linfield *(Greenwillow)*
1987
NELL'S QUILT by Susan Terris *(Farrar)*
1988
STEP INTO THE NIGHT by Joanne Ryder *(Four Winds)*
1989
No Award

1990
Up to 10
BABUSHKA'S DOLL by Patricia Polacco *(Simon & Schuster)*
11-16
THE FABULOUS FIFTY by Morton Grosser *(Atheneum)*

Delacorte Press Prize for a First Young Adult Novel ❧

This annual contest is open to American and Canadian writers who have not previously published a young adult novel. Submissions must have contemporary settings and be suitable for readers ages 12 to 18. The sponsor is Delacorte Press (Department BFYR, 666 Fifth Ave., New York, NY 10103). ($1,500 cash prize, and $6,000 advance against royalties for hardcover edition published by Delacorte Press and paperback edition published by Dell)

1983
CENTER LINE by Joyce Sweeney *(Delacorte)*

1984
WALK THROUGH COLD FIRE by Cin Forshay-Lunsford *(Delacorte)*

1985
THE IMPACT ZONE by Ray Maloney *(Delacorte)*

1986
No prizewinner

1987
CAL CAMERON BY DAY, SPIDER-MAN BY NIGHT by A. E. Cannon *(Delacorte)*

1988
OZZY ON THE OUTSIDE by R. E. Allen *(Delacorte)*

1989
HANK by James Sauer *(Delacorte)*

1990
LIZARD by Dennis Covington *(Delacorte)*

1991
SQUASHED by Joan Bauer *(Delacorte)*

Dutton Children's Books
Picture Book Competition 🕭

The purpose of the competition is to encourage and attract new and talented children's book illustrators to the field. Entrants may not have published books previously. They must be enrolled in an art school or institute of design, or be taking an art or design course in a college or university; recent (five years) graduates are also eligible. Detailed information about the specific format of submissions is available from the publisher sponsor (E. P. Dutton Children's Books, Attn.: Picture Book Competition, 375 Hudson St., New York, NY 10014). (First prize: $1,500, Second prize: $1,000, Third prize: $500; Dutton has an option to publish any prizewinner and offers an advance and royalties in addition to prize money upon exercising its option)

1986
MINERVA LOUISE by Janet Morgan Stoeke *(Dutton)*
1988
Winner was Annette Le Blanc; entry not published; later book to be published
1990
No winners

Margaret A. Edwards Award 🕭

Named for a youth services librarian who worked at the Enoch Pratt Free Library in Baltimore, MD, and wrote *The Fair Garden and the Swarm of Beasts: The Library and the Young Adult*, this award is sponsored by the Young Adult Library Services Association of the American Library Association (50 East Huron St., Chicago, IL 60611) in cooperation with *School Library Journal*, the donor of the stipend. Formerly the Young Adult Author Achievement Award, the award is for a living writer whose "book or books, over a period of time, have been accepted by young people as an authentic voice that continues to illuminate their experiences and emotions, giving insight into their lives." ($1,000 and citation)

1988   S. E. Hinton
1990   Richard Peck
1991   Robert Cormier
1992   Lois Duncan

Empire State Award for Excellence in Literature for Young People 🍂

This award is for a body of work "which represents excellence in children's or young adult literature and has made a significant contribution to literature for young people." Recipients must be residents of New York State. The sponsor is the Youth Services Section of the New York Library Association (252 Hudson Ave., Albany, NY 12210). (Medallion)

1990 Maurice Sendak
1991 Madeleine L'Engle

Joan Fassler Memorial Book Award 🍂

Sponsored by the Association for the Care of Children's Health (7910 Woodmont Ave., Bethesda, MD 20814), a multidisciplinary nonprofit membership organization of professionals and parents working together "to ensure that all aspects of children's health care are family-centered, psychosocially sound, and developmentally appropriate," this award is named for the late Joan Fassler, a child psychologist and children's trade book author. It is for a book that makes an "outstanding contribution to children's literature dealing with hospitalization, disease, disabling conditions, death, and dying." ($1,000 and plaque)

1989
SAYING GOODBYE TO GRANDMA by Jane Resh Thomas, ill. by Marcia Sewall (Clarion)
1990
HOW IT FEELS TO FIGHT FOR YOUR LIFE by Jill Krementz (Joy Street/Little, Brown)
1991
THE CANADA GEESE QUILT by Natalie Kinsey-Warnock (Cobblehill)

Carolyn W. Field Award ❧

This award is named for the former Coordinator of Children's Services at the Free Library of Philadelphia who has been designated by her state a "Distinguished Daughter of Pennsylvania." Sponsored by the Youth Services Division of the Pennsylvania Library Association (126 Locust St, Harrisburg, PA 17110), the award is given annually to a Pennsylvania author or illustrator for a distinguished children's book published in the preceding year. In the listing below, when there is more than one by-line, the name of the award recipient is followed by an asterisk. (Medal)

1984
SOME THINGS GO TOGETHER by Charlotte Zolotow, ill. by Karen Gundersheimer* *(Crowell)*
1985
SAINT GEORGE AND THE DRAGON retold by Margaret Hodges*, ill. by Trina Schart Hyman *(Little, Brown)*
1986
THE NEW BABY by Fred Rogers *(Putnam)*
1987
THE ILLYRIAN ADVENTURE by Lloyd Alexander *(Dutton)*
1988
LITTLE TREE by e. e. cummings, ill. by Deborah Kogan Ray * *(Crown)*
1989
CATWINGS by Ursula LeGuin, ill. by S. D. Schindler* *(Orchard)*
1990
BOX TURTLE AT LONG POND by William T. George*, ill. by Lindsay Barrett George* *(Greenwillow)*
1991
MANIAC MAGEE by Jerry Spinelli *(Little, Brown)*

Friends of American Writers Awards ❧

JUVENILE BOOK AWARD

Presented annually in the spring since 1960 by Friends of American Writers/Chicago, Young People's Literature Commission (1634 N. Wood St., #1, Chicago, IL 60622) the award was given to a single title through 1972. In 1973, the awards program expanded; first-place juvenile writing award winners are listed below. (An award for illustration was also presented from 1973-1977 and in 1979 and 1980 and those awards are listed.) The awards are for books published in the year preceding the award presentation. The winner must be a native or a resident, for at least five years, of one of thirteen Midwestern states or one of those states must be the locale of the winning book. (Various stipends)

1960
FIRST BOY ON THE MOON by Clifford B. Hicks *(Holt)*
1961
SEQUOYAH, YOUNG CHEROKEE GUIDE by Dorothea J. Snow *(Bobbs)*
1962
HOSTAGE TO ALEXANDER by Mary Evans Andrews *(McKay)*
1963
CATHIE AND THE PADDY BOY by Nora Tully MacAlvay *(Viking)*
1964
I JESSIE by Ruth Painter Randall *(Little, Brown)*
1965
THE FAR-OFF LAND by Rebecca Caudill *(Viking)*
1966-1968
No Awards
1969
JUD by Charles Raymond *(Houghton)*
1970
TRAILBLAZER: NEGRO NURSE IN THE AMERICAN RED CROSS by Jean Maddern Pitrone *(HBJ)*
1971
TOUCH OF LIGHT by Anne Neimark *(HBJ)*
1972
WAR WORK by Zibby Oneal *(Viking)*
1973
THE WINTER CAT by Howard Knotts *(Harper)*
Illustration: AUTHORIZED AUTUMN CHARTS OF THE UPPER RED CANOE RIVER COUNTRY by Peter Zachary Cohen, ill. by Tomie de Paola *(Atheneum)*
1974
SIX DAYS FROM SUNDAY by Betty Biesterveld *(Rand McNally)*
Illustration: THE LONG HUNGRY NIGHT by Elizabeth C. Foster and Slim Williams, ill. by Glo Coalson *(Atheneum)*

1975
THE TARTAR'S SWORD by Erich A. Kimmel *(Coward)*
Illustration: KONGA AND KUMBA by Alice Shick, ill. by
Joseph Cellini *(Dial)*
1976
FIRST STEP by Anne Snyder *(Holt)*
Illustration: THE DEVIL DID IT by Susan Jeschke *(Holt)*
1977
TOBY, GRANNY & GEORGE by Robbie Branscum
(Doubleday)
Illustration: LITTLE FOX GOES TO THE END OF THE
WORLD by Ann Tompert, ill. by John Wallner *(Crown)*
1978
THE DREAM RUNNER by Audree Distad *(Harper)*
1979
HARVEY, THE BEER CAN KING by Jamie Gilson *(Lothrop)*
Illustration: ON THE FOREST EDGE by Carol Lerner
(Morrow)
1980
BETWEEN DARK AND DAYLIGHT by Crystal Thrasher
(McElderry)
Illustration: THE KING AT THE DOOR by Brock Cole
(Doubleday)
1981
THE SNOWBIRD by Patricia Calvert *(Scribner)*
1982
BEYOND TWO RIVERS by David Kherdian *(Greenwillow)*
1983
THE LAND I LOST by Huynh Quang Nhuong *(Harper)*
1984
RASPBERRY ONE by Charles Ferry *(Houghton)*
1985
RODEO SUMMER by Judie Gulley *(Houghton)*
1986
WHERE THE PIRATES ARE by Tom Townsend *(Eakin)*
1987
ROVER AND COO COO by John Hay *(Green Tiger)*
1988
ISLAND OF PERIL by Raboo Rodgers *(Houghton)*
1989
THE SECRET FRIENDSHIP by Virginia Brosseit
(Winston-Derek)
1990
DYING SUN by Gary L. Blackwood *(Atheneum)*
1991
BOY IN THE MOON by Ron Koertge *(Joy Street/Little, Brown)*
NIGHT OWLS by Sharon P. Denslow, ill. by Jill Kastner *(Bradbury)*

Friends of Children and Literature (FOCAL) Award ❧

The Friends of Children and Literature (FOCAL) is a support group of the Central Library, Los Angeles Public Library (630 W. 5th St., Los Angeles, CA 90071). Its annual award is for the author or illustrator of a creative book that has enriched a child's appreciation for and knowledge of California. There are no restrictions as to the publication years of books considered for the award. (Hand-crafted puppet of a main character in the honored book; puppet holds a calligraphed scroll, with title, etc.; duplicate of puppet is presented to Central Library)

1980
PEDRO, THE ANGEL OF OLVERA STREET by Leo Politi
(Scribner)
1981
ISLAND OF THE BLUE DOLPHINS by Scott O'Dell
(Houghton)
1982
BLUE WILLOW by Doris Gates (Viking)
1983
BY THE GREAT HORN SPOON by Sid Fleischman (Atlantic-Little, Brown)
1984
DRAGONWINGS by Laurence Yep (Harper)
1985
JULIA AND THE HAND OF GOD by Eleanor Cameron
(Dutton)
1986
A JAR OF DREAMS by Yoshiko Uchida (McElderry)
1987
DEAR MR. HENSHAW by Beverly Cleary (Morrow)
1988
FAREWELL TO MANZANAR by Jeanne Wakatsuki Houston
(Houghton)
1989
A ROOM MADE OF WINDOWS by Eleanor Cameron
(Atlantic-Little, Brown)
1990
COME THE MORNING by Mark Jonathan Harris (Bradbury)
1991
THE GREAT AMERICAN GOLD RUSH by Rhoda Blumberg
(Bradbury)

Garden State Children's Book Awards ❧

Established in 1977 by the New Jersey Library Association Children's Services Section (116 W. State St., Trenton, NJ 08608) to give recognition to books of literary merit and also popularity with readers in the early and middle grades (2-5). The awards, given in three categories to both authors and illustrators, are selected by a committee of the Children's Services Section of the New Jersey Library Association. Only books published three years prior to the award year are considered. (Certificate)

ER—Easy-to-Read; *Y/F*—Younger Fiction; *Y/NF*—Younger Nonfiction

1977
ER
DINOSAUR TIME by Peggy Parish, ill. by Arnold Lobel *(Harper)*
Y/F
ENCYCLOPEDIA BROWN LENDS A HAND by Donald J. Sobol, ill. by Leonard Shortall *(Elsevier/Nelson)*
Y/NF
ON THE TRACK OF BIGFOOT by Marian T. Place *(Dodd)*
1978
ER
OWL AT HOME by Arnold Lobel *(Harper)*
Y/F
DORRIE'S BOOK by Marilyn Sachs, ill. by Anne Sachs *(Doubleday)*
Y/NF
HOW KITTENS GROW by Millicent Selsam, photos by Esther Bubley *(Four Winds)*
1979
ER
HATTIE RABBIT by Dick Gackenbach *(Harper)*
ER
HEATHER'S FEATHERS by Leatie Weiss, ill. by Ellen Weiss *(Watts)*
Y/F
NOBODY HAS TO BE A KID FOREVER by Hila Colman *(Crown)*
Y/NF
A VERY YOUNG DANCER by Jill Krementz *(Knopf)*
1980
ER
TEACH US, AMELIA BEDELIA by Peggy Parish, ill. by Lynn Sweat *(Greenwillow)*

Y/F
RAMONA AND HER FATHER by Beverly Cleary, ill. by Alan
Tiegreen *(Morrow)*
Y/NF
THE QUICKSAND BOOK by Tomie de Paola *(Holiday House)*

1981
ER
GRASSHOPPER ON THE ROAD by Arnold Lobel *(Harper)*
Y/F
THE GREAT GILLY HOPKINS by Katherine Paterson *(Crowell)*
Y/NF
TYRANNOSAURUS REX by Millicent Selsam *(Harper)*

1982
ER
MRS. GADDY AND THE GHOST by Wilson Gage, ill. by
Marylin Hafner *(Greenwillow)*
Y/F
RAMONA AND HER MOTHER by Beverly Cleary, ill. by Alan
Tiegreen *(Morrow)*
Y/NF
MUMMIES MADE IN EGYPT by Aliki *(Crowell)*

1983
ER
CLAMS CAN'T SING by James Stevenson *(Greenwillow)*
ER
COMMANDER TOAD IN SPACE by Jane Yolen, ill. by Bruce
Degen *(Coward)*
Y/F
SUPERFUDGE by Judy Blume *(Dutton)*
Y/NF
A SHOW OF HANDS: SAY IT IN SIGN LANGUAGE by Mary
Beth Sullivan and Linda Bourke, ill. by Linda Bourke *(Addison)*

1984
ER
NATE THE GREAT AND THE MISSING KEY by Marjorie
Sharmat, ill. by Marc Simont *(Coward)*
Y/F
RAMONA QUIMBY, AGE 8 by Beverly Cleary, ill. by Alan
Tiegreen *(Morrow)*
Y/NF
A LIGHT IN THE ATTIC by Shel Silverstein *(Harper)*

1985
ER
NATE THE GREAT AND THE SNOWY TRAIL by Marjorie
Sharmat, ill. by Marc Simont *(Coward)*
Y/F
RALPH S. MOUSE by Beverly Cleary, ill. by Paul O. Zelinsky
(Morrow)

Y/NF
IT'S BASIC: THE ABC'S OF COMPUTER PROGRAMMING by
Shelley Lipson, ill. by Janice Stapleton *(Holt)*
1986
ER
M & M AND THE BAD NEWS BABIES by Pat Ross, ill. by
Marylin Hafner *(Knopf)*
Y/F
DEAR MR. HENSHAW by Beverly Cleary, ill. by Paul O.
Zelinsky *(Morrow)*
Y/NF
DRAW 50 MONSTERS... by Lee J. Ames *(Doubleday)*
1987
ER
IN A DARK, DARK ROOM AND OTHER SCARY STORIES,
ill. by Dirk Zimmer *(Harper)*
Y/F
ANASTASIA, ASK YOUR ANALYST by Lois Lowry *(Houghton)*
Y/NF
THE NEW KID ON THE BLOCK by Jack Prelutsky, ill. by
James Stevenson *(Greenwillow)*
1988
ER
AMELIA BEDELIA GOES CAMPING by Peggy Parish, ill. by
Lynn Sweat *(Greenwillow)*
Y/F
SARAH, PLAIN AND TALL by Patricia MacLachlan *(Harper)*
Y/NF
HOW THEY BUILT THE STATUE OF LIBERTY by Mary J.
Shapiro, ill. by Huck Scarry *(Random)*
1989
ER
MERRY CHRISTMAS, AMELIA BEDELIA by Peggy Parish, ill.
by Lynn Sweat *(Greenwillow)*
Y/F
ANASTASIA HAS THE ANSWERS by Lois Lowry *(Houghton)*
Y/NF
TO SPACE AND BACK by Sally Ride, with Susan Okie
(Lothrop)
1990
ER
HENRY AND MUDGE IN PUDDLE TROUBLE by Cynthia
Rylant, ill. by Sucie Stevenson *(Bradbury)*
Y/F
NIGHTY-NIGHTMARE by James Howe, ill. by Leslie Morrill
(Atheneum)
Y/NF
KOKO'S STORY by Francine Patterson *(Scholastic)*

1991
ER
FOX ON THE JOB by James Marshall *(Dial)*
Y/F
THE BURNING QUESTIONS OF BINGO BROWN by Betsy
Byars *(Viking)*
Y/F
TEACHER'S PET by Johanna Hurwitz *(Morrow)*
Y/NF
VOLCANOES by Seymour Simon *(Morrow)*

Golden Kite Awards 🦋

Sponsored and administered by the Society of Children's Book
Writers (SCBW) (P.O. Box 296, Mar Vista Station, Los Angeles,
CA 90066), these awards are presented annually to those
members of SCBW whose award-year books of fiction, nonfiction
and picture-illustration "best exhibit excellence in writing or
illustration and genuinely appeal to the interests and concerns of
children." Originally an award for fiction *(F)* only, a nonfiction
(NF) category was added in 1977, and a picture-illustration *(PI)*
category in 1982. The year date in our listing is the publication
year. (Statuette)

1973
SUMMER OF MY GERMAN SOLDIER by Bette Greene *(Dial)*
1974
THE GIRL WHO CRIED FLOWERS by Jane Yolen *(Crowell)*
1975
THE GARDEN IS DOING FINE by Carol Farley *(Atheneum)*
1976
ONE MORE FLIGHT by Eve Bunting *(Warne)*
1977
F: THE GIRL WHO HAD NO NAME by Berniece Rabe
(Dutton)
NF: PEEPER, FIRST VOICE OF SPRING by Robert McClung
(Morrow)
1978
F: AND YOU GIVE ME A PAIN, ELAINE by Stella Pevsner
(Clarion)
NF: HOW I CAME TO BE A WRITER by Phyllis Reynolds
Naylor *(Atheneum)*
1979
F: THE MAGIC OF THE GLITS by C. S. Adler *(Macmillan)*

NF: RUNAWAY TEENS by Arnold Madison *(Elsevier/Nelson)*

1980

F: ARTHUR, FOR THE VERY FIRST TIME by Patricia MacLachlan *(Harper)*

NF: THE LIVES OF SPIDERS by Dorothy Hinshaw Patent *(Holiday House)*

1981

F: LITTLE LITTLE by M.E. Kerr *(Harper)*

NF: BLISSYMBOLICS by Elizabeth Helfman *(Lodestar)*

1982

F: RALPH S. MOUSE by Beverly Cleary *(Morrow)*

NF: CHIMNEY SWEEPS by James Cross Giblin *(Crowell)*

PI: GIORGIO'S VILLAGE by Tomie de Paola *(Putnam)*

1983

F: THE TEMPERING by Gloria Skurzynski *(Clarion)*

NF: THE ILLUSTRATED DINOSAUR DICTIONARY by Helen Roney Sattler *(Lothrop)*

PI: LITTLE RED RIDING HOOD by Trina Schart Hyman *(Holiday House)*

1984

F: TANCY by Belinda Hurmence *(Clarion)*

NF: WALLS: DEFENSES THROUGHOUT HISTORY by James Cross Giblin *(Little, Brown)*

PI: THE NAPPING HOUSE by Audrey Wood, ill. by Don Wood *(HBJ)*

1985

F: SARAH, PLAIN AND TALL by Patricia MacLachlan *(Harper)*

NF: COMMODORE PERRY IN THE LAND OF THE SHOGUN by Rhoda Blumberg *(Lothrop)*

PI: THE DONKEY'S DREAM by Barbara Helen Berger *(Philomel)*

1986

F: AFTER THE DANCING DAYS by Margaret I. Rostkowski *(Harper)*

NF: POVERTY IN AMERICA by Milton Meltzer *(Morrow)*

PI: ALPHABATICS by Suse MacDonald *(Bradbury)*

1987

F: RABBLE STARKEY by Lois Lowry *(Houghton)*

NF: THE INCREDIBLE JOURNEY OF LEWIS AND CLARK by Rhoda Blumberg *(Lothrop)*

PI: THE DEVIL & MOTHER CRUMP by Valerie Scho Carey, ill. by Arnold Lobel *(Harper)*

1988

F: BORROWED CHILDREN by George Ella Lyon *(Orchard)*

NF: LET THERE BE LIGHT: A BOOK ABOUT WINDOWS by James Cross Giblin *(Crowell)*

PI: FOREST OF DREAMS by Rosemary Wells, ill. by Susan Jeffers *(Dial)*

1989
F: JENNY OF THE TETONS by Kristiana Gregory *(Gulliver/HBJ)*
NF: PANAMA CANAL: GATEWAY TO THE WORLD by Judith St. George *(Putnam)*
PI: TOM THUMB by Richard Jesse Watson *(HBJ)*

1990
F: THE TRUE CONFESSIONS OF CHARLOTTE DOYLE by Avi *(Orchard)*
NF: THE BOY'S WAR: CONFEDERATE AND UNION SOLDIERS TALK ABOUT THE CIVIL WAR by Jim Murphy *(Clarion)*
PI: HOME PLACE by Crescent Dragonwagon, ill. by Jerry Pinkney *(Macmillan)*

1991
F: THE RAINCATCHERS by Jean Thesman *(Houghton)*
NF: THE WRIGHT BROTHERS: HOW THEY INVENTED THE AIRPLANE by Russell Freedman *(Holiday House)*
PI: MAMA, DO YOU LOVE ME? by Barbara M. Joosse, ill. by Barbara Lavallee *(Chronicle)*

Eva L. Gordon Award for Children's Science Literature ❧

This award is named for the late Eva L. Gordon, author, reviewer and professor of children's science literature at Cornell University. It honors the body of work of an author or illustrator whose science trade books exemplify "high standards of accuracy, readability, sensitivity to interrelationships, timeliness and joyousness while they extend either directly or subtly an invitation to the child to become involved." The sponsor is the American Nature Study Society (ANSS) (Helen Ross Russell, Chairman of Publications Committee, ANSS, 44 College Dr., Jersey City, NJ 07305). (Certificate)

1964   Millicent Selsam
1965   Edwin Way Teale
1966   Robert M. McClung
1967-1969   No Awards
1970   Jean Craighead George

1971 Verne Rockcastle
1972-1973 No Awards
1974 Phyllis Busch
1975 Jeanne Bendick
1976 Helen Ross Russell
1977 Herman and Nina Schneider
1978 George Mason
       Dorothy Shuttlesworth
1979 Ross Hutchins
1980 Glenn O. Blough
1981 Herbert Zim
1982 Peter Parnall
1983 Lawrence Pringle
1984 Seymour Simon
1985 Vicki Cobb
1986 Dorothy Hinshaw Patent
1987 Patricia Lauber
1988 Franklyn M. Branley
1989 Ada and Frank Graham
1990 Joanna Cole
1991 Jim Arnosky

Jefferson Cup Award ða

This annual award is named for the famous Virginian and third President of the United States, Thomas Jefferson, whose personal library provided the nucleus for the Library of Congress, Washington, DC. The award, administered by the Children's and Young Adult Round Table of the Virginia Library Association (669 So. Washington St., Alexandria, VA 22314) is for a distinguished book for young people in the fields of American history, biography or historical fiction, and published in the preceding year. (Silver-plated inscribed Jefferson Cup and a small honorarium)

1983
THE JEWISH AMERICANS: A HISTORY IN THEIR OWN WORDS, 1650-1950 by Milton Meltzer *(Crowell)*
1984
WHO SPEAKS FOR WOLF? by Paul Underwood Spencer *(Tribe of Two Press)*

1985
IN THE YEAR OF THE BOAR AND JACKIE ROBINSON by
Bette Bao Lord *(Harper)*

1986
SARAH, PLAIN AND TALL by Patricia MacLachlan *(Harper)*

1987
AFTER THE DANCING DAYS by Margaret I. Rostkowski
(Harper)

1988
LINCOLN: A PHOTOBIOGRAPHY by Russell Freedman
(Clarion)

1989
ANTHONY BURNS: THE DEFEAT AND TRIUMPH OF A
FUGITIVE SLAVE by Virginia Hamilton *(Knopf)*

1990
SHADES OF GRAY by Carolyn Reeder *(Macmillan)*

1991
FRANKLIN DELANO ROOSEVELT by Russell Freedman
(Clarion)

1992
THE WRIGHT BROTHERS: HOW THEY INVENTED THE
AIRPLANE by Russell Freedman *(Holiday House)*

Ezra Jack Keats New Writer Award ❧

Administered by the Early Childhood Resources and Information
Center of the New York Public Library (66 Leroy St., New
York, NY 10014), and funded by the Ezra Jack Keats
Foundation, this award is for a promising new writer of not
more than six published children's picture books "that reflect the
tradition of Ezra Jack Keats" (1916-1983), a Caldecott Medal
winner whose books often featured multicultural settings and
portrayed strong family relationships. Honorees need not have
illustrated the book(s) nominated for the award; books must
appeal to children ages 9 and under. The award is now given at
two-year intervals. (Medallion and honorarium)

1986
THE PATCHWORK QUILT by Valerie Flournoy, ill. by Jerry
Pinkney *(Dial)*

1987
JAMAICA'S FIND by Juanita Havill, ill. by Anne Sibley O'Brien
(Houghton)

1988
ANNA'S SPECIAL PRESENT by Yoriko Tsutsui, ill. by Akiko Hayashi *(Viking)*
1990
TELL ME A STORY, MAMA by Angela Johnson, ill. by David Soman *(Orchard)*

Keene State College Children's Literature Festival Award ❧

The award is for an author and/or illustrator who has made outstanding contributions over a period of years and whose "work shows variety and diversity while maintaining the highest standards in literature for children." (Keene State College Children's Literature Festival, 229 Main Street, Keene, NH 03431) (Honorarium and engraved Paul Revere bowl)

1986 Maurice Sendak
1987 Katherine Paterson
1988 Leo and Diane Dillon
1989 Barbara Cooney
1990 Betsy Byars
1991 Trina Schart Hyman

Kerlan Award ❧

Established in 1975 by the Twenty-Fifth Kerlan Anniversary Committee of the University of Minnesota (The Kerlan Collection, 109 Walter Library, Minneapolis, MN 55455), the award is given "in recognition of singular attainments in the creation of children's literature and in appreciation for generous donation of unique resources to the Kerlan Collection for the study of children's literature." (Plaque)

1975 Marie Hall Ets
      Elizabeth Coatsworth
      Marguerite Henry
1976 Roger Duvoisin
1977 Wanda Gág

1978 Carol Ryrie Brink
1979 Margot Zemach
1980 Glen Rounds
1981 Tomie de Paola
1982 Jean Craighead George
1983 Katherine Paterson
1984 Margaret Wise Brown (Also honored were Brown's editors and illustrators, represented by Clement Hurd, illustrator of Brown's GOODNIGHT MOON.)
1985 Eleanor Cameron
1986 Charlotte Zolotow
1987 Charles Mikolaycak
1988 Jane Yolen
1989 Gail E. Haley
1990 Madeleine L'Engle
1991 Leonard Everett Fisher
1992 Barbara Cooney

Coretta Scott King Awards

This award was designed "to commemorate and foster the life, works and dreams" of Dr. Martin Luther King, Jr., and to honor his wife Coretta Scott King "for her courage and determination to continue the work for peace and world brotherhood." The award is given annually to a black author *(A)* and, since 1974, to a black illustrator *(I)*, whose books, published in the preceding year, are outstanding, inspirational and educational contributions to literature for children and young people. The awards are administered by the Social Responsibilities Round Table, with the cooperation of the Association for Library Service to Children, of the American Library Association (50 E. Huron St., Chicago, IL 60611). (Citation, honorarium and an encyclopedia)

1970
MARTIN LUTHER KING, JR.: MAN OF PEACE by Lillie Patterson *(Garrard)*
1971
BLACK TROUBADOR: LANGSTON HUGHES by Charlemae Rollins *(Rand McNally)*
1972
17 BLACK ARTISTS by Elton C. Fax *(Dodd)*
1973
I NEVER HAD IT MADE by Jackie Robinson as told to Alfred Duckett *(Putnam)*

1974
A: RAY CHARLES by Sharon Bell Mathis *(Crowell)*
I: the same title, ill. by George Ford

1975
A: THE LEGEND OF AFRICANA by Dorothy Robinson *(Johnson)*
I: the same title, ill. by Herbert Temple

1976
A: DUEY'S TALE by Pearl Bailey *(HBJ)*
I: No Award

1977
A: THE STORY OF STEVIE WONDER by James Haskins *(Lothrop)*
I: No Award

1978
A: AFRICA DREAM by Eloise Greenfield *(Day/Crowell)*
I: the same title, ill. by Carole Bayard

1979
A: ESCAPE TO FREEDOM by Ossie Davis *(Viking)*
I: SOMETHING ON MY MIND by Nikki Grimes, ill. by Tom Feelings *(Dial)*

1980
A: THE YOUNG LANDLORDS by Walter Dean Myers *(Viking)*
I: CORNROWS by Camille Yarbrough, ill. by Carole Bayard *(Coward)*

1981
A: THIS LIFE by Sidney Poitier *(Knopf)*
I: BEAT THE STORY-DRUM, PUM-PUM by Ashley Bryan *(Atheneum)*

1982
A: LET THE CIRCLE BE UNBROKEN by Mildred D. Taylor *(Dial)*
I: MOTHER CROCODILE: AN UNCLE AMADOU TALE FROM SENEGAL adapted by Rosa Guy, ill. by John Steptoe *(Delacorte)*

1983
A: SWEET WHISPERS, BROTHER RUSH by Virginia Hamilton *(Philomel)*
I: BLACK CHILD by Peter Mugabane *(Knopf)*

1984
A: EVERETT ANDERSON'S GOOD-BYE by Lucille Clifton *(Holt)*
I: MY MAMA NEEDS ME by Mildred Pitts Walter, ill. by Pat Cummings *(Lothrop)*

1985
A: MOTOWN AND DIDI by Walter Dean Myers *(Viking)*
I: No Award

1986
A: THE PEOPLE COULD FLY: AMERICAN BLACK
FOLKTALES by Virginia Hamilton *(Knopf)*
I: THE PATCHWORK QUILT by Valerie Flournoy, ill. by
Jerry Pinkney *(Dial)*

1987
A: JUSTIN AND THE BEST BISCUITS IN THE WORLD by
Mildred Pitts Walter *(Lothrop)*
I: HALF A MOON AND ONE WHOLE STAR by Crescent
Dragonwagon, ill. by Jerry Pinkney *(Macmillan)*

1988
A: THE FRIENDSHIP by Mildred D. Taylor *(Dial)*
I: MUFARO'S BEAUTIFUL DAUGHTERS: AN AFRICAN
TALE by John Steptoe *(Lothrop)*

1989
A: FALLEN ANGELS by Walter Dean Myers *(Scholastic)*
I: MIRANDY AND BROTHER WIND by Patricia McKissack,
ill. by Jerry Pinkney *(Knopf)*

1990
A: A LONG HARD JOURNEY: THE STORY OF THE
PULLMAN PORTER by Patricia and Frederick McKissack *(Walker)*
I: NATHANIEL TALKING by Eloise Greenfield, ill. by Jan
Spivey Gilchrist *(Black Butterfly)*

1991
A: THE ROAD TO MEMPHIS by Mildred D. Taylor *(Dial)*
I: AÏDA told by Leontyne Price, ill. by Leo and Diane Dillon
(Gulliver/HBJ)

1992
A: NOW IS YOUR TIME!: THE AFRICAN AMERICAN
STRUGGLE FOR FREEDOM by Walter Dean Myers
(HarperCollins)
I: TAR BEACH by Faith Ringgold *(Crown)*

Knickerbocker Award for Juvenile Literature ❧

This award honors a living author currently residing in New
York State whose body of work is of superior quality and
supports the educational needs of students. Its sponsor is the
School Library Media Section of the New York Library
Association (252 Hudson Ave., Albany, NY 12210). (Crystal
trapezoid depicting children in a schoolhouse filled with books)

1991   Jean Craighead George

Judy Lopez Memorial Award 🍂

Sponsored by the Women's National Book Association/Los Angeles Chapter (P. O. Box 807, Burbank, CA 91503-0807), this award honors the memory of one if its founding members, who was active in publishing and bookselling professions, and who had a strong interest in literacy development. Eligible titles are "works of literary excellence for nine to twelve year olds, written by a citizen or resident of the United States." We list the award year; winners were published in the preceding year. (Medal and honorarium)

1986
PRAIRIE SONGS by Pam Conrad *(Harper)*
1987
COME A STRANGER by Cynthia Voigt *(Atheneum)*
1988
M. E. AND MORTON by Sylvia Cassedy *(Crowell)*
1989
THE TROUBLE WITH GRAMARY by Betty Levin *(Greenwillow)*
1990
THE WINTER ROOM by Gary Paulsen *(Orchard)*
1991
THE TRUE CONFESSIONS OF CHARLOTTE DOYLE by Avi *(Orchard)*

Lupine Award 🍂

Sponsored by the Children's and Young Adult's Services Section of the Maine Library Association (Local Government Center, Community Drive, Augusta, ME 04330), this award is for an outstanding contribution to children's literature from or about Maine, and published in the year before the award presentation. It takes its name from the glorious landscape depicted, among other places, in Barbara Cooney's *Miss Rumphius*. (Plate with picture of lupine; honoree selects a library as recipient of gift copy of book)

1990
BRICKYARD SUMMER by Paul Janeczko *(Orchard)*
1991
HATTIE AND THE WILD WAVES by Barbara Cooney *(Viking)*

David McCord
Children's Literature Citation 🍂

Sponsored by Framingham State College (Curriculum Library, Framingham State College, Framingham, MA 01701) and the Nobscot Reading Council of the International Reading Association, this award is for "significant contribution to excellence" in the field of children's books. It honors David McCord, first recipient of the National Council of Teachers of English Award for Excellence in Poetry for Children, and recipient of Harvard's first honorary degree of Doctor of Humane Letters. It was originally presented as part of notable anniversary observances of both its sponsors, and is designed to single out authors or illustrators whose work continues David McCord's traditions. (Engraved Jefferson cup, citation, and honorarium)

1986   Tomie dePaola
1987   Steven Kellogg
1988   Jean Fritz
1989   Peter Spier
1990   Barbara Cooney
1991   Rosemary Wells

Minnesota Book Awards 🍂
CHILDREN'S BOOK CATEGORIES

"The Minnesota Book Awards recognizes, promotes, and celebrates the rich variety of resident authors and illustrators who contribute to the state's quality of life. The intention of this awards program is to strengthen the linkages among the Minnesota community of the book between authors and illustrators, publishers, the mass media, booksellers, librarians, and other educators, and readers. In this awards program, identification of winners is subordinate to these greater aims." Awards are given in several categories; books suitable for young readers may be honored in other categories *(noted +)*, as well. The award "year" for the program changed in 1991. The sponsors are the Minnesota Center for the Book, Metronet, *Minnesota Reviews*, and—the source for information about the program—the Office of Library Development & Services (550 Cedar St., 440 Capitol Square Bldg., Saint Paul, MN 55101). (Certificate)

1988
Younger children: THE STAR MAIDEN: AN OJIBWAY TALE
by Barbara Juster Esbensen *(Little, Brown)*
Older children: HATCHET by Gary Paulsen *(Bradbury)*
1989
Children: GOING THE MOOSE WAY HOME by Jim Latimer
(Scribner)
Book arts +: THE ARCTIC WOLF: LIVING WITH THE
PACK by L. David Mech *(Voyageur)*
1991 (see introductory note)
Younger children: HOW THE GUINEA FOWL GOT HER
SPOTS: A SWAHILI TALE retold and ill. by Barbara Knutson
(Carolrhoda)
Older children: WOODSONG by Gary Paulsen *(Bradbury)*
Science fiction & fantasy +: DEALING WITH DRAGONS by
Patricia C. Wrede *(Jane Yolen/HBJ)*

Mountains and Plains Booksellers Association Awards ⮞

CHILDREN'S/YOUNG ADULT
BOOK CATEGORY

The Mountains and Plains Booksellers Association (805 LaPorte
Ave., Fort Collins, CO 80521) gives awards at its annual Trade
Show and Author Banquet to "regional" books and/or authors in
four categories, including an award for a book for young readers.

1990
BEARSTONE by Will Hobbs *(Atheneum)*
1991
CANYONS by Gary Paulsen *(Delacorte)*

National Council of Teachers of English Award for Excellence in Poetry for Children ⮞

Sponsored by the National Council of Teachers of English (1111
Kenyon Rd., Urbana, IL 61801), the award was given annually
1977-1982 to a living American poet in recognition of an
aggregate body of work for children ages 3-13. Currently, the

award is presented every three years. (Citation and medallion design of seal for dust jacket use)

1977   David McCord
1978   Aileen Fisher
1979   Karla Kuskin
1980   Myra Cohn Livingston
1981   Eve Merriam
1982   John Ciardi
1985   Lilian Moore
1988   Arnold Adoff
1991   Valerie Worth

National Jewish Book Awards ⪪
CHILDREN'S BOOK CATEGORIES

Sponsored by the JWB Jewish Book Council (15 E. 26th St., New York, NY 10010), this awards program is designed to promote American Jewish literary creativity and an appreciation of Jewish literature. The awards program includes several categories. Since 1952 a Children's Literature award has been given to the writer of a specific book or to an author for a cumulative contribution to Jewish juvenile literature. Beginning in 1983, an award for an Illustrated Children's Book (I) has been given when warranted. (Certificate and $750)

1952
ALL-OF-A-KIND FAMILY by Sydney Taylor *(Follett)*
1953
STAR LIGHT STORIES *(Bloch)* and STORIES OF KING DAVID *(Jewish Publication Society)* by Lillian S. Freehof
1954
THE JEWISH PEOPLE: BOOK THREE by Deborah Pessin *(United Synagogue Commission)*
1955
KING SOLOMON'S NAVY by Nora Benjamin Kubie *(Harper)*
1956
Sadie Rose Weilerstein
1957
Elma E. Levinger
1958
JEWISH JUNIOR ENCYCLOPEDIA by Naomi Ben Asher and Hayim Leaf *(Shengold)*

1959
BORDER HAWK: AUGUST BONDI by Lloyd Alexander
(Farrar)
1960
KEYS TO A MAGIC DOOR: ISAAC LEIB PERETZ by Sylvia
Rothchild *(Farrar)*
1961
DISCOVERING ISRAEL by Regina Tor *(Random)*
1962
TEN AND A KID by Sadie Rose Weilerstein *(Doubleday)*
1963
RETURN TO FREEDOM by Josephine Kamm *(Abelard)*
1964
A BOY OF OLD PRAGUE by Sulamith Ish-Kishor *(Pantheon)*
1965
WORLDS LOST AND FOUND by Dov Peretz Elkins and Azriel
Eisenberg *(Abelard)*
1966
THE DREYFUS AFFAIR by Betty Schechter *(Houghton)*
1967
THE STORY OF ISRAEL by Meyer Levin *(Putnam)*
1968-1969
No Awards
1970
MARTIN BUBER: WISDOM IN OUR TIME by Charlie May
Simon *(Dutton)*
THE STORY OF MASADA retold by Gerald Gottlieb *(Random)*
1971
JOURNEY TO AMERICA by Sonia Levitin *(Atheneum)*
1972
THE MASTER OF MIRACLE: A NEW NOVEL OF THE
GOLEM by Sulamith Ish-Kishor *(Harper)*
1973
THE UPSTAIRS ROOM by Johanna Reiss *(Crowell)*
1974
UNCLE MISHA'S PARTISANS by Yuri Suhl *(Four Winds)*
1975
THE HOLOCAUST: A HISTORY OF COURAGE AND
RESISTANCE by Bea Stadtler *(Behrman House)*
1976
HAYM SALOMON: LIBERTY'S SON by Shirley Milgrim
(Jewish Publication Society)
1977
RIFKA GROWS UP by Chaya Burstein *(Bonim Books/Hebrew
Publishing Co.)*

1978
NEVER TO FORGET: THE JEWS OF THE HOLOCAUST by
Milton Meltzer *(Harper)*
1979
JOSHUA: FIGHTER FOR BAR KOCHBA by Irene Narell
(Akiba Press)
1980
DITA SAXOVA by Arnost Lustig *(Harper)*
1981
A RUSSIAN FAREWELL by Leonard Everett Fisher *(Four
Winds)*
1982
THE NIGHT JOURNEY by Kathryn Lasky *(Warne)*
1983
KING OF THE SEVENTH GRADE by Barbara Cohen
(Lothrop)
I: YUSSEL'S PRAYER: A YOM KIPPUR STORY by Barbara
Cohen, ill. by Michael Deraney *(Lothrop)*
1984
THE JEWISH KIDS CATALOG by Chaya M. Burstein *(Jewish
Publication Society)*
1985
GOOD IF IT GOES by Gary Provost and Gail Levine-Freidus
(Bradbury)
I: MRS. MOSKOWITZ AND THE SABBATH CANDLESTICKS
by Amy Schwartz *(Jewish Publication Society)*
1986
IN KINDLING FLAME: THE STORY OF HANNAH SENESH,
1921-1944 by Linda Atkinson *(Lothrop)*
I: BROTHERS retold by Florence B. Freedman, ill. by Robert
Andrew Parker *(Harper)*
1987
MONDAY IN ODESSA by Eileen Bluestone Sherman *(Jewish
Publication Society)*
I: POEMS FOR JEWISH HOLIDAYS selected by Myra Cohn
Livingston, ill. by Lloyd Bloom *(Holiday House)*
1988
THE RETURN by Sonia Levitin *(Atheneum)*
I: EXODUS adapted from the Bible by Miriam Chaikin, ill. by
Charles Mikolaycak *(Holiday House)*
1989
THE DEVIL'S ARITHMETIC by Jane Yolen *(Viking)*
I: JUST ENOUGH IS PLENTY: A HANUKKAH TALE by
Barbara Diamond Goldin, ill. by Seymour Chwast *(Viking)*
1990
NUMBER THE STARS by Lois Lowry *(Houghton)*

I: BERCHICK by Esther Silverstein Blanc, ill. by Tennessee Dixon *(Volcano)*

1991
BECOMING GERSHONA by Nava Semel *(Viking)*
I: HANUKKAH! by Roni Schotter, ill. by Marylin Hafner *(Joy Street/Little, Brown)*

1992
THE MAN FROM THE OTHER SIDE by Uri Orlev, translated by Hillel Halkin *(Houghton)*
I: CHICKEN MAN by Michelle Edwards *(Lothrop)*

New England Book Awards

CHILDREN'S BOOK CATEGORY

This annual awards program is designed "to focus attention on the lifetime achievements of New England's outstanding community of writers, book illustrators, and book publishers." Achievement in children's literature is one of the areas honored. The sponsor and administrator is the New England Booksellers Association (45 Newbury St., Boston, MA 02116), which solicits nominations for the awards from its over 500 bookstore members. (Announcement, ceremony, and gift)

1990   Jan Brett
1991   Barbara Cooney
1992   Katherine Paterson

New Voices/New World Minority Fiction Contest

This contest is for "writers from ethnic minority backgrounds who have never published a children's book" and whose manuscripts should be for a picture book, for middle-grade readers, or for young adult readers. The sponsor is Joy Street Books/Little, Brown & Co. (34 Beacon St., Boston, MA 02108). ($5,000 cash award and a contract for publication to be negotiated with the sponsor)

1990
DUMPLING SOUP by Jama Kim Rattigan, ill. by Lillian Hsu-Flanders *(Joy Street/ Little, Brown)* (1992 title)

New York Academy of Sciences ?&
CHILDREN'S SCIENCE BOOK AWARDS

The New York Academy of Sciences (2 East 63rd St., New York, NY 10021) has presented awards for children's books "to encourage the writing of more high-quality books about science for children" and to "bring the importance of science to the attention of children and to adults who work with children, thus helping to promote a greater understanding of the role science plays in today's world." First given to one book, in the second year of the program awards were given in two categories, Younger (Y) and Older (O). As the program matured, illustrators were included as honorees if the author was not the illustrator. The program also included Special Awards for, for example, an outstanding series, outstanding photography, body of work, etc., as well as excellent Honorable Mention lists of titles highly regarded by the distinguished panel of judges reviewing submissions. Our listing is of the presentation year. The program was temporarily discontinued after the 1990 presentations; the New York Academy of Sciences plans to continue it in due course. (Citations, and also honoraria, shared between authors and illustrators when the award is for both)

1972
THE STARS AND SERENDIPITY by Robert Richardson
(Pantheon)

1973
Y: CITY LEAVES, CITY TREES by Edward Gallob (Scribner)
0: READING THE PAST by Leonard Cottrell (Crowell-Collier)

1974
Y: THE WEB IN THE GRASS by Berniece Freschet (Scribner)
0: A NATURAL HISTORY OF GIRAFFES by Dorcas MacClintock and Ugo Mochi (Scribner)

1975
Y: SEE WHAT I AM by Roger Duvoisin (Lothrop)
0: HUNTERS OF THE WHALE by Ruth Kirk and Richard D. Daugherty (Morrow)

1976
Y: EMPEROR PENGUIN by Jean-Claude Deguine (Stephen Greene)
0: DOCTOR IN THE ZOO by Bruce Buchenholz (Viking)

1977
Y: CORN IS MAIZE by Aliki (Crowell)
0: WATCHING THE WILD APES by Bettyann Kevles (Dutton)

1978
Y: WILD MOUSE by Irene Brady (Scribner)

0: GRAINS by Elizabeth Burton Brown *(Prentice-Hall)*

1979

Y: THE SMALLEST LIFE AROUND US by Lucia Anderson, ill. by Leigh Grant *(Crown)*

0: LASER LIGHT by Herman Schneider, ill. by Radu Vero *(McGraw-Hill)*

1980

Y: A SPACE STORY by Karla Kuskin, ill. by Marc Simont *(Harper)*

0: BUILDING: THE FIGHT AGAINST GRAVITY by Mario Salvadori, ill. by Saralinda Hooker and Christopher Ragus *(McElderry)*

1981

Y: BET YOU CAN'T! by Vicki Cobb and Kathy Darling, ill. by Martha Weston *(Lothrop)*

0: MOVING HEAVY THINGS by Jan Adkins *(Houghton)*

1982

Y: MESSING AROUND WITH WATER PUMPS AND SIPHONS by Bernie Zubrowski, ill. by Steve Lindblom *(Little, Brown)*

1983

Y: THE SNAIL'S SPELL by Joanne Ryder, ill. by Lynne Cherry *(Warne)*

0: THE BROOKLYN BRIDGE: THEY SAID IT COULDN'T BE BUILT by Judith St. George *(Putnam)*

1984

Y: OAK & COMPANY by Richard Mabey, ill. by Clare Roberts *(Greenwillow)*

0: VOLCANO WEATHER by Henry Stommel and Elizabeth Stommel *(Seven Seas)*

1985

Y: THE SECRET LANGUAGE OF SNOW by Terry Tempest Williams and Ted Major, ill. by Jennifer Dewey *(Sierra Club/Pantheon)*

0: THE DAYWATCHERS by Peter Parnall *(Macmillan)*

1986

Y: THE BIG STRETCH by Ada and Frank Graham, ill. by Richard Rosenblum *(Knopf)*

0: BREAKTHROUGH: THE TRUE STORY OF PENICILLIN by Francine Jacobs *(Dodd)*

1987

Y: WHEN SHEEP CANNOT SLEEP: THE COUNTING BOOK by Satoshi Kitamura *(Farrar)*

0: THE EVOLUTION BOOK by Sara Stein, photog. by Rona Beame *(Workman)*

1988

Y: ICEBERGS AND GLACIERS by Seymour Simon *(Morrow)*

O: EXPLORING THE NIGHT SKY by Terence Dickinson, ill. by John Bianchi *(Camden)*

1989
No presentations

1990
Y: THE SIERRA CLUB WAYFINDING BOOK by Vicki McVey, ill. by Martha Weston *(Sierra Club/Little, Brown)*
O: DIGGING DINOSAURS by John R. Horner and James Gorman, ill. by Donna Braginetz and Kris Ellingsen *(Workman)*

New York Times Best Illustrated Children's Books of the Year 🕬

Sponsored by *The New York Times* (229 W. 43rd St., New York, NY 10036), this annual selection of best illustrated children's books of the year by a panel of three judges was initiated in 1952. (Certificate)

1952
THE ANIMAL FAIR by Alice and Martin Provensen *(Golden)*
BEASTS AND NONSENSE by Marie Hall Ets *(Viking)*
THE DOGCATCHER'S DOG by Andre Dugo *(Holt)*
FIVE LITTLE MONKEYS by Juliet Kepes *(Houghton)*
THE HAPPY PLACE by Ludwig Bemelmans *(Little, Brown)*
A HOLE IS TO DIG by Ruth Krauss, ill. by Maurice Sendak *(Harper)*
THE MAGIC CURRANT BUN by John Symonds, ill. by André Francois *(Lippincott)*

1953
FAST IS NOT A LADYBUG by Miriam Schlein, ill. by Leonard Kessler *(Scott)*
FLORINA AND THE WILD BIRD by Selina Chonz, ill. by Alois Carigiet *(Walck)*
THE GOLDEN BIBLE FOR CHILDREN: THE NEW TESTAMENT edited by Elsa Jane Werner, ill. by Alice and Martin Provensen *(Golden)*
GREEN EYES by A. Birnbaum *(Golden)*
A HERO BY MISTAKE by Anita Brenner, ill. by Jean Charlot *(Scott)*
LUCKY BLACKY by Eunice Lackey, ill. by Winifred Greene *(Watts)*
MADELINE'S RESCUE by Ludwig Bemelmans *(Viking)*
MOTHER GOOSE RIDDLE RHYMES by Joseph Low *(HBJ)*
PITSCHI by Hans Fischer *(HBJ)*

WHO GAVE US? by Madeleine Gekiere *(Pantheon)*

1954

ANDY SAYS BONJOUR by Pat Diska, ill. by Chris Jenkyns *(Vanguard)*

THE ANIMAL FROLIC by 12th century Japanese artist, probably Toba Sojo *(Putnam)*

CIRCUS RUCKUS by Will, ill. by Nicolas *(HBJ)*

THE HAPPY LION by Louise Fatio, ill. by Roger Duvoisin *(McGraw-Hill)*

HEAVY IS A HIPPOPOTAMUS by Miriam Schlein, ill. by Leonard Kessler *(Scott)*

I'LL BE YOU AND YOU BE ME by Ruth Krauss, ill. by Maurice Sendak *(Harper)*

JENNY'S BIRTHDAY BOOK by Esther Averill *(Harper)*

A KISS IS ROUND by Blossom Budney, ill. by Vladimir Bobri *(Lothrop)*

THE SUN LOOKS DOWN by Miriam Schlein, ill. by Abner Graboff *(Abelard)*

THE WET WORLD by Norma Simon, ill. by Jane Miller *(Lippincott)*

1955

BEASTS FROM A BRUSH by Juliet Kepes *(Pantheon)*

CHAGA by Will, ill. by Nicolas *(HBJ)*

THE HAPPY LION IN AFRICA by Louise Fatio, ill. by Roger Duvoisin *(McGraw-Hill)*

A LITTLE HOUSE OF YOUR OWN by Beatrice Schenk de Regniers, ill. by Irene Haas *(HBJ)*

PARSLEY by Ludwig Bemelmans *(Harper)*

RUMPLESTILTSKIN by Jan B. Balet *(Rand McNally)*

SEE AND SAY by Antonio Frasconi *(HBJ)*

SWITCH ON THE NIGHT by Ray Bradbury, ill. by Madeleine Gekiere *(Pantheon)*

THE THREE KINGS OF SABA by Alf Evers, ill. by Helen Sewell *(Lippincott)*

UNCLE BEN'S WHALE by Walter D. Edmonds, ill. by William Gropper *(Dodd)*

1956

BABAR'S FAIR by Laurent De Brunhoff *(Random)*

CROCODILE TEARS by André Francois *(Universe)*

I KNOW A LOT OF THINGS by Ann Rand, ill. by Paul Rand *(HBJ)*

I WANT TO PAINT MY BATHROOM BLUE by Ruth Krauss, ill. by Maurice Sendak *(Harper)*

I WILL TELL YOU OF A TOWN by Alistair Reid, ill. by Walter Lorraine *(Houghton)*

JONAH THE FISHERMAN by Reiner Zimnik *(Pantheon)*

LITTLE BIG-FEATHER by Joseph Longstretch, ill. by Helen Borten *(Abelard)*

THE LITTLE ELEPHANT by Ylla *(Harper)*

REALLY SPRING by Gene Zion, ill. by Margaret Bloy Graham *(Harper)*

WAS IT A GOOD TRADE? by Beatrice Schenk de Regniers, ill. by Irene Haas *(HBJ)*

1957

BIG RED BUS by Ethel Kessler, ill. by Leonard Kessler *(Doubleday)*

THE BIRTHDAY PARTY by Ruth Krauss, ill. by Maurice Sendak *(Harper)*

CURIOUS GEORGE GETS A MEDAL by H.A. Rey *(Houghton)*

DEAR GARBAGE MAN by Gene Zion, ill. by Margaret Bloy Graham *(Harper)*

FAINT GEORGE by Robert E. Barry *(Houghton)*

THE FISHERMAN AND HIS WIFE by the Brothers Grimm, ill. by Madeleine Geikiere *(Pantheon)*

THE FRIENDLY BEASTS by Laura Baker, ill. by Nicholas Sidjakov *(Parnassus)*

THE RED BALLOON by Albert Lamorisse *(Doubleday)*

SPARKLE AND SPIN by Ann Rand, ill. by Paul Rand *(HBJ)*

THE UNHAPPY HIPPOPOTAMUS by Nancy Moore, ill. by Edward Leight *(Vanguard)*

1958

ALL ABOARD by Mary Britton Miller, ill. by Bill Sokol *(Pantheon)*

CHOUCHOU by Francoise *(Scribner)*

THE DADDY DAYS by Norma Simon, ill. by Abner Graboff *(Abelard)*

A FRIEND IS SOMEONE WHO LIKES YOU by Joan Walsh Anglund *(HBJ)*

THE GIANT GOLDEN BOOK OF ANIMALS by Anne Terry White, ill. by W. Suschitzy *(Golden)*

THE HOUSE THAT JACK BUILT by Antonio Frasconi *(HBJ)*

HOW TO HIDE A HIPPOPOTAMUS by Volney Croswell *(Dodd)*

THE MAGIC FEATHER DUSTER by Will, ill. by Nicolas Mordvinoff *(HBJ)*

ROLAND by Nelly Stephane, ill. by André Francois *(HBJ)*

WHAT DO YOU SAY, DEAR? by Sesyle Joslin, ill. by Maurice Sendak *(Scott)*

1959

ANIMAL BABIES by Arthur Gregor, ill. by Ylla *(Harper)*

FATHER BEAR COMES HOME by Else Holmelund Minarik, ill. by Maurice Sendak *(Harper)*

THE FIRST NOEL by Alice and Martin Provensen *(Golden)*

FULL OF WONDER by Ann Kirn *(World)*

THE GIRL IN THE WHITE HAT by W.T. Cummings *(McGraw-Hill)*

KASIMIR'S JOURNEY by Monroe Stearns, ill. by Marlene Reidel *(Lippincott)*

LITTLE BLUE AND LITTLE YELLOW by Leo Lionni *(Astor-Honor)*

PABLO PAINTS A PICTURE by Warren Miller, ill. by Edward Sorel *(Little, Brown)*

THE REASON FOR THE PELICAN by John Ciardi, ill. by Madeleine Gekiere *(Lippincott)*

THIS IS LONDON by Miroslav Sasek *(Macmillan)*

1960

A B C by Bruno Munari *(World)*

THE ADVENTURES OF ULYSSES by Jacque le Marchand, ill. by André Francois *(Criterion)*

BABOUSHKA AND THE THREE KINGS by Ruth Robbins, ill. by Nicholas Sidjakov *(Parnassus)*

INCH BY INCH by Leo Lionni *(Astor-Honor)*

OPEN HOUSE FOR BUTTERFLIES by Ruth Krauss, ill. by Maurice Sendak *(Harper)*

SCRAPPY THE PUP by John Ciardi, ill. by Jane Miller *(Lippincott)*

THE SHADOW BOOK by Beatrice Schenk de Regniers, ill. by Isabel Gordon *(HBJ)*

THIS IS NEW YORK by Miroslav Sasek *(Macmillan)*

26 WAYS TO BE SOMEBODY ELSE by Devorah Boxer *(Pantheon)*

TWO LITTLE BIRDS AND THREE by Juliet Kepes *(Houghton)*

1961

THE BIG BOOK OF ANIMAL STORIES edited by Margaret Green, ill. by Janusz Grabianski *(Watts)*

DEAR RAT by Julia Cunningham, ill. by Walter Lorraine *(Houghton)*

THE HAPPY HUNTER by Roger Duvoisin *(Lothrop)*

LISTEN—THE BIRDS by Mary Britton Miller, ill. by Evaline Ness *(Pantheon)*

MY TIME OF YEAR by Katherine Dow, ill. by Walter Erhard *(Walck)*

ONCE A MOUSE...by Marcia Brown *(Scribner)*

SANDPIPERS by Edith Thacher Hurd, ill. by Lucienne Bloch *(Crowell)*

THE SNOW AND THE SUN by Antonio Frasconi *(HBJ)*

UMBRELLAS, HATS, AND WHEELS by Ann Rand, ill. by Jerome Snyder *(HBJ)*

THE WING ON A FLEA by Ed Emberley *(Little, Brown)*

1962

BOOKS! by Murray McCain, ill. by John Alcorn *(Simon & Schuster)*

THE EMPEROR AND THE DRUMMER BOY by Ruth Robbins, ill. by Nicholas Sidjakov *(Parnassus)*

GENNARINO by Nicola Simbari *(Lippincott)*

THE ISLAND OF FISH IN THE TREES by Eva-Lis Wuorio, ill. by Edward Ardizzone *(World)*

KAY-KAY COMES HOME by Nicholas Samstag, ill. by Ben Shahn *(Astor-Honor)*
LITTLE OWL by Reiner Zimnik, ill. by Hanne Axmann *(Atheneum)*
THE PRINCESSES by Sally P. Johnson, ill. by Beni Montresor *(Harper)*
THE SINGING HILL by Meindert DeJong, ill. by Maurice Sendak *(Harper)*
THE TALE OF A WOOD by Henry B. Kane *(Knopf)*
THE THREE ROBBERS by Tomi Ungerer *(Atheneum)*

1963
THE GREAT PICTURE ROBBERY by Leon Harris, ill. by Joseph Schindelman *(Atheneum)*
GWENDOLYN AND THE WEATHERCOCK by Nancy Sherman, ill. by Edward Sorel *(Golden)*
A HOLIDAY FOR MISTER MUSTER by Arnold Lobel *(Harper)*
HURLY BURLY AND THE KNIGHTS by Milton Rugoff, ill. by Emanuele Luzzati *(Platt & Munk)*
JOHN J. PLENTY AND FIDDLER DAN by John Ciardi, ill. by Madeleine Gekiere *(Lippincott)*
KAREN'S CURIOSITY by Alice and Martin Provensen *(Golden)*
ONCE UPON A TOTEM by Christie Harris, ill. by John Frazer Mills *(Atheneum)*
PLUNKETY PLUNK by Peter J. Lippman *(Farrar)*
SWIMMY by Leo Lionni *(Pantheon)*
WHERE THE WILD THINGS ARE by Maurice Sendak *(Harper)*

1964
THE BAT-POET by Randall Jarrell, ill. by Maurice Sendak *(Macmillan)*
CASEY AT THE BAT by E.L. Thayer, ill. by Leonard Everett Fisher *(Watts)*
THE CHARGE OF THE LIGHT BRIGADE by Alfred Lord Tennyson, ill. by Alice and Martin Provensen *(Golden)*
EXACTLY ALIKE by Evaline Ness *(Scribner)*
THE GIRAFFE OF KING CHARLES X by Miche Wynants *(McGraw-Hill)*
THE HAPPY OWLS by Celestino Piatti *(Atheneum)*
I'LL SHOW YOU CATS by C.N. Bonsall, ill. by Ylla *(Harper)*
THE LIFE OF A QUEEN by Colette Portal *(Braziller)*
RAIN MAKES APPLESAUCE by Julian Scheer, ill. by Marvin Bileck *(Holiday House)*
THE WAVE by Margaret Hodges, ill. by Blair Lent *(Houghton)*

1965
ALBERIC THE WISE AND OTHER JOURNEYS by Norton Juster, ill. by Domenico Gnoli *(Pantheon)*
THE ANIMAL FAMILY by Randall Jarrell, ill. by Maurice Sendak *(Pantheon)*

A DOUBLE DISCOVERY by Evaline Ness *(Scribner)*
HIDE AND SEEK FOG by Alvin Tresselt, ill. by Roger Duvoisin
(Lothrop)
KANGAROO & KANGROO by K. Braun, ill. by Jim McMullan
(Doubleday)
PLEASE SHARE THAT PEANUT! by Sesyle Joslin, i!l. by
Simms Taback *(HBJ)*
PUNCH & JUDY by Ed Emberley *(Little, Brown)*
SVEN'S BRIDGE by Anita Lobel *(Harper)*
1966
ANANSE THE SPIDER by Peggy Appiah, ill. by Peggy Wilson
(Pantheon)
ANIMAL ABC by Celestino Piatti *(Atheneum)*
A BOY WENT OUT TO GATHER PEARS by Felix Hoffmann
(HBJ)
THE JAZZ MAN by Mary H. Weik, ill. by Ann Grifalconi
(Atheneum)
THE MAGIC FLUTE by Stephen Spender, ill. by Beni
Montresor *(Putnam)*
THE MONSTER DEN by John Ciardi, ill. by Edward Gorey
(Lippincott)
NOTHING EVER HAPPENS ON MY BLOCK by Ellen Raskin
(Atheneum)
SHAW'S FORTUNE by Edwin Tunis *(World)*
WONDERFUL TIME by Phyllis McGinley, ill. by John Alcorn
(Lippincott)
ZLATEH THE GOAT AND OTHER STORIES by Isaac
Bashevis Singer, ill. by Maurice Sendak *(Harper)*
1967
ANIMALS OF MANY LANDS by Hanns Reich *(Hill & Wang)*
BRIAN WILDSMITH'S BIRDS by Brian Wildsmith *(Watts)*
A DOG'S BOOK OF BUGS by Elizabeth Griffin, ill. by Peter
Parnall *(Atheneum)*
FABLES OF AESOP by Sir Roger L'Estrange, ill. by Alexander
Calder *(Dover)*
FREDERICK by Leo Lionni *(Pantheon)*
THE HONEYBEES by Franklin Russell, ill. by Collette Portal
(Knopf)
HUBERT by Wendy Stang and Susan Richards, ill. by Robert L.
Anderson *(Quist)*
KNEE-DEEP IN THUNDER by Sheila Moon, ill. by Peter
Parnall *(Atheneum)*
SEASHORE STORY by Taro Yashima *(Viking)*
1968
HARRIET AND THE PROMISED LAND by Jacob Lawrence
(Windmill/Simon & Schuster)
A KISS FOR LITTLE BEAR by Else Holmelund Minarik, ill. by
Maurice Sendak *(Harper)*

MALACHI MUDGE by Edward Cecil, ill. by Peter Parnall (*McGraw-Hill*)

MISTER CORBETT'S GHOST by Leon Garfield, ill. by Alan E. Cober (*Pantheon*)

THE REAL TIN FLOWER by Aliki Barnstone, ill. by Paul Giovanopoulos (*Crowell-Collier*)

THE SECRET JOURNEY OF HUGO THE BRAT by Francois Ruy-Vidal, ill. by Nicole Claveloux (*Quist*)

SPECTACLES by Ellen Raskin (*Atheneum*)

STORY NUMBER 1 by Eugene Ionesco, ill. by Etienne Delessert (*Quist*)

TALKING WITHOUT WORDS by Marie Hall Ets (*Viking*)

THE VERY OBLIGING FLOWERS by Claude Roy, ill. by Alain LeFoll (*Grove*)

1969

ARM IN ARM by Remy Charlip (*Four Winds*)

BANG BANG YOU'RE DEAD by Louise Fitzhugh and Sandra Scoppetone, ill. by Louise Fitzhugh (*Harper*)

BIRDS by Juliet Kepes (*Walker*)

THE CIRCUS IN THE MIST by Bruno Munari (*World*)

THE DONG WITH A LUMINOUS NOSE by Edward Lear, ill. by Edward Gorey (*Scott*)

FREE AS A FROG by Elizabeth Hodges, ill. by Paul Giovanopoulos (*Addison*)

LIGHT PRINCESS by George MacDonald, ill. by Maurice Sendak (*Farrar*)

SARA'S GRANNY AND THE GROODLE by Joan Gill, ill. by Seymour Chwast (*Doubleday*)

WHAT IS IT FOR? by Henry Humphrey (*Simon & Schuster*)

WINTER'S EVE by Natalia M. Belting, ill. by Alan E. Cober (*Holt*)

1970

ALALA by Guy Monreal, ill. by Nicole Claveloux (*Quist*)

FINDING A POEM by Eve Merriam, ill. by Seymour Chwast (*Atheneum*)

THE GNU AND THE GURU GO BEHIND THE BEYOND by Peggy Clifford, ill. by Eric von Schmidt (*Houghton*)

HELP, HELP, THE GLOBOLINKS by Gian-Carlo Menotti, adapted by Leigh Dean, ill. by Milton Glaser (*McGraw-Hill*)

IN THE NIGHT KITCHEN by Maurice Sendak (*Harper*)

LIFT EVERY VOICE AND SING by James Weldon Johnson and J. Rosamond, ill. by Mozelle Thompson (*Hawthorn*)

MATILDA WHO TOLD LIES AND WAS BURNED TO DEATH by Hillaire Belloc, ill. by Steven Kellogg (*Dial*)

TIMOTHY'S HORSE by Vladimir Mayakovsky, adapted by Guy Daniels, ill. by Flavio Constantini (*Pantheon*)

TOPSY-TURVIES: PICTURES TO STRETCH THE IMAGINATION by Mitsumasa Anno (*Weatherhill*)

YOU ARE RI-DI-CU-LOUS by André Francois *(Pantheon)*
1971
AMOS & BORIS by William Steig *(Farrar)*
BEAR CIRCUS by William Pène du Bois *(Viking)*
THE BEAST OF MONSIEUR RACINE by Tomi Ungerer
(Farrar)
CHANGES, CHANGES by Pat Hutchins *(Macmillan)*
LOOK AGAIN! by Tana Hoban *(Macmillan)*
LOOK WHAT I CAN DO by Jose Aruego *(Scribner)*
THE MAGIC TEARS by Jack Sendak, ill. by Mitchell Miller
(Harper)
MR. GUMPY'S OUTING by John Burningham *(Holt)*
ONE DANCING DRUM by Gail Kredenser and Stanley Mack,
ill. by Stanley Mack *(Phillips)*
THE SHRINKING OF TREEHORN by Florence Parry Heide,
ill. by Edward Gorey *(Holiday House)*
1972
BEHIND THE WHEEL by Edward Koren *(Holt)*
COUNT AND SEE by Tana Hoban *(Macmillan)*
GEORGE AND MARTHA by James Marshall *(Houghton)*
HOSIE'S ALPHABET by Hosea, Tobias and Lisa Baskin, ill. by
Leonard Baskin *(Viking)*
JUST SO STORIES by Rudyard Kipling, ill. by Etienne Delessert
(Doubleday)
A LITTLE SCHUBERT by M.B. Goffstein *(Harper)*
MISS JASTER'S GARDEN by N.M. Bodecker *(Golden)*
MOUSE CAFÉ by Patricia Coombs *(Lothrop)*
SIMON BOOM GIVES A WEDDING by Yuri Suhl, ill. by
Margot Zemach *(Four Winds)*
WHERE'S AL? by Byron Barton *(Seabury)*
1973
CATHEDRAL by David Macaulay *(Houghton)*
THE EMPEROR'S NEW CLOTHES by Hans Christian
Andersen, ill. by Monika Laimgruber *(Addison)*
HECTOR PENGUIN by Louise Fatio, ill. by Roger Duvoisin
(McGraw-Hill)
THE JUNIPER TREE AND OTHER TALES FROM GRIMM
ill. by Maurice Sendak *(Farrar)*
KING GRISLY-BEARD ill. by Maurice Sendak *(Farrar)*
NUMBER 24 by Guy Billout *(Quist)*
A PRAIRIE BOY'S WINTER by William Kurelek *(Houghton)*
THE SILVER PONY by Lynd Ward *(Houghton)*
TIM'S LAST VOYAGE by Edward Ardizzone *(Walck)*
1974
THE GIRL WHO CRIED FLOWERS by Jane Yolen, ill. by
David Palladini *(Crowell)*
A HOME by Lennart Rudstrom, ill. by Carl Larsson *(Putnam)*

LUMBERJACK by William Kurelek *(Houghton)*
THE MAN WHO TOOK THE INDOORS OUT by Arnold Lobel *(Harper)*
MISS SUZY'S BIRTHDAY by Miriam Young, ill. by Arnold Lobel *(Parents)*
ROSIE AND MICHAEL by Judith Viorst, ill. by Lorna Tomei *(Atheneum)*
A STORYBOOK by Tomi Ungerer *(Watts)*
THERE WAS AN OLD WOMAN by Steven Kellogg *(Four Winds)*

1975
ANNO'S ALPHABET by Mitsumasa Anno *(Crowell)*
A BOOK OF A-MAZE-MENTS by Jean Seisser and France de Ranchin *(Quist)*
MR. MICHAEL MOUSE UNFOLDS HIS TALE by Walter Crane *(Merrimack)*
THE PIG-TALE by Lewis Carroll, ill. by Leonard B. Lubin *(Little, Brown)*
THERE'S A SOUND IN THE SEA...A CHILD'S EYE VIEW OF THE WHALE collected by Tamar Griggs *(Scrimshaw)*
THIRTEEN by Remy Charlip and Jerry Joyner *(Four Winds)*
THE TUTTI-FRUTTI CASE by Harry Allard, ill. by James Marshall *(Prentice-Hall)*

1976
AS RIGHT AS RIGHT CAN BE by Anne Rose, ill. by Arnold Lobel *(Dial)*
ASHANTI TO ZULU by Margaret Musgrove, ill. by Leo and Diane Dillon *(Dial)*
THE BEAR AND THE FLY by Paula Winter *(Crown)*
EVERYONE KNOWS WHAT A DRAGON LOOKS LIKE by Jay Williams, ill. by Mercer Mayer *(Four Winds)*
FLY BY NIGHT by Randall Jarrell, ill. by Maurice Sendak *(Farrar)*
LITTLE THOUGH I BE by Joseph Low *(McGraw-Hill)*
MERRY EVER AFTER by Joe Lasker *(Viking)*
THE MOTHER GOOSE BOOK by Alice and Martin Provensen *(Random)*
A NEAR THING FOR CAPTAIN NAJORK by Russell Hoban, ill. by Quentin Blake *(Atheneum)*

1977
THE CHURCH MICE ADRIFT by Graham Oakley *(Atheneum)*
COME AWAY FROM THE WATER, SHIRLEY by John Burningham *(Crowell)*
IT COULD ALWAYS BE WORSE: A YIDDISH FOLK TALE retold and ill. by Margot Zemach *(Farrar)*
JACK AND THE WONDER BEANS by James Still, ill. by Margot Tomes *(Putnam)*

MERRY MERRY, FIBruary by Doris Orgel, ill. by Arnold Lobel
(Parents)
MY VILLAGE, STURBRIDGE by Gary Bowen, wood engravings
designed by Gary Bowen and engraved by Randy Miller *(Farrar)*
NOAH'S ARK by Peter Spier *(Doubleday)*
THE SURPRISE PICNIC by John S. Goodall *(McElderry)*
WHEN THE WIND BLEW by Margaret Wise Brown, ill. by
Geoffrey Hayes *(Harper)*

1978
CLOUDY WITH A CHANCE OF MEATBALLS by Judi Barrett,
ill. by Ron Barrett *(Atheneum)*
THE FORBIDDEN FOREST by William Pène du Bois *(Harper)*
THE GREAT SONG BOOK edited by Timothy John, music
editor Peter Hankey, ill. by Tomi Ungerer *(Doubleday/Benn)*
HANUKAH MONEY by Sholem Aleichem, ill. by Uri Shulevitz
(Greenwillow)
THE LEGEND OF SCARFACE: A BLACKFEET INDIAN
TALE by Robert San Souci, ill. by Daniel San Souci *(Doubleday)*
THE NUTCRACKERS AND THE SUGAR-TONGS by Edward
Lear, ill. by Marcia Sewall *(Atlantic-Little, Brown)*
ODETTE: A BIRD IN PARIS by Kay Fender, ill. by Phillipe
Dumas *(Prentice-Hall)*
A PEACEABLE KINGDOM: THE SHAKER ABECEDARIUS,
ill. by Alice and Martin Provensen *(Viking)*
THERE ONCE WAS A WOMAN WHO MARRIED A MAN by
Norma Farber, ill. by Lydia Dabcovich *(Addison)*
THIS LITTLE PIG-A-WIG AND OTHER RHYMES ABOUT
PIGS chosen by Lenore Blegvad, ill. by Erik Blegvad *(McElderry)*

1979
BY CAMEL OR BY CAR: A LOOK AT TRANSPORTATION
by Guy Billout *(Prentice-Hall)*
THE GARDEN OF ABDUL GASAZI by Chris Van Allsburg
(Houghton)
HAPPY BIRTHDAY OLIVER! by Pierre Le-Tan *(Random)*
KING KRAKUS AND THE DRAGON by Janina Domanska
(Greenwillow)
THE LONG DIVE by Mr. and Mrs. Smith *(Atheneum/Cape)*
NATURAL HISTORY by M.B. Goffstein *(Farrar)*
OX-CART MAN by Donald Hall, ill. by Barbara Cooney
(Viking)
THE TALE OF FANCY NANCY: A SPANISH FOLK TALE
adapted by Marion Koenig, ill. by Klaus Ensikat
(Chatto/Merrimack)
TILLY'S HOUSE by Faith Jaques *(McElderry)*
THE TREASURE by Uri Shulevitz *(Farrar)*

1980
AN ARTIST by M.B. Goffstein *(Harper)*

A CHILD'S CHRISTMAS IN WALES by Dylan Thomas, ill. by Edward Ardizzone *(Godine)*

GORKY RISES by William Steig *(Farrar)*

THE HEADLESS HORSEMAN RIDES TONIGHT: MORE POEMS TO TROUBLE YOUR SLEEP by Jack Prelutsky, ill. by Arnold Lobel *(Greenwillow)*

HOWARD by James Stevenson *(Greenwillow)*

THE LUCKY YAK by Annetta Lawson, ill. by Allen Say *(Parnassus)*

MR. MILLER THE DOG by Helme Heine *(McElderry)*

STONE & STEEL: A BOOK ABOUT ENGINEERING by Guy Billout *(Prentice-Hall)*

UNBUILDING by David Macaulay *(Houghton)*

THE WONDERFUL TRAVELS AND ADVENTURES OF BARON MÜNCHHAUSEN by Peter Nickl, ill. by Binette Schroeder *(Chatto/Merrimack)*

1981

THE CRANE WIFE retold by Sumiko Yagawa, ill. by Suekichi Akaba *(Morrow)*

FLIGHT: A PANORAMA OF AVIATION by Melvin B. Zisfein, ill. by Robert Andrew Parker *(Pantheon)*

JUMANJI by Chris Van Allsburg *(Houghton)*

THE MAID AND THE MOUSE AND THE ODD-SHAPED HOUSE: A STORY IN RHYME by Paul O. Zelinsky *(Dodd)*

ON MARKET STREET by Arnold Lobel, ill. by Anita Lobel *(Greenwillow)*

MY MOM TRAVELS A LOT by Caroline Feller Bauer, ill. by Nancy Winslow Parker *(Warne)*

THE NOSE TREE adapted and ill. by Warwick Hutton *(McElderry)*

OUTSIDE OVER THERE by Maurice Sendak *(Harper)*

THE STORY OF MRS. BRUBECK: AND HOW SHE LOOKED FOR TROUBLE AND WHERE SHE FOUND HIM by Lore Segal, ill. by Marcia Sewall *(Pantheon)*

WHERE THE BUFFALOES BEGIN by Olaf Baker, ill. by Stephen Gammell *(Warne)*

1982

ANNO'S BRITAIN by Mitsumasa Anno *(Philomel)*

BEN'S DREAM by Chris Van Allsburg *(Houghton)*

THE GIFT OF THE MAGI by O. Henry, lettering by Michael Neugebauer, ill. by Lisbeth Zwerger *(Picture Book Studio)*

MY UNCLE by Jenny Thorne *(McElderry)*

PADDY GOES TRAVELING by John S. Goodall *(McElderry)*

RAINBOWS ARE MADE: POEMS BY CARL SANDBURG edited by Lee Bennett Hopkins, ill. by Fritz Eichenberg *(HBJ)*

SMILE, ERNEST AND CELESTINE by Gabrielle Vincent *(Greenwillow)*

SQUID AND SPIDER: A LOOK AT THE ANIMAL KINGDOM by Guy Billout *(Prentice-Hall)*

THE STRANGE APPEARANCE OF HOWARD CRANEBILL,
JR. by Henrik Drescher *(Lothrop)*
THE TINY VISITOR by Oscar de Mejo *(Pantheon)*

1983
THE FAVERSHAMS by Roy Gerrard *(Farrar)*
LEONARD BASKIN'S MINIATURE NATURAL HISTORY:
FIRST SERIES by Leonard Baskin *(Pantheon)*
LITTLE RED CAP retold and ill. by Lisbeth Zwerger *(Morrow)*
ROUND TRIP by Ann Jonas *(Greenwillow)*
SIMON'S BOOK by Henrik Drescher *(Lothrop)*
TOOLS by Ken Robbins *(Four Winds)*
TWELVE CATS FOR CHRISTMAS by Martin Leman *(Pelham/
Merrimack)*
UP A TREE by Ed Young *(Harper)*
THE WRECK OF THE ZEPHYR by Chris Van Allsburg
(Houghton)

1984
ANIMAL ALPHABET by Bert Kitchen *(Dial)*
BABUSHKA retold and ill. by Charles Mikolaycak *(Holiday
House)*
IF THERE WERE DREAMS TO SELL compiled by Barbara
Lalicki, ill. by Margot Tomes *(Lothrop)*
JONAH AND THE GREAT FISH retold and ill. by Warwick
Hutton *(McElderry)*
THE MYSTERIES OF HARRIS BURDICK by Chris Van
Allsburg *(Houghton)*
THE NAPPING HOUSE by Audrey Wood, ill. by Don Wood
(HBJ)
THE NUTCRACKER by E.T.A. Hoffman, ill. by Maurice
Sendak *(Crown)*
SAINT GEORGE AND THE DRAGON retold by Margaret
Hodges, ill. by Trina Schart Hyman *(Little, Brown)*
SIR CEDRIC by Roy Gerrard *(Farrar)*
WHERE THE RIVER BEGINS by Thomas Locker *(Dial)*

1985
GORILLA by Anthony Browne *(Knopf)*
GRANPA by John Burningham *(Crown)*
HAZEL'S AMAZING MOTHER by Rosemary Wells *(Dial)*
THE INSIDE-OUTSIDE BOOK OF NEW YORK CITY by
Roxie Munro *(Dodd)*
THE LEGEND OF ROSEPETAL by Clemens Brentano, ill. by
Lisbeth Zwerger *(Picture Book Studio)*
THE NIGHTINGALE by Hans Christian Andersen, ill. by Demi
(HBJ)
THE POLAR EXPRESS by Chris Van Allsburg *(Houghton)*
THE PEOPLE COULD FLY: AMERICAN BLACK FOLKTALES
by Virginia Hamilton, ill. by Leo and Diane Dillon *(Knopf)*

THE RELATIVES CAME by Cynthia Rylant, ill. by Stephen Gammell *(Bradbury)*

THE STORY OF MRS. LOVEWRIGHT AND PURRLESS HER CAT by Lore Segal, ill. by Paul O. Zelinksy *(Knopf)*

1986

BRAVE IRENE by William Steig *(Farrar)*

CHERRIES AND CHERRY PITS by Vera B. Williams *(Greenwillow)*

FLYING by Donald Crews *(Greenwillow)*

MOLLY'S NEW WASHING MACHINE by Laura Geringer, ill. by Petra Mathers *(Harper)*

ONE MORNING by Canna Funakoshi, ill. by Yohji Izawa *(Picture Book Studio)*

THE OWL SCATTERER by Howard Norman, ill. by Michael McCurdy *(Atlantic-Little, Brown)*

PIGS FROM A TO Z by Arthur Geisert *(Houghton)*

REMBRANDT TAKES A WALK by Mark Strand, ill. by Red Grooms *(Clarkson Potter)*

THE STRANGER by Chris Van Allsburg *(Houghton)*

THE UGLY DUCKLING by Hans Christian Andersen, ill. by Robert Van Nutt *(Knopf)*

1987

THE CREMATION OF SAM McGEE by Robert W. Service, ill. by Ted Harrison *(Greenwillow)*

FOX'S DREAM by Tejima *(Philomel)*

HANDTALK BIRTHDAY by Remy Charlip and Mary Beth Miller, photog. by George Ancona *(Four Winds)*

HALLOWEEN ABC by Eve Merriam, ill. by Lane Smith *(Macmillan)*

IN COAL COUNTRY by Judith Hendershot, ill. by Thomas B. Allen *(Knopf)*

JUMP AGAIN! by Joel Chandler Harris, adapted by Van Dyke Parks, ill. by Barry Moser *(HBJ)*

THE MOUNTAINS OF TIBET by Mordicai Gerstein *(Harper)*

RAINBOW RHINO by Peter Sis *(Knopf)*

17 KINGS AND 42 ELEPHANTS by Margaret Mahy, ill. by Patricia MacCarthy *(Dial)*

THE YELLOW UMBRELLA by Henrik Drescher *(Bradbury)*

1988

CATS ARE CATS compiled by Nancy Larrick, ill. by Ed Young *(Philomel)*

FIRE CAME TO THE EARTH PEOPLE by Susan L. Roth *(St. Martin's)*

I WANT TO BE AN ASTRONAUT by Byron Barton *(Crowell)*

LOOK! LOOK! LOOK! by Tana Hoban *(Greenwillow)*

A RIVER DREAM by Allen Say *(Houghton)*

SHAKA: KING OF THE ZULUS by Diane Stanley and Peter Vennema, ill. by Diane Stanley *(Morrow)*

SIR FRANCIS DRAKE: HIS DARING DEEDS by Roy Gerrard
(Farrar)
STRINGBEAN'S TRIP TO THE SHINING SEA by Vera B.
Williams, ill. by Vera B. Williams and Jennifer Williams
(Greenwillow)
SWAN SKY by Tejima *(Philomel)*
THEODOR AND MR. BALBINI by Petra Mathers *(Harper)*

1989
THE DANCING SKELETON by Cynthia C. DeFelice, ill. by
Robert Andrew Parker *(Macmillan)*
DOES GOD HAVE A BIG TOE? STORIES ABOUT STORIES
IN THE BIBLE by Marc Gellman, ill. by Oscar de Mejo
(Harper)
THE HEARTACHES OF A FRENCH CAT by Barbara
McClintock *(Godine)*
HOW PIZZA CAME TO QUEENS by Dayal Kaur Khalsa
(Clarkson Potter)
NICHOLAS CRICKET by Joyce Maxner, ill. by William Joyce
(Harper)
OLSON'S MEAT PIES by Peter Cohen, ill. by Olof Landstrom
(R & S)
PEACOCK PIE: A BOOK OF RHYMES by Walter de la Mare,
ill. by Louise Brierley *(Holt)*
THESEUS AND THE MINOTAUR by Warwick Hutton
(McElderry)
TURTLE IN JULY by Marilyn Singer, ill. by Jerry Pinkney
(Macmillan)
WHALES by Seymour Simon, ill. with photogs. *(Crowell)*

1990
BEACH BALL by Peter Sis *(Greenwillow)*
BENEATH A BLUE UMBRELLA by Jack Prelutsky, ill. by
Garth Williams *(Greenwillow)*
A CHRISTMAS CAROL by Charles Dickens, ill. by Roberto
Innocenti *(Stewart, Tabori & Chang)*
THE DANCING PALM TREE: AND OTHER NIGERIAN
FOLKTALES by Barbara K. Walker, ill. by Helen Siegl *(Texas
Tech)*
FISH EYES: A BOOK YOU CAN COUNT ON by Lois Ehlert
(HBJ)
THE FOOL AND THE FISH: A TALE FROM RUSSIA by
Alexander Nikolayevich Afanasyev, retold by Lenny Hort, ill. by
Gennady Spirin *(Dial)*
I'M FLYING! by Alan Wade, ill. by Petra Mathers *(Knopf)*
ONE GORILLA: A COUNTING BOOK by Atsuko Morozumi
(Farrar)
THE TALE OF THE MANDARIN DUCKS by Katherine
Paterson, ill. by Leo and Diane Dillon *(Lodestar)*

WAR BOY: A COUNTRY CHILDHOOD by Michael Foreman *(Arcade)*

1991
ANOTHER CELEBRATED DANCING BEAR by Gladys Scheffrin-Falk, ill. by Barbara Garrison *(Scribner)*
DIEGO by Jonah Winter, ill. by Jeanette Winter *(Knopf)*
FOLLOW THE DREAM by Peter Sis *(Knopf)*
LITTLE RED RIDING HOOD by Charles Perrault, ill. by Beni Montresor *(Doubleday)*
THE MARVELOUS JOURNEY THROUGH THE NIGHT by Helme Heine *(Farrar)*
OLD MOTHER HUBBARD AND HER WONDERFUL DOG by James Marshall *(Farrar)*
OOH-LA-LA: (MAX IN LOVE) by Maira Kalman *(Viking)*
PUNCH IN NEW YORK by Alice Provensen *(Viking)*
TAR BEACH by Faith Ringgold *(Crown)*
WHAT CAN RABBIT HEAR? by Lucy Cousins *(Tambourine)*

John Newbery Medal ❧

Donated by the Frederic G. Melcher family, the Newbery Medal has been awarded annually since 1922 under the supervision of the Association for Library Service to Children of the American Library Association (50 E. Huron St., Chicago, IL 60611) to the author of the most distinguished contribution to literature for children published in the U.S. during the preceding year. Announced in January, the award is limited to residents or citizens of the U.S. (Medal)

1922
THE STORY OF MANKIND by Hendrik Willem van Loon *(Liveright)*
HONOR BOOKS
CEDRIC THE FORESTER by Bernard Marshall *(Appleton)*
THE GOLDEN FLEECE AND THE HEROES WHO LIVED BEFORE ACHILLES by Padraic Colum *(Macmillan)*
THE GREAT QUEST by Charles Hawes *(Little, Brown)*
THE OLD TOBACCO SHOP by William Bowen *(Macmillan)*
WINDY HILL by Cornelia Meigs *(Macmillan)*
1923
THE VOYAGES OF DOCTOR DOLITTLE by Hugh Lofting *(Lippincott)*

HONOR BOOK
No Record

1924
THE DARK FRIGATE by Charles Hawes *(Atlantic-Little, Brown)*
HONOR BOOK
No Record

1925
TALES FROM SILVER LANDS by Charles Finger *(Doubleday)*
HONOR BOOKS
DREAM COACH by Anne Parrish *(Macmillan)*
NICHOLAS by Anne Carroll Moore *(Putnam)*

1926
SHEN OF THE SEA by Arthur Bowie Chrisman *(Dutton)*
HONOR BOOK
VOYAGERS by Padraic Colum *(Macmillan)*

1927
SMOKY, THE COWHORSE by Will James *(Scribner)*
HONOR BOOK
No Record

1928
GAYNECK, THE STORY OF A PIGEON by Dhan Gopal Mukerji *(Dutton)*
HONOR BOOKS
DOWNRIGHT DENCEY by Caroline Snedeker *(Doubleday)*
THE WONDER SMITH AND HIS SON by Ella Young *(Longmans)*

1929
THE TRUMPETER OF KRAKOW by Eric P. Kelly *(Macmillan)*
HONOR BOOKS
THE BOY WHO WAS by Grace Hallock *(Dutton)*
CLEARING WEATHER by Cornelia Meigs *(Little, Brown)*
MILLIONS OF CATS by Wanda Gág *(Coward)*
PIGTAIL OF AH LEE BEN LOO by John Bennett *(Longmans)*
RUNAWAY PAPOOSE by Grace Moon *(Doubleday)*
TOD OF THE FENS by Elinor Whitney *(Macmillan)*

1930
HITTY, HER FIRST HUNDRED YEARS by Rachel Field *(Macmillan)*
HONOR BOOKS
DAUGHTER OF THE SEINE by Jeanette Eaton *(Harper)*
JUMPING-OFF PLACE by Marian Hurd McNeely *(Longmans)*
LITTLE BLACKNOSE by Hildegarde Swift *(HBJ)*
PRAN OF ALBANIA by Elizabeth Miller *(Doubleday)*
TANGLE-COATED HORSE AND OTHER TALES by Ella Young *(Longmans)* ·
VAINO by Julia Davis Adams *(Dutton)*

1931
THE CAT WHO WENT TO HEAVEN by Elizabeth
Coatsworth *(Macmillan)*
HONOR BOOKS
THE DARK STAR OF ITZA by Alida Malkus *(HBJ)*
FLOATING ISLAND by Anne Parrish *(Harper)*
GARRAM THE HUNTER by Herbert Best *(Doubleday)*
MEGGY MACINTOSH by Elizabeth Janet Gray *(Doubleday)*
MOUNTAINS ARE FREE by Julia Davis Adams *(Dutton)*
OOD-LE-UK THE WANDERER by Alice Lide and Margaret
Johansen *(Little, Brown)*
QUEER PERSON by Ralph Hubbard *(Doubleday)*
SPICE AND THE DEVIL'S CAKE by Agnes Hewes *(Knopf)*

1932
WATERLESS MOUNTAIN by Laura Adams Armer *(Longmans)*
HONOR BOOKS
BOY OF THE SOUTH SEAS by Eunice Tietjens *(Coward)*
CALICO BUSH by Rachel Field *(Macmillan)*
THE FAIRY CIRCUS by Dorothy P. Lathrop *(Macmillan)*
JANE'S ISLAND by Marjorie Allee *(Houghton)*
OUT OF THE FLAME by Eloise Lownsbery *(Longmans)*
TRUCE OF THE WOLF AND OTHER TALES OF OLD
ITALY by Mary Gould Davis *(HBJ)*

1933
YOUNG FU OF THE UPPER YANGTZE by Elizabeth Lewis
(Winston)
HONOR BOOKS
CHILDREN OF THE SOIL by Nora Burglon *(Doubleday)*
THE RAILROAD TO FREEDOM by Hildegarde Swift *(HBJ)*
SWIFT RIVERS by Cornelia Meigs *(Little, Brown)*

1934
INVINCIBLE LOUISA by Cornelia Meigs *(Little, Brown)*
HONOR BOOKS
ABC BUNNY by Wanda Gág *(Coward)*
APPRENTICE OF FLORENCE by Anne Kyle *(Houghton)*
BIG TREE OF BUNLAHY by Padraic Colum *(Macmillan)*
THE FORGOTTEN DAUGHTER by Caroline Snedeker
(Doubleday)
GLORY OF THE SEAS by Agnes Hewes *(Knopf)*
NEW LAND by Sarah Schmidt *(McBride)*
SWORDS OF STEEL by Elsie Singmaster *(Houghton)*
WINGED GIRL OF KNOSSOS by Erik Berry *(Appleton)*

1935
DOBRY by Monica Shannon *(Viking)*
HONOR BOOKS
DAVY CROCKETT by Constance Rourke *(HBJ)*
DAY ON SKATES by Hilda Van Stockum *(Harper)*

PAGEANT OF CHINESE HISTORY by Elizabeth Seeger *(Longmans)*

1936
CADDIE WOODLAWN by Carol Ryrie Brink *(Macmillan)*
HONOR BOOKS
ALL SAIL SET by Armstrong Sperry *(Winston)*
THE GOOD MASTER by Kate Seredy *(Viking)*
HONK, THE MOOSE by Phil Stong *(Dodd)*
YOUNG WALTER SCOTT by Elizabeth Janet Gray *(Viking)*

1937
ROLLER SKATES by Ruth Sawyer *(Viking)*
HONOR BOOKS
AUDUBON by Constance Rourke *(HBJ)*
THE CODFISH MUSKET by Agnes Hewes *(Doubleday)*
GOLDEN BASKET by Ludwig Bemelmans *(Viking)*
PHEBE FAIRCHILD: HER BOOK by Lois Lenski *(Stokes)*
WHISTLER'S VAN by Idwal Jones *(Viking)*
WINTERBOUND by Margery Bianco *(Viking)*

1938
THE WHITE STAG by Kate Seredy *(Viking)*
HONOR BOOKS
BRIGHT ISLAND by Mabel Robinson *(Random)*
ON THE BANKS OF PLUM CREEK by Laura Ingalls Wilder *(Harper)*
PECOS BILL by James Cloyd Bowman *(Little, Brown)*

1939
THIMBLE SUMMER by Elizabeth Enright *(Rinehart)*
HONOR BOOKS
HELLO THE BOAT! by Phyllis Crawford *(Holt)*
LEADER BY DESTINY: GEORGE WASHINGTON, MAN AND PATRIOT by Jeanette Eaton *(HBJ)*
MR. POPPER'S PENGUINS by Richard and Florence Atwater *(Little, Brown)*
NINO by Valenti Angelo *(Viking)*
PENN by Elizabeth Janet Gray *(Viking)*

1940
DANIEL BOONE by James Daugherty *(Viking)*
HONOR BOOKS
BOY WITH A PACK by Stephen W. Meader *(HBJ)*
BY THE SHORES OF SILVER LAKE by Laura Ingalls Wilder *(Harper)*
RUNNER OF THE MOUNTAIN TOPS by Mabel Robinson *(Random)*
THE SINGING TREE by Kate Seredy *(Viking)*

1941
CALL IT COURAGE by Armstrong Sperry *(Macmillan)*

HONOR BOOKS
BLUE WILLOW by Doris Gates *(Viking)*
THE LONG WINTER by Laura Ingalls Wilder *(Harper)*
NANSEN by Anna Gertrude Hall *(Viking)*
YOUNG MAC OF FORT VANCOUVER by Mary Jane Carr *(Crowell)*

1942
THE MATCHLOCK GUN by Walter D. Edmonds *(Dodd)*
HONOR BOOKS
DOWN RYTON WATER by Eva Roe Gaggin *(Viking)*
GEORGE WASHINGTON'S WORLD by Genevieve Foster *(Scribner)*
INDIAN CAPTIVE: THE STORY OF MARY JEMISON by Lois Lenski *(Lippincott)*
LITTLE TOWN ON THE PRAIRIE by Laura Ingalls Wilder *(Harper)*

1943
ADAM OF THE ROAD by Elizabeth Janet Gray *(Viking)*
HONOR BOOKS
HAVE YOU SEEN TOM THUMB? by Mabel Leigh Hunt *(Lippincott)*
THE MIDDLE MOFFAT by Eleanor Estes *(HBJ)*

1944
JOHNNY TREMAIN by Esther Forbes *(Houghton)*
HONOR BOOKS
FOG MAGIC by Julia Sauer *(Viking)*
MOUNTAIN BORN by Elizabath Yates *(Coward)*
RUFUS M. by Eleanor Estes *(HBJ)*
THESE HAPPY GOLDEN YEARS by Laura Ingalls Wilder *(Harper)*

1945
RABBIT HILL by Robert Lawson *(Viking)*
HONOR BOOKS
ABRAHAM LINCOLN'S WORLD by Genevieve Foster *(Scribner)*
THE HUNDRED DRESSES by Eleanor Estes *(HBJ)*
LONE JOURNEY: THE LIFE OF ROGER WILLIAMS by Jeanette Eaton *(HBJ)*
THE SILVER PENCIL by Alice Dalgliesh *(Scribner)*

1946
STRAWBERRY GIRL by Lois Lenski *(Lippincott)*
HONOR BOOKS
BHIMSA, THE DANCING BEAR by Christine Weston *(Scribner)*
JUSTIN MORGAN HAD A HORSE by Marguerite Henry *(Rand McNally)*
THE MOVED-OUTERS by Florence Crannell Means *(Houghton)*
NEW FOUND WORLD by Katherine Shippen *(Viking)*

1947
MISS HICKORY by Carolyn Sherwin Bailey *(Viking)*
HONOR BOOKS
THE AVION MY UNCLE FLEW by Cyrus Fisher *(Appleton)*
BIG TREE by Mary and Conrad Buff *(Viking)*
THE HEAVENLY TENANTS by William Maxwell *(Harper)*
THE HIDDEN TREASURE OF GLASTON by Eleanore Jewett
(Viking)
WONDERFUL YEAR by Nancy Barnes *(Messner)*

1948
THE TWENTY-ONE BALLOONS by William Pène du Bois
(Viking)
HONOR BOOKS
THE COW-TAIL SWITCH, AND OTHER WEST AFRICAN
STORIES by Harold Courlander *(Holt)*
LI LUN, LAD OF COURAGE by Carolyn Treffinger *(Abingdon)*
MISTY OF CHINCOTEAGUE by Marguerite Henry *(Rand
McNally)*
PANCAKES—PARIS by Claire Huchet Bishop *(Viking)*
THE QUAINT AND CURIOUS QUEST OF JOHNNY
LONGFOOT by Catherine Besterman *(Bobbs)*

1949
KING OF THE WIND by Marguerite Henry *(Rand McNally)*
HONOR BOOKS
DAUGHTER OF THE MOUNTAINS by Louise Rankin
(Viking)
MY FATHER'S DRAGON by Ruth S. Gannett *(Random)*
SEABIRD by Holling C. Holling *(Houghton)*
STORY OF THE NEGRO by Arna Bontemps *(Knopf)*

1950
THE DOOR IN THE WALL by Marguerite de Angeli
(Doubleday)
HONOR BOOKS
THE BLUE CAT OF CASTLE TOWN by Catherine Coblentz
(Longmans)
GEORGE WASHINGTON by Genevieve Foster *(Scribner)*
KILDEE HOUSE by Rutherford Montgomery *(Doubleday)*
SONG OF THE PINES by Walter and Marion Havighurst
(Winston)
TREE OF FREEDOM by Rebecca Caudill *(Viking)*

1951
AMOS FORTUNE, FREE MAN by Elizabeth Yates *(Dutton)*
HONOR BOOKS
ABRAHAM LINCOLN, FRIEND OF THE PEOPLE by Clara
Ingram Judson *(Follett)*
BETTER KNOWN AS JOHNNY APPLESEED by Mabel Leigh
Hunt *(Lippincott)*

GANDHI, FIGHTER WITHOUT A SWORD by Jeanette Eaton *(Morrow)*

THE STORY OF APPLEBY CAPPLE by Anne Parrish *(Harper)*

1952

GINGER PYE by Eleanor Estes *(HBJ)*

HONOR BOOKS

AMERICANS BEFORE COLUMBUS by Elizabeth Baity *(Viking)*

THE APPLE AND THE ARROW by Mary and Conrad Buff *(Houghton)*

THE DEFENDER by Nicholas Kalashnikoff *(Scribner)*

THE LIGHT AT TERN ROCKS by Julia Sauer *(Viking)*

MINN OF THE MISSISSIPPI by Holling C. Holling *(Houghton)*

1953

SECRET OF THE ANDES by Ann Nolan Clark *(Viking)*

HONOR BOOKS

THE BEARS ON HEMLOCK MOUNTAIN by Alice Dalgliesh *(Scribner)*

BIRTHDAYS OF FREEDOM, VOL. 1 by Genevieve Foster *(Scribner)*

CHARLOTTE'S WEB by E.B. White *(Harper)*

MOCCASIN TRAIL by Eloise McGraw *(Coward)*

RED SAILS TO CAPRI by Ann Weil *(Viking)*

1954

...AND NOW MIGUEL by Joseph Krumgold *(Crowell)*

HONOR BOOKS

ALL ALONE by Claire Huchet Bishop *(Viking)*

HURRY HOME CANDY by Meindert DeJong *(Harper)*

MAGIC MAIZE by Mary and Conrad Buff *(Houghton)*

SHADRACH by Meindert DeJong *(Harper)*

THEODORE ROOSEVELT, FIGHTING PATRIOT by Clara Ingram Judson *(Follett)*

1955

THE WHEEL ON THE SCHOOL by Meindert DeJong *(Harper)*

HONOR BOOKS

BANNER IN THE SKY by James Ullman *(Lippincott)*

COURAGE OF SARAH NOBLE by Alice Dalgliesh *(Scribner)*

1956

CARRY ON, MR. BOWDITCH by Jean Lee Latham *(Houghton)*

HONOR BOOKS

THE GOLDEN NAME DAY by Jennie Lindquist *(Harper)*

MEN, MICROSCOPES, AND LIVING THINGS by Katherine Shippen *(Viking)*

THE SECRET RIVER by Marjorie Kinnan Rawlings *(Scribner)*

1957

MIRACLES ON MAPLE HILL by Virginia Sorensen *(HBJ)*

HONOR BOOKS
BLACK FOX OF LORNE by Marguerite de Angeli *(Doubleday)*
THE CORN GROWS RIPE by Dorothy Rhoads *(Viking)*
THE HOUSE OF SIXTY FATHERS by Meindert DeJong
(Harper)
MR. JUSTICE HOLMES by Clara Ingram Judson *(Follett)*
OLD YELLER by Fred Gipson *(Harper)*
1958
RIFLES FOR WATIE by Harold Keith *(Crowell)*
HONOR BOOKS
GONE-AWAY LAKE by Elizabeth Enright *(HBJ)*
THE GREAT WHEEL by Robert Lawson *(Viking)*
THE HORSECATCHER by Mari Sandoz *(Westminster)*
TOM PAINE, FREEDOM'S APOSTLE by Leo Gurko *(Crowell)*
1959
THE WITCH OF BLACKBIRD POND by Elizabeth George
Speare *(Houghton)*
HONOR BOOKS
ALONG CAME A DOG by Meindert DeJong *(Harper)*
CHUCARO: WILD PONY OF THE PAMPA by Francis Kalnay
(HBJ)
THE FAMILY UNDER THE BRIDGE by Natalie Savage
Carlson *(Harper)*
THE PERILOUS ROAD by William O. Steele *(HBJ)*
1960
ONION JOHN by Joseph Krumgold *(Crowell)*
HONOR BOOKS
AMERICA IS BORN by Gerald W. Johnson *(Morrow)*
THE GAMMAGE CUP by Carol Kendall *(HBJ)*
MY SIDE OF THE MOUNTAIN by Jean Craighead George
(Dutton)
1961
ISLAND OF THE BLUE DOLPHINS by Scott O'Dell
(Houghton)
HONOR BOOKS
AMERICA MOVES FORWARD by Gerald W. Johnson
(Morrow)
THE CRICKET IN TIMES SQUARE by George Selden *(Farrar)*
OLD RAMON by Jack Schaefer *(Houghton)*
1962
THE BRONZE BOW by Elizabeth George Speare *(Houghton)*
HONOR BOOKS
BELLING THE TIGER by Mary Stolz *(Harper)*
FRONTIER LIVING by Edwin Tunis *(World)*
THE GOLDEN GOBLET by Eloise McGraw *(Coward)*
1963
A WRINKLE IN TIME by Madeleine L'Engle *(Farrar)*
HONOR BOOKS
MEN OF ATHENS by Olivia Coolidge *(Houghton)*

THISTLE AND THYME by Sorche Nic Leodhas *(Holt)*

1964

IT'S LIKE THIS, CAT by Emily Cheney Neville *(Harper)*

HONOR BOOKS

THE LONER by Ester Wier *(McKay)*

RASCAL by Sterling North *(Dutton)*

1965

SHADOW OF A BULL by Maia Wojciechowska *(Atheneum)*

HONOR BOOKS

ACROSS FIVE APRILS by Irene Hunt *(Follett)*

1966

I, JUAN DE PAREJA by Elizabeth Borten de Treviño *(Farrar)*

HONOR BOOKS

THE ANIMAL FAMILY by Randall Jarrell *(Pantheon)*

THE BLACK CAULDRON by Lloyd Alexander *(Holt)*

THE NOONDAY FRIENDS by Mary Stolz *(Harper)*

1967

UP A ROAD SLOWLY by Irene Hunt *(Follett)*

HONOR BOOKS

THE JAZZ MAN by Mary H. Weik *(Atheneum)*

THE KING'S FIFTH by Scott O'Dell *(Houghton)*

ZLATEH THE GOAT AND OTHER STORIES by Isaac
Bashevis Singer *(Harper)*

1968

FROM THE MIXED-UP FILES OF MRS. BASIL E.
FRANKWEILER by E.L. Konigsburg *(Atheneum)*

HONOR BOOKS

THE BLACK PEARL by Scott O'Dell *(Houghton)*

THE EGYPT GAME by Zilpha Keatley Snyder *(Atheneum)*

THE FEARSOME INN by Isaac Bashevis Singer *(Scribner)*

JENNIFER, HECATE, MACBETH, WILLIAM McKINLEY,
AND ME, ELIZABETH by E.L. Konigsburg *(Atheneum)*

1969

THE HIGH KING by Lloyd Alexander *(Holt)*

HONOR BOOKS

TO BE A SLAVE by Julius Lester *(Dial)*

WHEN SHLEMIEL WENT TO WARSAW & OTHER
STORIES by Isaac Bashevis Singer *(Farrar)*

1970

SOUNDER by William H. Armstrong *(Harper)*

HONOR BOOKS

JOURNEY OUTSIDE by Mary Q. Steele *(Viking)*

THE MANY WAYS OF SEEING: AN INTRODUCTION TO
THE PLEASURES OF ART by Janet Gaylord Moore *(World)*

OUR EDDIE by Sulamith Ish-Kishor *(Pantheon)*

1971

SUMMER OF THE SWANS by Betsy Byars *(Viking)*

HONOR BOOKS
ENCHANTRESS FROM THE STARS by Sylvia Louise Engdahl
(Atheneum)
KNEE-KNOCK RISE by Natalie Babbitt *(Farrar)*
SING DOWN THE MOON by Scott O'Dell *(Houghton)*
1972
MRS. FRISBY AND THE RATS OF NIMH by Robert C.
O'Brien *(Atheneum)*
HONOR BOOKS
ANNIE AND THE OLD ONE by Miska Miles *(Atlantic-Little,
Brown)*
THE HEADLESS CUPID by Zilpha Keatley Snyder *(Atheneum)*
INCIDENT AT HAWK'S HILL by Allan W. Eckert *(Little,
Brown)*
THE PLANET OF JUNIOR BROWN by Virginia Hamilton
(Macmillan)
THE TOMBS OF ATUAN by Ursula K. Le Guin *(Atheneum)*
1973
JULIE OF THE WOLVES by Jean Craighead George *(Harper)*
HONOR BOOKS
FROG AND TOAD TOGETHER by Arnold Lobel *(Harper)*
THE UPSTAIRS ROOM by Johanna Reiss *(Crowell)*
THE WITCHES OF WORM by Zilpha Keatley Snyder
(Atheneum)
1974
THE SLAVE DANCER by Paula Fox *(Bradbury)*
HONOR BOOK
THE DARK IS RISING by Susan Cooper *(McElderry)*
1975
M. C. HIGGINS, THE GREAT by Virginia Hamilton
(Macmillan)
HONOR BOOKS
FIGGS & PHANTOMS by Ellen Raskin *(Dutton)*
MY BROTHER SAM IS DEAD by James Lincoln Collier and
Christopher Collier *(Four Winds)*
THE PERILOUS GARD by Elizabeth Marie Pope *(Houghton)*
PHILIP HALL LIKES ME, I RECKON MAYBE by Bette Greene
(Dial)
1976
THE GREY KING by Susan Cooper *(McElderry)*
HONOR BOOKS
DRAGONWINGS by Laurence Yep *(Harper)*
THE HUNDRED PENNY BOX by Sharon Bell Mathis *(Viking)*
1977
ROLL OF THUNDER, HEAR MY CRY by Mildred D. Taylor
(Dial)
HONOR BOOKS
ABEL'S ISLAND by William Steig *(Farrar)*

A STRING IN THE HARP by Nancy Bond *(McElderry)*

1978
BRIDGE TO TERABITHIA by Katherine Paterson *(Crowell)*
HONOR BOOKS
ANPAO: AN AMERICAN INDIAN ODYSSEY by Jamake
Highwater *(Lippincott)*
RAMONA AND HER FATHER by Beverly Cleary *(Morrow)*

1979
THE WESTING GAME by Ellen Raskin *(Dutton)*
HONOR BOOKS
THE GREAT GILLY HOPKINS by Katherine Paterson *(Crowell)*

1980
A GATHERING OF DAYS: A NEW ENGLAND GIRL'S
JOURNAL, 1830-32 by Joan W. Blos *(Scribner)*
HONOR BOOK
THE ROAD FROM HOME: THE STORY OF AN
ARMENIAN GIRL by David Kherdian *(Greenwillow)*

1981
JACOB HAVE I LOVED by Katherine Paterson *(Crowell)*
HONOR BOOKS
THE FLEDGLING by Jane Langton *(Harper)*
A RING OF ENDLESS LIGHT by Madeleine L'Engle *(Farrar)*

1982
A VISIT TO WILLIAM BLAKE'S INN: POEMS FOR
INNOCENT AND EXPERIENCED TRAVELERS by Nancy
Willard *(HBJ)*
HONOR BOOKS
RAMONA QUIMBY, AGE 8 by Beverly Cleary *(Morrow)*
UPON THE HEAD OF THE GOAT: A CHILDHOOD IN
HUNGARY, 1939-1944 by Aranka Siegal *(Farrar)*

1983
DICEY'S SONG by Cynthia Voigt *(Atheneum)*
HONOR BOOKS
THE BLUE SWORD by Robin McKinley *(Greenwillow)*
DOCTOR DE SOTO by William Steig *(Farrar)*
GRAVEN IMAGES by Paul Fleischman *(Harper)*
HOMESICK: MY OWN STORY by Jean Fritz *(Putnam)*
SWEET WHISPERS, BROTHER RUSH by Virginia Hamilton
(Philomel)

1984
DEAR MR. HENSHAW by Beverly Cleary *(Morrow)*
HONOR BOOKS
THE SIGN OF THE BEAVER by Elizabeth George Speare
(Houghton)
A SOLITARY BLUE by Cynthia Voigt *(Atheneum)*
SUGARING TIME by Kathryn Lasky *(Macmillan)*
THE WISH GIVER by Bill Brittain *(Harper)*

1985
THE HERO AND THE CROWN by Robin McKinley
(Greenwillow)
HONOR BOOKS
LIKE JAKE AND ME by Mavis Jukes *(Knopf)*
THE MOVES MAKE THE MAN by Bruce Brooks *(Harper)*
ONE-EYED CAT by Paula Fox *(Bradbury)*
1986
SARAH, PLAIN AND TALL by Patricia MacLachlan *(Harper)*
HONOR BOOKS
COMMODORE PERRY IN THE LAND OF THE SHOGUN by
Rhoda Blumberg *(Lothrop)*
DOGSONG by Gary Paulsen *(Bradbury)*
1987
THE WHIPPING BOY by Sid Fleischman *(Greenwillow)*
HONOR BOOKS
A FINE WHITE DUST by Cynthia Rylant *(Bradbury)*
ON MY HONOR by Marion Dane Bauer *(Clarion)*
VOLCANO: THE ERUPTION AND HEALING OF MOUNT
ST. HELENS by Patricia Lauber *(Bradbury)*
1988
LINCOLN: A PHOTOBIOGRAPHY by Russell Freedman
(Clarion)
HONOR BOOKS
AFTER THE RAIN by Norma Fox Mazer *(Morrow)*
HATCHET by Gary Paulsen *(Bradbury)*
1989
JOYFUL NOISE: POEMS FOR TWO VOICES by Paul
Fleischman *(Harper)*
HONOR BOOKS
IN THE BEGINNING: CREATION STORIES FROM
AROUND THE WORLD by Virginia Hamilton *(HBJ)*
SCORPIONS by Walter Dean Myers *(Harper)*
1990
NUMBER THE STARS by Lois Lowry *(Houghton)*
HONOR BOOKS
AFTERNOON OF THE ELVES by Janet Taylor Lisle *(Orchard)*
SHABANU: DAUGHTER OF THE WIND by Suzanne Fisher
Staples *(Knopf)*
THE WINTER ROOM by Gary Paulsen *(Orchard)*
1991
MANIAC MAGEE by Jerry Spinelli *(Little, Brown)*
HONOR BOOK
THE TRUE CONFESSIONS OF CHARLOTTE DOYLE by Avi
(Orchard)
1992
SHILOH by Phyllis Reynolds Naylor *(Atheneum)*

HONOR BOOKS
NOTHING BUT THE TRUTH: A DOCUMENTARY NOVEL
by Avi *(Orchard)*
THE WRIGHT BROTHERS: HOW THEY INVENTED THE
AIRPLANE by Russell Freedman *(Holiday House)*

North Carolina Literary and Historical Association Awards 🐦

AMERICAN ASSOCIATION OF UNIVERSITY WOMEN (AAUW) AWARD IN JUVENILE LITERATURE, NORTH CAROLINA DIVISION, AAUW

Given annually in November through the North Carolina Literary and Historical Association (109 E. Jones St., Raleigh, NC 27611). Author must have maintained legal or physical residence in state for three years. (Cup)

1953
PEANUT by Ruth and Latrobe Carroll *(Walck)*

1954
PENNY ROSE by Mebane Holloman Burgwyn *(Walck)*

1955
DIGBY, THE ONLY DOG by Ruth and Latrobe Carroll *(Walck)*

1956
FIDDLER'S FANCY by Julia Montgomery Street *(Follett)*

1957
TAFFY OF TORPEDO JUNCTION by Nell Wise Wechter *(Blair)*

1958
THE SECRET CIRCLE by Ina B. Forbus *(Viking)*

1959
CAPTAIN GHOST by Thelma Harrington Bell *(Viking)*

1960
STONEWALL JACKSON by Jonathan Daniels *(Random)*

1961
BEAVER BUSINESS: AN ALMANAC by Glen Rounds *(Prentice-Hall)*

1962
RIFLES AT RAMSOUR'S MILL by Manly Wade Wellman *(Washburn)*

1963
DULCIE'S WHALE by Julia Montgomery Street *(Bobbs)*
1964
THE BAT-POET by Randall Jarrell *(Macmillan)*
1965
THE FORGOTTEN DOOR by Alexander Key *(Westminster)*
1966
NORTH CAROLINA PARADE by Julia Montgomery Street and
Richard Walser *(U. of North Carolina)*
1967
THE SNAKE TREE by Glen Rounds *(World)*
1968
A BIOGRAPHY OF THOMAS WOLFE by Neal F. Austin
(Roger Beacham)
1969
BUGLES AT THE BORDER by Mary Gillett *(Blair)*
1970
THE CRACKAJACK PONY by Mebane Holoman Burgwyn
(Lippincott)
1971
PURRO AND THE PRATTLEBERRIES by Suzanne Newton
(Westminster)
1972
No Award
1973
THE PEOPLE OF NORTH CAROLINA by Barbara M.
Parramore *(Sadlier)*
1974
C/O ARNOLD'S CORNERS by Suzanne Newton *(Westminster)*
1975
THE MAGIC MEADOW by Alexander Key *(Westminster)*
1976
MR. YOWDER AND THE LION ROAR CAPSULES by Glen
Rounds *(Holiday House)*
1977
THE CITY ROSE by Ruth White Miller *(McGraw-Hill)*
1978
WHAT ARE YOU UP TO, WILLIAM THOMAS? by Suzanne
Newton *(Westminster)*
1979
REUBELLA AND THE OLD FOCUS HOME by Suzanne
Newton *(Westminster)*
1980
SAFE AS THE GRAVE by Caroline B. Cooney *(Coward)*
1981
No Award

1982
M. V. SEXTON by Suzanne Newton *(Viking)*

1983
WILD APPALOOSA by Glen Rounds *(Holiday House)*

1984
TANCY by Belinda Hurmence *(Clarion)*

1985
THE SUMMER THAT LASTED FOREVER by Catherine Petroski *(Houghton)*

1986
GOLDEN GIRL by Nancy Tilly *(Farrar)*

1987
PERMANENT CONNECTIONS by Sue Ellen Bridgers *(Harper)*

1988
EATING CROW by Lila Hopkins *(Watts)*

1989
THE NIGHTWALKER by Belinda Hurmence *(Clarion)*

1990
TALKING TURKEY by Lila Hopkins *(Watts)*

1991
WHERE ARE YOU WHEN I NEED YOU? by Suzanne Newton *(Viking)*

Scott O'Dell Award for Historical Fiction &

Originated and donated by Scott O'Dell (1898-1989), author of several honored children's books and recipient in 1972 of the Hans Christian Andersen Award of the International Board on Books for Young People (IBBY) for the body of his work, this award is for a distinguished work of historical fiction. The winning titles must be published in English for children or young adults by a U.S. publisher, and be set in the New World, i.e., North, Central, or South America. The award was established in 1981, but not given until the selection committee determined there was an appropriate recipient. Administration and selection are by an Advisory Board chaired by Zena Sutherland (1418 East 57th St., Chicago, IL 60637). ($5,000)

1984
THE SIGN OF THE BEAVER by Elizabeth George Speare *(Houghton)*

1985
THE FIGHTING GROUND by Avi *(Lippincott)*

1986
SARAH, PLAIN AND TALL by Patricia MacLachlan *(Harper)*
1987
STREAMS TO THE RIVER, RIVER TO THE SEA by Scott O'Dell *(Houghton)*
Note: The award committee, with Scott O'Dell's agreement, selected the Children's Book Council as the recipient of the cash award.
1988
CHARLEY SKEDADDLE by Patricia Beatty *(Morrow)*
1989
THE HONORABLE PRISON by Lyll Becerra de Jenkins *(Lodestar)*
1990
SHADES OF GRAY by Carolyn Reeder *(Macmillan)*
1991
A TIME OF TROUBLES by Pieter van Raven *(Scribner)*
1992
STEPPING ON THE CRACKS by Mary Downing Hahn *(Clarion)*

Ohioana Book Awards 🦩

JUVENILE (OR YOUNG ADULT) BOOK CATEGORY

Awarded annually by the Ohioana Library Association (Room 1105, 65 S. Front St., Columbus, OH 43215-0334) to an Ohio author who has written an outstanding book published in the preceding year or for the body of work of an Ohio author. Author must have been born in Ohio or lived there a minimum of five years. (Medal)

1943
BIBI: THE BAKER'S HORSE by Anna Bird Stewart *(Lippincott)*
1944
BAYOU SUZETTE by Lois Lenski *(Stokes)*
1945
ONE GOD: THE WAYS WE WORSHIP HIM by Florence Mary Fitch *(Lothrop)*
1946
THE WHITE DEER by James Thurber *(HBJ)*
1947
THE SNOW OWL'S SECRET by Harriet Torrey Evatt *(Bobbs)*
1948
LI LUN, LAD OF COURAGE by Carolyn Treffinger *(Abingdon)*

1949
BLUEBERRIES FOR SAL by Robert McCloskey *(Viking)*
1950
SONG OF THE PINES by Walter and Marion Havighurst
(Winston)
1951-1953
No Awards
1954
TINKER'S TIM AND THE WITCHES by Bertha C. Anderson
(Little, Brown)
1955
PREHISTORIC ANIMALS by William E. Scheele *(World)*
1956
THE FABULOUS FIREWORK FAMILY by James Flora *(HBJ)*
1957
KNIGHT'S CASTLE by Edward McMaken Eager *(HBJ)*
1958
TIME OF WONDER by Robert McCloskey *(Viking)*
1959
AMERICA'S OWN MARK TWAIN by Jeanette Eaton *(Morrow)*
1960
THE GAMMAGE CUP by Carol Kendall *(HBJ)*
1961
OLD RAMON by Jack Schaefer *(Houghton)*
1962
SHIPS, SHOALS AND AMPHORAS by Suzanne de Borhegyi
(Holt)
1963
SEVEN-DAY MAGIC by Edward McMaken Eager *(HBJ)*
1964-1966
No Awards
1967
WALK A NARROW BRIDGE by Dale Fife *(Coward)*
1968
FOCUS THE BRIGHT LAND by Elisabeth Hamilton Friermood
(Doubleday)
1969
THE HOUSE OF DIES DREAR by Virginia Hamilton
(Macmillan)
1970
THE NORMAN ROCKWELL STORYBOOK by Jan Wahl
(Windmill/Simon & Schuster)
1971
OHIO by Marion Renick *(Coward)*
1972
WINDS by Mary O'Neill *(Doubleday)*

1973-1975
No Awards

1976
WITCH OF THE CUMBERLANDS by Mary Jo Stephens
(Houghton)

1977
DEEP IN THE FOREST by Brinton Turkle *(Dutton)*
ISLAND TIME by Brinton Turkle *(Lippincott)*

1978
POOR TOM'S GHOST by Jane Louise Curry *(McElderry)*

1979
ZOAR BLUE by Janet Hickman *(Macmillan)*

1980
Body of work of Andre Norton

1981
THE LIBERATION OF TANSY WARNER by Stephanie S.
Tolan *(Scribner)*

1982
ANOTHER HEAVEN, ANOTHER EARTH by H. M. Hoover
(Viking)

1983
No Award

1984
Body of work of Virginia Hamilton

1985 -1986
No Awards

1987
THE LOTUS CUP by Jane Louise Curry *(McElderry)*

1988
Body of work of Joseph Slate

1989
THE TSAR & THE AMAZING COW by J. Patrick Lewis *(Dial)*

1990
BUT I'LL BE BACK AGAIN: AN ALBUM by Cynthia Rylant
(Orchard)

1991
Lifetime career medal to Virginia Hamilton
Body of work of Mildred D. Taylor
WITH A NAME LIKE LULU, WHO NEEDS MORE
TROUBLE? by Tricia Springstubb *(Delacorte)*

Oklahoma Book Awards 🦃
CHILDREN'S AND YOUNG ADULT CATEGORY

Sponsored by the Oklahoma Center for the Book (200 Northeast 18th St., Oklahoma City, OK 73105), this awards program has five categories, including one for Children's and Young Adult books, comprising fiction, nonfiction or poetry. "Books considered for this award must have an Oklahoma-based theme or have been written by an author who resides or has resided in Oklahoma." (Medallion and citation)

1990
TYRANNOSAURUS REX AND ITS KIN: THE MESOZOIC MONSTERS by Helen Roney Sattler *(Lothrop)*
1991
A CAPITAL FOR THE NATION by Stan Hoig *(Cobblehill)*
1992
HILLBACK TO BOGGY by Jess and Bonnie Speer *(Reliance)*

Orbis Pictus Award for Outstanding Nonfiction for Children 🦃

Commemorating the work of "that brave old man, Johannes Amos Commenius, the fame of whose worth has been trumpeted as far as more than three languages could carry it," and whose book *Orbis Pictus (The World in Pictures)* is historically considered to be the first work created exclusively for children, this award honors distinction in nonfiction for children. An undertaking of and administered by the Committee on Using Nonfiction in the Elementary Language Arts Classroom of the National Council of Teachers of English (1111 Kenyon Rd., Urbana, IL 61801), the committee considers "accuracy, organization, design, writing style, and usefulness for classroom teaching in grades K-8" in selecting the winner, up to five Honor Books, and a longer annual listing of "Outstanding Nonfiction Choices for Children." Our listing is of the award presentation year; winners were published in the previous year. (Plaque)

1990
THE GREAT LITTLE MADISON by Jean Fritz *(Putnam)*
1991
FRANKLIN DELANO ROOSEVELT by Russell Freedman *(Clarion)*

1992
FLIGHT: THE JOURNEY OF CHARLES LINDBERGH by
Robert Burleigh, ill. by Mike Wimmer *(Philomel)*

Outstanding Pennsylvania Author Award ❧

The purpose of this award "is to recognize a Pennsylvania author who has made outstanding contributions in the field of literature." The author must be from Pennsylvania originally, or must currently live in Pennsylvania, or write about the state. Books for readers from the first school years through high school are considered. The sponsor is Pennsylvania School Librarians Association (112 Nursery La., Lancaster, PA 17603) (Certificate)

1975 Marguerite De Angeli
1976 Lloyd Alexander
1977 Margaret Hodges
1978 Jean Fritz
1979 Carolyn Haywood
1980 Walter Farley
1981 Harriet May Savitz
1982 James A. Michener
1983 Robin Brancato
1984 Muriel Feelings
1985 Barbara Robinson
1986 Barbara Brenner
1987 Lucille Wallower
1988 Fred Rogers
1989 Marc Brown
1990 Carolyn Meyer
1991 Aliki

Parenting's Reading-Magic Awards ❧

Parenting (501 Second St., San Francisco, CA 94107), a magazine with a circulation of about 800,000, presents awards for excellence in children's literature. "From lists compiled for

Parenting by a panel of noted experts in the field of children's books," *Parenting* selects ten best books and—a most appealing feature of this award program—recognizes over 40 other titles for excellence. "The list of winners includes a wide range of titles, which are characterized by age: first books, up to age 5; picture books, ages 4 to 8; first readers, ages 5 to 8; middle readers, ages 9 to 12; and nonfiction books, which vary in age." This feature is published as a multi-page foldout in the December/January issues of *Parenting*. (Certificate)

1988
THE BOY OF THE THREE-YEAR NAP retold by Dianne Snyder, ill. by Allen Say *(Houghton)*
A CARIBOU ALPHABET by Mary Beth Owens *(Dog Ear Press)*
CATWINGS by Ursula K. LeGuin, ill. by S. D. Schindler *(Orchard)*
DEAR MILI by Wilhelm Grimm, translated by Ralph Manheim, ill. by Maurice Sendak *(Farrar)*
A GIRL FROM YAMHILL: A MEMOIR by Beverly Cleary *(Morrow)*
HENRY by Nina Bawden *(Lothrop)*
MORE TALES OF UNCLE REMUS: FURTHER ADVENTURES OF BRER RABBIT, HIS FRIENDS, ENEMIES, AND OTHERS retold by Julius Lester, ill. by Jerry Pinkney *(Dial)*
THE THREE AND MANY WISHES OF JASON REID by Hazel J. Hutchins *(Viking)*
TOM AND PIPPO (series) by Helen Oxenbury *(Aladdin)*
WHERE THE FOREST MEETS THE SEA by Jeannie Baker *(Greenwillow)*
1989
BILL PEET: AN AUTOBIOGRAPHY by Bill Peet *(Houghton)*
EATING THE ALPHABET: FRUITS AND VEGETABLES FROM A TO Z by Lois Ehlert *(HBJ)*
INSPIRATIONS: STORIES ABOUT WOMEN ARTISTS by Leslie Sills *(Whitman)*
MOUSE PAINT by Ellen Stoll Walsh *(HBJ)*
THE PUP GREW UP! by Samuel Marshak, translated by Richard Pevear, ill. by Vladimir Radunsky *(Holt)*
QUENTIN BLAKE'S ABC by Quentin Blake *(Knopf)*
THE RAINBOW PEOPLE by Laurence Yep *(Harper)*
VALENTINE & ORSON by Nancy Ekholm Burkert *(Farrar)*
WE'RE GOING ON A BEAR HUNT retold by Michael Rosen, ill. by Helen Oxenbury *(McElderry)*
YOUNG LIONS by Toshi Yoshida *(Philomel)*
1990
BASEBALL IN APRIL by Gary Soto *(HBJ)*
THE BUCK STOPS HERE by Alice Provensen *(HarperCollins)*
COUSINS by Virginia Hamilton *(Philomel)*

EL CHINO by Allen Say *(Houghton)*
GOOD QUEEN BESS by Diane Stanley and Peter Vennema, ill. by Diane Stanley *(Four Winds)*
PUSS IN BOOTS by Charles Perrault, translated by Malcolm Arthur, ill. by Fred Marcellino *(Farrar)*
SHREK! by William Steig *(Farrar)*
TEHANU by Ursula K. LeGuin *(Atheneum)*
THE WHEELS ON THE BUS by Paul O. Zelinsky *(Dutton)*
WHITE PEAK FARM by Berlie Doherty *(Orchard)*
1991
AKI AND THE FOX by Akiko Hayashi *(Doubleday)*
CLOWNING AROUND by Cathryn Falwell *(Orchard)*
DOG; CAT; DUCK; *and* BEAR by Juan Wijngaard *(Crown)*
HOW THE OX STAR FELL FROM HEAVEN retold and ill. by Lily Toy Hong *(Whitman)*
PUNCH IN NEW YORK by Alice Provensen *(Viking)*
STARS COME OUT WITHIN by Jean Little *(Viking)*
STRIDER by Beverly Cleary *(Morrow)*
TUESDAY by David Wiesner *(Clarion)*
A WAVE IN HER POCKET by Lynn Joseph, ill. by Brian Pinkney *(Clarion)*
THE WRIGHT BROTHERS by Russell Freedman *(Holiday House)*

PEN/Norma Klein Award 🐾

This award commemorates Norma Klein (1938-1989), author of more than thirty novels for teenagers and adults. Presented biennially, the prize recognizes "an emerging voice of literary merit among American writers of children's fiction...new authors whose books, for elementary school to adult readers, demonstrate the adventuresome and innovative spirit that characterizes the best children's literature and Norma Klein's own work (but need not resemble her novels stylistically)." The award is administered by PEN American Center (568 Broadway, New York, NY 10012), whose Children's Book Committee Norma Klein served as co-chairman. PEN International is a world association of writers with centers in Europe, Asia, Africa, Australia, and the Americas. ($3,000)

1991
Cynthia Grant, author of PHOENIX RISING *(Atheneum)* and other novels

Phoenix Award ॐ

This award, originated and sponsored by the Children's Literature Association (22 Harvest Lane, Battle Creek, MI 49017), an organization encouraging the study of children's literature, is for "a book for children published twenty years earlier which did not win a major award at the time of its publication but which, from the perspective of time, is deemed worthy of special recognition for its literary quality." Only titles originally published in English are considered. The winners' first publishers appear in our listing; a book's U. S. publisher is also listed if the winner was first published abroad. (Statue)

1985
THE MARK OF THE HORSE LORD by Rosemary Sutcliff *(U. K.: Oxford, 1965; U. S.: Walck, 1965)*

1986
QUEENIE PEAVY by Robert Burch *(Viking, 1966)*

1987
SMITH by Leon Garfield *(U. K.: Constable, 1967; U. S.: Pantheon, 1967)*

1988
THE RIDER AND HIS HORSE by Erik Christian Haugaard *(Houghton, 1968)*

1989
THE NIGHT WATCHMEN by Helen Cresswell *(U. K.: Faber, 1969; U. S.: Macmillan, 1969)*

1990
ENCHANTRESS FROM THE STARS by Sylvia Louise Engdahl *(Atheneum, 1970)*

1991
A LONG WAY FROM VERONA by Jane Gardam *(U. K.: Hamish Hamilton, 1971; U. S.: Macmillan, 1971)*

1992
A SOUND OF CHARIOTS by Mollie Hunter *(U. K.: Hamish Hamilton, 1972; U. S.: Harper, 1972)*

Please Touch Book Award ॐ

This annual award is designed to encourage the publishing of books for children three and younger that provide enjoyment and learning. The award is sponsored by the Please Touch Museum for Children (210 N. 21st St., Philadelphia, PA 19103). (Medal)

1985
WHAT'S INSIDE? by Duanne Daughtry *(Knopf)*
1986
IS IT LARGER? IS IT SMALLER? by Tana Hoban
(Greenwillow)
1987
WHO'S COUNTING? by Nancy Tafuri *(Greenwillow)*
1988
CLAUDE AND SUN by Matt Novak *(Bradbury)*
1989
WHO'S SICK TODAY? by Lynne Cherry *(Dutton)*
1990
DINOSAURS, DINOSAURS by Byron Barton *(Crowell)*
1991
MAISY GOES TO BED by Lucy Cousins *(Little, Brown)*

Edgar Allan Poe Awards ⅋
BEST JUVENILE AND YOUNG ADULT NOVEL CATEGORIES

The Mystery Writers of America (236 West 27th St., New York, NY 10001) honors the best work in the mystery, crime, suspense, and intrigue fields in several media each year. An award for "Best Juvenile Novel" was added to the program in 1962, "Best Young Adult Novel" in 1989. In our listing, we use the codes *"J"* and *"Y/A"* as of 1989. The event at which the awards are presented is called the "Edgars," the mystery world's equivalent of Hollywood's "Oscars." (Ceramic bust of Poe)

1962
THE MYSTERY OF THE HAUNTED POOL by Phyllis A.
Whitney *(Westminster)*
1963
THE PHANTOM OF WALKAWAY HILL by Edward Fenton
(Doubleday)
1964
CUTLASS ISLAND by Scott Corbett *(Atlantic-Little, Brown)*
1965
THE MYSTERY OF THE HIDDEN HAND by Phyllis A.
Whitney *(Westminster)*
1966
THE MYSTERY AT CRANE'S LANDING by Marcella Thum
(Dodd)
1967
THE MYSTERY OF 22 EAST by Leon Ware *(Westminster)*

1968
SINBAD AND ME by Kin Platt *(Chilton)*
1969
SIGNPOST TO TERROR by Gretchen Sprague *(Dodd)*
1970
THE HOUSE OF DIES DREAR by Virginia Hamilton
(Macmillan)
1971
DANGER AT BLACK DYKE by Winifred Finlay *(Phillips)*
1972
THE INTRUDER by John Rowe Townsend *(Lippincott)*
1973
NIGHT FALL by Joan Aiken *(Holt)*
1974
DEATHWATCH by Robb White *(Doubleday)*
1975
THE LONG BLACK COAT by Jay Bennett *(Delacorte)*
1976
THE DANGLING WITNESS by Jay Bennett *(Delacorte)*
1977
Z FOR ZACHARIAH by Robert C. O'Brien *(Atheneum)*
1978
ARE YOU IN THE HOUSE ALONE? by Richard Peck *(Viking)*
1979
ALONE IN WOLF HOLLOW by Dana Brookins *(Clarion)*
1980
THE KIDNAPPING OF CHRISTINA LATTIMORE by Joan
Lowery Nixon *(HBJ)*
1981
THE SEANCE by Joan Lowery Nixon *(HBJ)*
1982
TAKING TERRI MUELLER by Norma Fox Mazer *(Avon)*
1983
THE MURDER OF HOUND DOG BATES by Robbie
Branscum *(Viking)*
1984
THE CALLENDER PAPERS by Cynthia Voigt *(Atheneum)*
1985
NIGHT CRY by Phyllis Reynolds Naylor *(Atheneum)*
1986
THE SANDMAN'S EYES by Patricia Windsor *(Delacorte)*
1987
THE OTHER SIDE OF THE DARK by Joan Lowery Nixon
(Delacorte)

1988
LUCY FOREVER AND MISS ROSETREE, SHRINKS by Susan
Shreve *(Holt)*
1989
J: MEGAN'S ISLAND by Willo Davis Roberts *(Atheneum)*
Y/A: INCIDENT AT LORING GROVES by Sonia Levitin *(Dial)*
1990
J: No Award
Y/A: SHOW ME THE EVIDENCE by Alane Ferguson
(Bradbury)
1991
J: STONEWORDS by Pam Conrad *(HarperCollins)*
Y/A: MOTE by Chap Reaver *(Delacorte)*

Redbook Children's Picturebook Awards 🍂

Redbook, a monthly magazine with about four million readers,
many of them young mothers, selects "the 10 best new
picturebooks for kids" that appears as a fully annotated and
illustrated list in its December issues. In its first years, the list
was separated into various categories; subsequently *Redbook*'s
judges have selected "ten winners." The titles selected have been
books that "open up new worlds to a child, offer interesting and
exciting ideas, stimulate the imagination, and give hours and
hours of enjoyment." (*Redbook*, 224 West 57th St., New York,
NY 10019). (Certificate)

1984
Hardcover
I KNOW A LADY by Charlotte Zolotow, ill. by James Stevenson
(Greenwillow)
I'M COMING TO GET YOU by Tony Ross *(Dial)*
THE MYSTERIES OF HARRIS BURDICK by Chris Van
Allsburg *(Houghton)*
YELLOW & PINK by William Steig *(Farrar)*
Paperback
THE EMPEROR'S NEW CLOTHES by Hans Christian
Andersen, retold and ill. by Nadine Bernard Westcott *(Atlantic)*
MOON MAN by Tomi Ungerer *(Harper)*
WHERE THE WILD THINGS ARE by Maurice Sendak
(Harper)
Pop-ups
THE CAR by Ray Marshall and John Bradley *(Viking)*

LEONARDO DA VINCI by Alice and Martin Provensen
(Viking)
SAILING SHIPS by Ron van der Meer and Alan McGowan
(Viking)

1985
Hardcover
ANNIE AND THE WILD ANIMALS by Jan Brett *(Houghton)*
IN OUR HOUSE by Anne Rockwell *(Crowell)*
THE POLAR EXPRESS by Chris Van Allsburg *(Houghton)*
SOLOMON THE RUSTY NAIL by William Steig *(Farrar)*
THERE WAS AN OLD WOMAN by Stephen Wyllie, ill. by
Maureen Roffey *(Harper)*
WATCH THE STARS COME OUT by Riki Levinson, ill. by
Diane Goode *(Dutton)*
Paperback
FREIGHT TRAIN by Donald Crews *(Puffin)*
IN THE NIGHT KITCHEN by Maurice Sendak *(Harper)*
MISS RUMPHIUS by Barbara Cooney *(Puffin)*
WILLIAM'S DOLL by Charlotte Zolotow, ill. by William Pène
du Bois *(Harper)*

1986
Hardcover
ABIYOYO: BASED ON A SOUTH AFRICAN LULLABY AND
FOLK STORY by Pete Seeger, ill. by Michael Hays *(Macmillan)*
BRAVE IRENE by William Steig *(Farrar)*
THE LITTLE BOOKMOBILE: COLORS, NUMBERS, AND
SHAPES, ON WHEELS by Suzanne Green, ill. by Daisuke Yokoi
(Doubleday)
RUMPELSTILTSKIN by Paul O. Zelinsky *(Dutton)*
A TOURNAMENT OF KNIGHTS by Joe Lasker *(Crowell)*
A YEAR OF BEASTS by Ashley Wolff *(Dutton)*
Paperback
ANNO'S COUNTING BOOK by Mitsumasa Anno *(Harper)*
THE GUINEA PIG ABC by Kate Duke *(Dutton)*
THE SNOWMAN by Raymond Briggs *(Random)*
WHAT DO YOU SAY, DEAR? A BOOK OF MANNERS FOR
ALL OCCASIONS by Sesyle Joslin, ill. by Maurice Sendak
(Harper)

1987
Hardcover
CREATURES OF THE DESERT WORLD *and* STRANGE
ANIMALS OF THE SEA *(National Geographic)*
HIGHER ON THE DOOR by James Stephenson *(Greenwillow)*
HUMPHREY'S BEAR by Jan Wahl, ill. by William Joyce *(Holt)*
JUMP AGAIN! MORE ADVENTURES OF BRER RABBIT by
Joel Chandler Harris, adapted by Van Dyke Parks, ill. by Barry
Moser *(HBJ)*

THE LOATHSOME DRAGON retold by David Wiesner and Kim Kahng, ill. by David Wiesner *(Putnam)*

THE MIDNIGHT FARM by Reeve Lindbergh, ill. by Susan Jeffers *(Dial)*

MONKEY'S CRAZY HOTEL by Stephen Wyllie, ill. by Maureen Roffey *(Harper)*

THE MONSTER BED by Jeanne Willis, ill. by Susan Varley *(Lothrop)*

A PLACE FOR BEN by Jeanne Titherington *(Greenwillow)* Paperback

THE WILD SWANS by Hans Christian Andersen, retold by Amy Ehrlich, ill. by Susan Jeffers *(Dial)*

1988

ANIMALS SHOWING OFF *and* CREATURES OF LONG AGO: DINOSAURS *(National Geographic)*

BLOSSOM COMES HOME by James Herriot, ill. by Ruth Brown *(St. Martin's)*

COMPANY'S COMING by Arthur Yorinks, ill. by David Small *(Crown)*

THE ENCHANTER'S DAUGHTER by Antonia Barber, ill. by Errol Le Cain *(Farrar)*

HOW MANY BUGS IN A BOX? by David A. Carter *(Simon & Schuster)*

THE INCREDIBLE PAINTING OF FELIX CLOUSSEAU by Jon Agee *(Farrar)*

JUNGLEWALK by Nancy Tafuri *(Greenwillow)*

THE SCAREBIRD by Sid Fleischman, ill. by Peter Sis *(Greenwillow)*

SPINKY SULKS by William Steig *(Farrar)*

TAIL FEATHERS FROM MOTHER GOOSE: THE OPIE RHYME BOOK compiled by Peter and Iona Opie *(Little, Brown)*

1989

ANIMALS ANIMALS compiled by Laura Whipple, ill. by Eric Carle *(Philomel)*

ANNABEL'S HOUSE by Norman Messenger *(Orchard)*

A CHILD'S GARDEN OF VERSES by Robert Louis Stevenson, various illustrators *(Chronicle)*

FRIEND OR FROG by Marjorie Priceman *(Houghton)*

THE LITTLE MERMAID by Hans Christian Andersen, ill. by Katie Thamer Treherne *(HBJ)*

MOUSE PAINT by Ellen Stoll Walsh *(HBJ)*

MY FIRST COOKBOOK by Angela Wilkes, photog. by David Johnson *(Knopf)*

NIGHT NOISES by Mem Fox, ill. by Terry Denton *(Gulliver/HBJ)*

SKIP TO MY LOU adapted and ill. by Nadine Bernard Westcott *(Joy Street/Little, Brown)*

TENREC'S TWIGS by Bert Kitchen *(Philomel)*

1990

AESOP'S FABLES compiled by Russell Ash and Bernard Higton, various illustrators *(Chronicle)*

BENJAMIN'S BARN by Reeve Lindbergh, ill. by Susan Jeffers *(Dial)*

CHARLIE ANDERSON by Barbara Abercrombie, ill. by Mark Graham *(McElderry)*

FEATHERS FOR LUNCH by Lois Ehlert *(HBJ)*

MANY MOONS by James Thurber, ill. by Marc Simont *(HBJ)*

TEAMMATES by Peter Golenbock, ill. by Paul Bacon *(HBJ)*

TRAIN SONG by Diane Siebert, ill. by Mike Wimmer *(Crowell)*

THE UGLY DUCKLING retold and ill. by Troy Howell *(Putnam)*

THE VERY QUIET CRICKET by Eric Carle *(Philomel)*

THE WHEELS ON THE BUS adapted and ill. by Paul 0. Zelinsky *(Dutton)*

1991

A IS FOR ANIMALS by David Pelham *(Simon & Schuster)*

BORREGUITA AND THE COYOTE by Verna Aardema, ill. by Petra Mathers *(Knopf)*

THE FISH WHO COULD WISH by John Bush, ill. by Korky Paul *(Kane/Miller)*

IN THE TALL, TALL GRASS by Denise Fleming *(Holt)*

THE MINPINS by Roald Dahl *(Viking)*

POLAR BEAR, POLAR BEAR by Bill Martin Jr., ill. by Eric Carle *(Holt)*

SEE HOW THEY GROW: FROG/PUPPY/KITTEN/DUCK photographed by Jane Burton, Kim Taylor and Barrie Watts *(Lodestar)*

THE STORY OF CHRISTMAS: WORDS FROM THE GOSPELS OF MATTHEW AND LUKE by Jane Ray *(Dial)*

TEN LITTLE RABBITS by Virginia Grossman, ill. by Sylvia Long *(Chronicle)*

WHITE IS THE MOON by Valerie Greeley *(Macmillan)*

Carl Sandburg Literary Arts Awards 🎗

CHILDREN'S LITERATURE CATEGORY

This annual awards program, named for the famous Illinois poet and biographer, includes a children's literature category. The recipients are authors who are natives of or live in the six-county Chicago metropolitan area. The award is sponsored by the Friends of the Chicago Public Library (Harold Washington Library Center, 400 South State St. 9S-7, Chicago, IL 60605) (Medal and $1,000)

1980
CUTE IS A FOUR-LETTER WORD by Stella Pevsner *(Clarion)*
1981
DO BANANAS CHEW GUM? by Jamie Gilson *(Lothrop)*
1982
BEHIND THE SCENES AT THE HORSE HOSPITAL by Fern Brown *(Whitman)*
1983
WAIT, SKATES! by Mildred Johnson *(Children's Press)*
1984
PITCHER PLANTS, THE ELEGANT INSECT TRAPS by Carol Lerner *(Morrow)*
1985
THE SEARCH FOR GRISSI by Mary Frances Shura *(Dodd)*
1986
THATCHER PAYNE-IN-THE-NECK by Betty Bates *(Holiday House)*
1987
ELI'S GHOST by Betsy Hearne *(McElderry)*
1988
THE GOATS by Brock Cole *(Farrar)*
1989
A CIRCLE UNBROKEN by Sollace Hotze *(Clarion)*
1990
THE HOUSE ON WALENSKA STREET by Charlotte Herman *(Dutton)*
1991
THE BRIDGE DANCERS by Carol Saller *(Carolrhoda)*

School Library Media Specialists of Southeastern New York Award ❧

This annual award for an author or illustrator living in a seven-county region of Southeastern New York State for a body of work that is an outstanding contribution to children's and/or young adult literature is sponsored by School Library Media Specialists of Southeastern New York, an affiliate of the School Library Media Section, New York Library Association. As the administration of this program changes annually, there is not a continuing address to contact for additional information. (Engraved plate)

1980   Eleanor Clymer
1981   Jean Craighead George
1982   Leonard Kessler
1983   Susan Beth Pfeffer
1984   Jean Fritz
1985   Paul Galdone
1986   Alice and Martin Provensen
1987   Charlotte Zolotow
1988   Judie Angell
1989   Scott O'Dell
1990   Susan Jeffers
1991   Lilian Moore
1992   Nancy Willard

Society of Midland Authors Book Awards 🥀

CHILDREN'S FICTION & NONFICTION CATEGORIES

Beginning in 1961, the Society of Midland Authors (c/o Jim
Bowman, 152 N. Scoville, Oak Park, IL 60302) presented an
annual award named in honor of the distinguished writer and
Laura Ingalls Wilder Medalist, Clara Ingram Judson. That award
was for an outstanding children's book of the year written by a
native or resident of the Midwest. This awards program   •
continued through 1970. Thereafter, the Society presented an
award for children's books from time to time. Currently, the
Society sponsors an awards program that includes children's
fiction (F) and nonfiction (NF) categories. The authors and/or
subject matter of books receiving the awards have a connection
with the twelve-state American Midland. A Midland author is
one who now resides in the Midland, who grew up there, or
whose book has a Midland setting. (Plaque and $300)

1961
GAUDENZIA: PRIDE OF THE PALIO by Marguerite Henry
(Rand)
1962
THE DRAGON TREE by Val Gendron (McKay)
1963
TO LIGHT A SINGLE CANDLE by Beverly Butler (Dodd)

1964
GEORGE SHANNON: YOUNG EXPLORER WITH LEWIS AND CLARK by Virginia S. Eifert *(Dodd)*
1965
ACROSS FIVE APRILS by Irene Hunt *(Follett)*
1966
A CERTAIN SMALL SHEPHERD by Rebecca Caudill *(Holt)*
1967
THE LIVING COMMUNITY: A VENTURE INTO ECOLOGY by S. Carl Hirsch *(Viking)*
1968
THE COUNT WHO WISHED HE WERE A PEASANT by Morris Philipson *(Pantheon)*
1969
THE ILLINOIS RIVER by James Ayars *(Holt)*
1970
WIZARD OF THE DOME: R. BUCKMINSTER FULLER by Sidney Rosen *(Little, Brown)*
1971-1975
No Awards
1976
HE AND SHE by S. Carl Hirsch *(Lippincott)*
1977
OUR SNOWMAN HAD OLIVE EYES by Charlotte Herman *(Dutton)*
1978
AND YOU GIVE ME A PAIN, ELAINE by Stella Pevsner *(Clarion)*
THE ORPHANS by Berniece Rabe *(Dutton)*
1979-1981
No Awards
1982
MOON AND ME by Hadley Irwin *(McElderry)*
1983
JOEL: GROWING UP A FARM MAN by Patricia and Jack Demuth *(Dodd)*
1984
LOVE IN A DIFFERENT KEY by Marjorie Franco *(Houghton)*
1985
F: TRACKER by Gary Paulsen *(Bradbury)*
NF: WAITING TO WALTZ: A CHILDHOOD by Cynthia Rylant *(Bradbury)*
1986
PRAIRIE SONGS by Pam Conrad *(Harper)*
1987
MRS. PORTREE'S PONY by Lynn Hall *(Scribner)*

1988
F: VIEW FROM THE PIGHOUSE ROOF by Violet Olsen
(Atheneum)
NF: MAGGIE BY MY SIDE by Beverly Butler *(Dodd)*
1989
F: SONG AND DANCE MAN by Karen Ackerman *(Knopf)*
NF: A series of books about dinosaurs by Janet Riehecky *(Child's World)*
1990
No Awards
1991
F: ROBODAD by Alden R. Carter *(Putnam)*
NF: WOODSONG by Gary Paulsen *(Bradbury)*

Southern California Council on Literature for Children and Young People Awards 🙰

The Southern California Council on Literature for Children and Young People (P.O. Box 5249, North Hollywood, CA 91616) gives awards to authors and illustrators living in Southern California. Areas in which awards are given vary from year to year. The listing below includes only the awards relating to literature. The program also includes an award for services to book promotion and literature, now called the Dorothy C. McKenzie Award, in honor of SCCLCYP's founder. Specific books listed were published in the year before the award year. (Plaque)

1961
Notable book: ISLAND OF THE BLUE DOLPHINS by Scott O'Dell *(Houghton)*
Significant contribution in the field of illustration: MOY MOY by Leo Politi *(Scribner)*
Comprehensive contribution of lasting value: Conrad and Mary Buff, Lucille and Holling C. Holling
1962
Notable book: LEGEND OF BILLY BLUESAGE by Jonreed Lauritzen *(Little, Brown)*
A significant contribution in the field of illustration: COME AGAIN, PELICAN by Don Freeman *(Viking)*
Distinguished contribution to the field of children's literature: Clyde Robert Bulla

1963

Notable book: FROM THE EAGLE'S WING by Hildegard Hoyt Swift *(Morrow)*

Distinguished contribution to the field of children's literature: W.W. and Irene Robinson

1964

Notable book: BY THE GREAT HORN SPOON by Sid Fleischman *(Atlantic-Little, Brown)*

Significant contribution in the field of illustration: WILD WINGS OVER THE MARSHES by Lucielle N. and William D. Stratton, ill. by Bernard Garbutt *(Golden Gate)*

Distinguished contribution to the fields of illustration and writing: Taro Yashima

1965

Notable book: A DAWN IN THE TREES: THOMAS JEFFERSON, THE YEARS 1776 TO 1789 by Leonard Wibberley *(Farrar)*

Distinguished contribution to the field of children's literature: Eleanor Cameron

1966

Notable book: DORP DEAD by Julia Cunningham *(Pantheon)*

Comprehensive contribution of lasting value to the field of children's literature: Carol Ryrie Brink

1967

Notable book: THE ROYAL DIRK by John and Patricia Beatty *(Morrow)*

Significant contribution in the field of illustration: FAREWELL TO SHADY GLADE by Bill Peet *(Houghton)*

Comprehensive contribution of lasting value to the field of children's literature: Margot Benary-Isbert

1968

Significant contribution to the field of illustration: SEASHORE STORY by Taro Yashima *(Viking)*

Significant contribution to the field of literature for young people: Lorenz Graham

Comprehensive contribution of lasting value in the field of literature for children and young people: Myra Cohn Livingston

Significant contribution to the field of informational books for children and young people: Charles Coombs

1969

Notable book: THE BEARS AND I by Robert Franklin Leslie *(Dutton)*

Comprehensive contribution of lasting value for children and young people: Harriet Huntingdon

1970

Notable book: THE CAY by Theodore Taylor *(Doubleday)*

Significant contribution in the field of illustration: NEW MOON COVE by Ann Atwood *(Scribner)*

Distinguished contribution to the field of folklore: Richard Chase

1971

Notable book: THE DAYBREAKERS by Jane Louise Curry *(HBJ)*

Significant contribution in the field of illustration: BOBBY SHAFTO'S GONE TO SEA by Graham Booth, ill. by Mark Taylor *(Golden Gate)*

Comprehensive contribution of lasting value to the field of children's literature: Margaret Leighton

1972

Notable book: ANOTHER PLACE, ANOTHER SPRING by Adrienne Jones *(Houghton)*

Comprehensive contribution of lasting value to the literature for children and young people: Sid Fleischman

Distinguished contribution exhibiting the fusion of poetry and photography: Ann Atwood and Mark Pines of Lyceum Productions

1973

Notable book: THE MALIBU AND OTHER POEMS by Myra Cohn Livingston *(McElderry)*

Comprehensive contribution of lasting value to the field of children's literature: Marguerite Henry

1974

Distinguished work of fiction: CHLORIS AND THE CREEPS by Kin Platt *(Chilton)*

Distinguished work of nonfiction: JUAREZ, A SON OF THE PEOPLE by Jean Rouverol *(Macmillan)*

Comprehensive contribution of lasting value to the field of children's literature: Patricia Beatty

Special contribution to children's literature: Theodor S. Geisel *(Dr. Seuss)*

1975

Distinguished work of fiction: SO, NOTHING IS FOREVER by Adrienne Jones *(Houghton)*

Distinguished work of nonfiction: BEFORE THE SUPREME COURT: THE STORY OF BELVA ANN LOCKWOOD by Terry Dunnahoo *(Houghton)*

Significant contribution to the field of illustration: SON OF THUNDER by Ethel K. McHale, ill. by Ruth Bornstein *(Children's Press)*

1976

Notable book: SHOESHINE GIRL by Clyde Robert Bulla *(Crowell)*

Significant contribution in the field of illustration for total concept and illustration: WILL'S QUILL by Don Freeman *(Viking)*

Significant contribution in the field of illustration: LITTLE PIECES OF THE WEST WIND by Christian Garrison, ill. by Diane Goode *(Bradbury)*; THE SELCHIE'S SEED by Sulamith Oppenheim, ill. by Diane Goode *(Bradbury)*

Significant contribution for excellence in a series: The HENRY books by Mark Taylor *(Atheneum)*

Distinguished contribution to the field of children's literature: Helen Hinkley Jones

1977

Notable book of fiction: THE MARK OF CONTE by Sonia Levitin *(Atheneum)*

Significant contribution to the field of illustration: LITTLE GORILLA by Ruth Bornstein *(Clarion)*

Significant contribution for excellence in a series: TREEGATE CHRONICLES by Leonard Wibberley *(Farrar)*

1978

Best work of fiction: GHOST SUMMER by Eve Bunting *(Warne)*

Distinguished contribution to the field of children's literature: Theodore Taylor

1979

Distinguished work of fiction: ALONE IN WOLF HOLLOW by Dana Brookins *(Clarion)*

Significant contribution to the field of illustration: THE DREAM EATER by Christian Garrison, ill. by Diane Goode *(Bradbury)*

Significant contribution for a body of work: Jane Louise Curry

1980

Distinguished work of nonfiction: THE SNOW MONKEY AT HOME by Margaret Rau *(Knopf)*

Special recognition for a contribution of cultural significance: BEYOND THE EAST WIND; KHMERS, TIGERS AND TALISMANS; ENCIRCLED KINGDOM (Trilogy) by Jewell Rinehart Coburn and Duong Van Quyen *(Burn, Hart)*

Significant contribution for a body of work: Frank Bonham

1981

Notable work of fiction: STONE FOX by John Reynolds Gardiner *(Crowell)*

Distinguished body of work: Sonia Levitin

1982

Distinguished work of fiction: WHICH WAY COURAGE by Eiveen Weiman *(Atheneum)*

Significant contribution for excellence in a series: The JEWISH HOLIDAYS books by Malka Drucker *(Holiday House)*

Distinguished body of work: Julia Cunningham

1983

Distinguished work of fiction: JONATHAN DOWN UNDER by Patricia Beatty *(Morrow)*

Distinguished work of nonfiction: WINDOWS IN SPACE by Ann Elwood and Linda Wood *(Walker)*

Special recognition for excellence in a series: DORIS FEIN mysteries by T. Ernesto Bethancourt *(Holiday House)*

Special recognition for a contribution of cultural significance: STORY FOR A BLACK NIGHT by Clayton Bess *(Houghton)*

1984
Distinguished work of fiction: NADIA THE WILLFUL by Sue Alexander *(Pantheon)*
Recognition of merit for a first novel: ELEMENT OF TIME by Kathy Livoni *(HBJ)*
Distinguished body of work: Adrienne Jones

1985
Notable work of fiction: PRUNE by Raymond Royal Ross *(Atheneum)*
Notable work of nonfiction: TOO FAT? TOO THIN? DO YOU HAVE A CHOICE? by Caroline Arnold *(Morrow)*
Significant contribution in the field of illustration: THE NAPPING HOUSE by Audrey Wood, ill. by Don Wood *(HBJ)*

1986
Notable work of fiction: A PLACE FOR ALLIE by M. V. Carey *(Dodd)*
Notable work of nonfiction: THE COMET AND YOU by Edwin Krupp and Robin Rector Krupp *(Macmillan)*
Excellence in a series for young people with underdeveloped reading skills: LIPPINCOTT PAGE TURNERS by Eve Bunting *(Lippincott)*

1987
Distinguished work of nonfiction: I LIFT MY LAMP: EMMA LAZARUS AND THE STATUE OF LIBERTY by Nancy Smiler Levinson *(Lodestar)*
Notable achievement in photojournalism: MOTORCYCLE ON PATROL: THE STORY OF A HIGHWAY OFFICER by Joan and Richard Hewett *(Clarion)*
Outstanding contribution of lasting value in a body of work: Clyde Robert Bulla

1988
Excellence in illustration: THE FLAME OF PEACE: A TALE OF THE AZTECS by Deborah Nourse Lattimore *(Harper)*
Outstanding work of fiction for children: LILA ON THE LANDING by Sue Alexander *(Clarion)*
Outstanding work of fiction for young adults: INVINCIBLE SUMMER by Jean Ferris *(Farrar)*

1989
Outstanding literary quality in a picture book: YONDER by Tony Johnston (ill. by Lloyd Bloom) *(Dial)*
Outstanding work of fiction for children: DEAR BABY by Joanne Rocklin *(Macmillan)*
Outstanding work of fiction for young adults: A SUDDEN SILENCE by Eve Bunting *(HBJ)*
Special recognition for excellence in a poetry quartet: EARTH SONGS (1986), SEA SONGS (1986), SKY SONGS (1984), SPACE SONGS (1988) by Myra Cohn Livingston *(Holiday House)*

1990
Distinguished work of fiction for children: THE WEDNESDAY
SURPRISE by Eve Bunting *(Clarion)*
Distinguished work of fiction for young adults: WRESTLING
WITH HONOR by David Klass *(Lodestar)*
Distinguished work of nonfiction: ONCE UPON A HORSE by
Suzanne Jurmain *(Lothrop)*
Notable book celebrating a creative life: BILL PEET: AN
AUTOBIOGRAPHY by Bill Peet *(Houghton)*
1991
Distinguished work of illustrating and writing: THE DRAGON'S
ROBE by Deborah Nourse Lattimore *(HarperCollins)*
Distinguished work of fiction: THE WALL by Eve Bunting
(Clarion)
Distinguished work of fiction for young adults: DIXIE STORMS
by Barbara Hall *(HBJ)*
Distinguished work of nonfiction: CHRISTOPHER COLUMBUS:
VOYAGER TO THE UNKNOWN by Nancy Smiler Levinson
(Lodestar)

Southwest Book Awards ❧

"The Southwest Book Awards were instituted in 1971 to
encourage the writing and publication of outstanding literature
about the Southwest." In the early years of the program, books
in numerous categories were honored. Currently, there are only
three categories: Arts and Letters, History and Biography, and
Nonfiction. Children's and young adult books are considered for
honors in all three areas. "Southwest" is defined as Texas, west
of the Pecos River, Northern Mexico, Southern New Mexico,
and Eastern and Southern Arizona. The awards are sponsored by
the Border Regional Library Association (P. O. Box 5342, El
Paso, TX 79901). (Certificate)

1971
THE SPIDER, THE CAVE, AND THE POTTERY BOWL by
Eleanor Clymer *(Atheneum)*
1972
WHEN CLAY SINGS by Byrd Baylor, ill. by Tom Bahti
(Scribner)
1975
THE DESERT IS THEIRS by Byrd Baylor, ill. by Peter Parnall
(Scribner)
MANY WINTERS by Nancy Wood *(Doubleday)*

1976
HAWK, I'M YOUR BROTHER by Byrd Baylor, ill. by Peter Parnall *(Scribner)*

1979
TARANTULAS by Joan Berg Victor *(Dodd)*

1982
DESERT VOICES by Byrd Baylor, ill. by Peter Parnall *(Scribner)*

1985
GRANDMOTHER'S ADOBE DOLLHOUSE by Mary Lou M. Smith *(New Mexico Magazine)*

1986
PECOS BILL by Steven Kellogg *(Morrow)*

1987
DOCTOR COYOTE: A NATIVE AMERICAN AESOP'S FABLES by John Bierhorst, ill. by Wendy Watson *(Macmillan)*
THE PUEBLO by Charlotte and David Yue *(Houghton)*

1988
DAWN SEEKERS by Carol Hamilton, ill. by Jeremy Guitar *(Whitman)*

1989
DESERT GIANT: THE WORLD OF THE SAGUARO CACTUS by Barbara Bash *(Sierra Club/ Little, Brown)*

1990
AGAVE BLOOMS JUST ONCE by Gisela Jernigan, ill. by E. Wesley Jernigan *(Harbinger)*

1991
ROXABOXEN by Alice McLerran, ill. by Barbara Cooney *(Lothrop)*

State Historical Society of Wisconsin Book Awards 🔔

JUVENILE BOOK CATEGORY

The State Historical Society of Wisconsin (816 State St., Madison, WI 53706) is the sponsor of an annual awards program. In years in which an award is presented for a children's book, the honored title is judged to have made a contribution to readers' knowledge of the State of Wisconsin. (Certificate)

1966
FEATHER IN THE WIND by Beverly Butler *(Dodd)*

1967
SPAN ACROSS THE RIVER by Donald Emerson *(McKay)*

1968
No Award

1969
NINE LIVES OF MOSES ON THE OREGON TRAIL by
Marion Fuller Archer *(Whitman)*

1970
No Award

1971
HIGGINS OF THE RAILROAD MUSEUM by Ethelyn M.
Parkinson *(Abingdon)*

1972-1974
No Awards

1975
SONGS OF THE CHIPPEWA edited by John Bierhorst *(Farrar)*

1976
No Award

1977
CUTOVER COUNTRY: JOLIE'S STORY by Jolie Paylin *(Iowa
State University Press)*

1978-1982
No Awards

1983
FIRST FARM IN THE VALLEY: ANNA'S STORY by Anne
Pellowski *(Philomel)*

1984
THE CHILD OF TWO MOTHERS by Malcolm and Margaret
Rosholt *(Rosholt House)*

1985
No Award

1986
RAILROADS OF SOUTHERN & SOUTHWESTERN
WISCONSIN: DEVELOPMENT TO DECLINE by Daniel J.
Lanz *(Ski Printers)*

1987
No Award

1988
THE STORY OF OLD ABE by Malcolm and Margaret Rosholt
(Rosholt House)

1989-1990
No Awards

1991
ADVENTURES OF THE NORTHWOODS (series) by Lois
Walfrid Johnson *(Bethany House)*

George G. Stone Center for Children's Books Recognition of Merit Award ❧

Given annually since 1965 at the Claremont Reading Conference (Claremont Graduate School, Claremont, CA 91711) to an author or illustrator of a children's book or for a body of work for the "power to please and to expand the awareness of children and teachers as they have shared the book in their classrooms." (The Center is named for a benefactor.) (Scroll)

1965
CRICKET SONGS translated by Harry Behn *(HBJ)*

1966
CALENDAR MOON by Natalia M. Belting *(Holt)*

1967
DURANGO STREET by Frank Bonham *(Dutton)*

1968
WHITE BIRD by Clyde Robert Bulla *(Crowell)*

1969
MY SIDE OF THE MOUNTAIN by Jean Craighead George *(Dutton)*

1970
CHARLOTTE'S WEB by E.B. White *(Harper)*

1971
THE PHANTOM TOLLBOOTH by Norton Juster *(Random)*

1972
BY THE GREAT HORN SPOON by Sid Fleischman *(Atlantic Little, Brown)*

1973
THE EGYPT GAME by Zilpha Keatley Snyder *(Atheneum)*

1974
QUEENIE PEAVY by Robert Burch *(Viking)*

1975
INCIDENT AT HAWK'S HILL by Allan W. Eckert *(Little, Brown)*

1976
Body of work of Leo Lionni

1977
THE WHITE MOUNTAINS *(The Tripods Trilogy)* by John Christopher *(Macmillan)*

1978
FROG AND TOAD books by Arnold Lobel *(Harper)*

1979
Body of work of Natalie Babbitt
1980
TEETONCEY STORIES *(The Cape Hatteras Trilogy)*
by Theodore Taylor *(Doubleday)*
1981
No Award
1982
Body of work of Mary Stolz
1983
Body of work of Beverly Cleary
1984
A LIGHT IN THE ATTIC by Shel Silverstein *(Harper)*
WHERE THE SIDEWALK ENDS by Shel Silverstein *(Harper)*
1985
Body of work of Bill Peet
1986
Body of work of Tana Hoban
1987
STONE FOX by John Reynolds Gardiner *(Crowell)*
1988
ALEXANDER AND THE TERRIBLE, HORRIBLE, NO
GOOD, VERY BAD DAY by Judith Viorst *(Atheneum)*
1989
THE BEARS' HOUSE by Marilyn Sachs *(Dutton)*
FRAN ELLEN'S HOUSE by Marilyn Sachs *(Dutton)*
1990
HONEY, I LOVE AND OTHER LOVE POEMS by Eloise
Greenfield *(Crowell)*
1991
LET THE CIRCLE BE UNBROKEN by Mildred D. Taylor
(Dial)
THE ROAD TO MEMPHIS by Mildred D. Taylor *(Dial)*
ROLL OF THUNDER, HEAR MY CRY by Mildred D. Taylor
(Dial)

Joan G. Sugarman
Children's Book Award ❧

This award honors excellence in writing for children by authors
who are residents of Washington, DC, Virginia, or Maryland.
Joan G. Sugarman, a children's book author and librarian,
established the award in honor of her late husband, Norman A.

Sugarman. Originally presented each year, the award is now a biennial one, administered by the Washington Independent Writers Legal and Educational Fund (220 Woodward Bldg., 733 15th St., NW, Washington, DC 20005), a nonprofit organization founded "to defend First Amendment cases and address other concerns of independent writers." ($1,000)

1988
BEETLES, LIGHTLY TOASTED by Phyllis Reynolds Naylor (*Atheneum*)
1989
TREE BY LEAF by Cynthia Voigt *(Atheneum)*
1990
SHABANU: DAUGHTER OF THE WIND by Suzanne Fisher Staples *(Knopf)*
1992
STEPPING ON THE CRACKS by Mary Downing Hahn *(Clarion)*

Sydney Taylor Book Awards ❧

The Sydney Taylor Book Awards are part of the awards program of the Association of Jewish Libraries (AJL) (c/o National Foundation for Jewish Culture, 330 Seventh Ave., 21st floor, New York, NY 10001). AJL first gave an award for children's books in 1969, for a book published in 1968. Then called the Shirley Kravitz Award, this honors program originated as an activity of AJL's School and Center Division. In 1975 AJL integrated its award for books for young readers into the overall Association of Jewish Libraries Awards program, establishing a separate category for children's books. Another distinction was added to the AJL Awards for 1978: the Sydney Taylor Body of Work Award for an author. It honored the memory of the creator of the warmly appreciated series of "All-of-a-Kind Family" books about Jewish family life in New York's Lower East Side in the early part of the 20th century. As of the program relating to 1981 books, there were provisions for awards for a book for older children, and also a book for younger children. By 1985—featuring 1984 titles—the entire AJL program honoring children's books deemed by a committee of professional Judaica librarians to have made outstanding contributions to Jewish literature for young readers was renamed the Sydney Taylor Book Awards. In addition to honoring published works and authors for a body of work, AJL also sponsors an annual Sydney Taylor Manuscript Award for unpublished authors. In the listing below, honorees are preceded by 0 = book for older readers, Y = book for younger readers, and B = body of work. In some years, it is apparent, awards have not been given in all categories. (Plaque and honorarium)

1968
0: THE ENDLESS STEPPE by Esther Hautzig *(Crowell)*
1969
0: OUR EDDIE by Sulamith Ish-Kishor *(Pantheon)*
1970
0: THE YEAR by Suzanne Lange *(Phillips)*
1971
B: Isaac Bashevis Singer
1972
B: Molly Cone
1973
0: UNCLE MISHA'S PARTISANS by Yuri Suhl *(Four Winds)*
1974
No Award
1975
0: WAITING FOR MAMA by Marietta Moskin *(Coward)*
1976
0: NEVER TO FORGET: THE JEWS OF THE HOLOCAUST by Milton Meltzer *(Harper)*
1977
0: EXIT FROM HOME by Anita Heyman *(Crown)*
1978
0: THE DEVIL IN VIENNA by Doris Orgel *(Dial)*
B: Sydney Taylor (posthumously)
1979
0: IKE AND MAMA AND THE BLOCK WEDDING by Carol Snyder *(Coward)*
B: Marilyn Hirsch
1980
0: A RUSSIAN FAREWELL by Leonard Everett Fisher *(Four Winds)*
B: Sadie Rose Weilerstein
1981
0: THE NIGHT JOURNEY by Kathryn Lasky *(Warne)*
Y: YUSSEL'S PRAYER: A YOM KIPPUR STORY by Barbara Cohen *(Lothrop)*
B: Barbara Cohen
1982
0: CALL ME RUTH by Marilyn Sachs *(Doubleday)*
Y: CASTLE ON HESTER STREET by Linda Heller *(Jewish Publication Society)*

1983
0: IN THE MOUTH OF THE WOLF by Rose Zar *(Jewish Publication Society)*
Y: BUBBIE, ME AND MEMORIES by Barbara Pomerantz *(Union of American Hebrew Congregations)*

1984
0: THE ISLAND ON BIRD STREET by Uri Orlev, translated by Hillel Halkin *(Houghton)*
Y: MRS. MOSKOWITZ AND THE SABBATH CANDLESTICKS by Amy Schwartz *(Jewish Publication Society)*
B: Miriam Chaikin

1985
0: IKE AND MAMA AND THE SEVEN SURPRISES by Carol Snyder *(Lothrop)*
Y: BROTHERS by Florence B. Freedman, ill. by Robert Andrew Parker *(Harper)*
B: Carol Snyder

1986
0: BEYOND THE HIGH WHITE WALL by Nancy Pitt *(Scribner)*
Y: JOSEPH WHO LOVED THE SABBATH by Marilyn Hirsh, ill. by Devis Grebu *(Viking)*

1987
0: THE RETURN by Sonia Levitin *(Atheneum)*
Y: THE NUMBER ON MY GRANDFATHER'S ARM by David A. Adler, photog. by Rose Eichenbaum *(Union of American Hebrew Congregations)*

1988
0: THE DEVIL'S ARITHMETIC by Jane Yolen *(Viking)*
Y: THE KEEPING QUILT by Patricia Polacco *(Simon & Schuster)*

1989
0: NUMBER THE STARS by Lois Lowry *(Houghton)*
Y: BERCHICK by Esther Silverstein Blanc, ill. by Tennessee Dixon *(Volcano)*
B: Yaffa Ganz

1990
0: MY GRANDMOTHER'S STORIES by Adele Geras, ill. by Jael Jorden *(Knopf)*
Y: THE CHANUKKAH GUEST by Eric Kimmel, ill. by Giori Carmi *(Holiday House)*

University of Southern Mississippi Medallion 🔔

This award is given annually in the spring at the University of Southern Mississippi Children's Book Festival (School of Library Service, Hattiesburg, MS 39406) to a writer or illustrator who has made an outstanding contribution to the field of children's literature. The awards program is a project of the de Grummond Children's Literature Research Collection of the university's McCain Library. (Silver medallion)

1969 Lois Lenski
1970 Ernest H. Shepard
1971 Roger Duvoisin
1972 Marcia Brown
1973 Lynd Ward
1974 Taro Yashima
1975 Barbara Cooney
1976 Scott O'Dell
1977 Adrienne Adams
1978 Madeleine L'Engle
1979 Leonard Everett Fisher
1980 Ezra Jack Keats
1981 Maurice Sendak
1982 Beverly Cleary
1983 Katherine Paterson
1984 Peter Spier
1985 Arnold Lobel
1986 Jean Craighead George
1987 Paula Fox
1988 Jean Fritz
1989 Lee Bennett Hopkins
1990 Charlotte Zolotow
1991 Richard Peck

Washington Post/Childrens' Book Guild Nonfiction Award 🔔

This awards program was initially a project of the Childrens' Book Guild, a Washington DC-area association of authors, illustrators, editors and a variety of other children's literature specialists. As of 1983, the *Washington Post* (1150 15th St., NW, Washington, DC 20071) joined with the Guild as a co-sponsor of the award, which is given to an author or illustrator for a body of work in informational books for young readers. (Inscribed paperweight and a cash award)

1977 David Macaulay
1978 Millicent Selsam
1979 Jean Fritz
1980 Shirley Glubok
1981 Milton Meltzer
1982 Tana Hoban
1983 Patricia Lauber
1984 Jill Krementz
1985 Isaac Asimov
1986 Kathryn Lasky
1987 Gail Gibbons
1988 Jim Arnosky
1989 Leonard Everett Fisher
1990 Brent Ashabranner
1991 Joanna Cole
1992 Russell Freedman

Western Heritage Awards ❧
JUVENILE BOOK CATEGORY

Given annually by the National Cowboy Hall of Fame and Western Heritage Center (1700 N.E. 63rd St., Oklahoma City, OK 73111) to a juvenile book that best portrays the authentic American West. (Bronze *Wrangler* trophy)

1962
KING OF THE MOUNTAIN by Gene Caesar *(Dutton)*
1963
THE BOOK OF THE WEST by Charles Clifton *(Bobbs)*
1964
KILLER-OF-DEATH by Betty Baker *(Harper)*
1965
THE GREATEST CATTLE DRIVE by Paul Wellman *(Houghton)*
1966
LAND RUSH by Carl C. Hodges *(Duell-Sloan)*

1967
MUSTANG by Marguerite Henry *(Rand McNally)*
1968
DOWN THE RIVERS, WESTWARD HO! by Eric Scott
(Meredith)
1969
EDGE OF TWO WORLDS by Weyman Jones *(Dial)*
1970
AN AWFUL NAME TO LIVE UP TO by Jossie Hosford
(Meredith)
1971
AND ONE WAS A WOODEN INDIAN by Betty Baker
(Macmillan)
1972
THE BLACK MUSTANGER by Richard Wormser *(Morrow)*
1973
FAMOUS AMERICAN EXPLORERS by Bern Keating *(Rand McNally)*
1974
No Award
1975
SUSY'S SCOUNDREL by Harold Keith *(Crowell)*
1976
OWL IN THE CEDAR TREE by Natachee Scott Momaday
(Northland Press)
1977-1978
No Awards
1979
THE OBSTINATE LAND by Harold Keith *(Crowell)*
1980
THE *LITTLE HOUSE* COOKBOOK by Barbara Walker
(Harper)
1981-1983
No Awards
1984
CHILDREN OF THE WILD WEST by Russell Freedman
(Clarion)
1985
No Award
1986
HAPPILY MAY I WALK: AMERICAN INDIANS AND
ALASKA NATIVES TODAY by Arlene Hirschfelder *(Scribner)*
1987
THE COVERED WAGON AND OTHER ADVENTURES by
Lynn H. Scott *(University of Nebraska)*

1988
STAY PUT, ROBBIE McAMIS by Frances G. Tunbo *(Texas Christian University)*

1989
LETTERS TO OMA by Marj Gurasich *(Texas Christian University)*

1990
BUNKHOUSE JOURNAL by Diane Johnston Hamm *(Scribner)*

1991
MONSTER SLAYER: A NAVAJO FOLKTALE retold by Vee Brown, ill. by Baje Whitethorne *(Northland)*

Western Writers of America Spur Awards 🌿

BEST WESTERN JUVENILE CATEGORIES

The Spur Awards aim to encourage "high achievement in literature and art that portray the history and heritage of The American West." They are given to works in many categories, including novels, historical novels, nonfiction, short fiction and nonfiction, cover art, scripts for both motion pictures and television, and include awards for fiction and nonfiction books for young readers. If the quality of the entries is high for both fiction *(F)* and nonfiction *(NF)* juveniles, two awards are presented. In some years, only one award is presented to a juvenile book. In addition to the Spur Awards, the sponsor (Western Writers of America, Inc., Attn.: Betty Ketcham, Secretary-Treasurer, P. O. Box 823, Sheridan, WY 82801) administers the Medicine Pipe Bearer's Award for a first novel, for which juveniles are eligible. The year cited is the year in which books were published. (Spurs and a plaque)

1953
SAGEBRUSH SORREL by Frank C. Robertson *(Nelson)*

1954
YOUNG HERO OF THE RANGE by Stephen Payne *(Lantern)*

1955
No Award

1956
TRAPPING THE SILVER BEAVER by Charles Niehuis *(Dodd)*

1957
WOLF BROTHER by James Kjelgaard *(Holiday House)*

1958
STEAMBOAT UP THE MISSOURI by Dale White *(Viking)*
1959
F: THEIR SHINING HOUR by Romona Maher Weeks *(John Day)*
NF: HOLD BACK THE HUNTER by Dale White *(Marion T. Place)*
1960
THE HORSE TALKER by Jeanne Williams *(Prentice-Hall)*
1961
No Award
1962
THE WESTERN HORSE by Natlee Kenoyer *(Meredith)*
1963
BY THE GREAT HORN SPOON by Sid Fleischman *(Atlantic-Little, Brown)*
THE STORY CATCHER by Mari Sandoz *(Westminster)*
1964
RIDE A NORTHBOUND HORSE by Richard Wormser *(Morrow)*
1965
THE STUBBORN ONE by Rutherford Montgomery *(Duell-Sloan)*
1966
F: THE BURNING GLASS by Annabel and Edgar Johnson *(Harper)*
NF: VALLEY OF THE SMALLEST by Aileen Fisher *(Crowell)*
1967
F: THE DUNDERHEAD WAR by Betty Baker *(Harper)*
HALF BREED by Evelyn Lampman *(Doubleday)*
NF: TO THE PACIFIC WITH LEWIS AND CLARK by Ralph Andrist and E.R. Bingham *(Harper)*
1968
F: MIDDL'UN by Elizabeth Burleson *(Follett)*
NF: RIFLES AND WARBONNETS by Marian T. Place *(Washburn)*
1969
F: THE MEEKER MASSACRE by Lewis D. Patten and Wayne D. Overholser *(Cowles)*
NF: CONQUISTADORS AND PUEBLOS by Olga Hall-Quest *(Dutton)*
1970
F: CAYUSE COURAGE by Evelyn Lampman *(HBJ)*
NF: RETREAT TO THE BEAR PAW by Marian T. Place *(Four Winds)*
SEARCH FOR SEVEN CITIES by John Upton Terrell *(HBJ)*

1971
F: THE BLACK MUSTANGER by Richard Wormser *(Morrow)*
NF: LORDS OF THE EARTH by Jules Loh *(Crowell-Collier)*

1972
F: ONLY EARTH AND SKY LAST FOREVER by Nathaniel Benchley *(Harper)*
NF: THE TIGUAS by Stan Steiner *(Crowell-Collier)*

1973
F: FREEDOM TRAIL by Jean Williams *(Putnam)*
NF: RED POWER ON THE RIO GRANDE by Franklin Folsom *(Follett)*

1974
SUSY'S SCOUNDREL by Harold Keith *(Crowell)*

1975
F: DUST OF THE EARTH by Vera and Bill Cleaver *(Lippincott)*
NF: LAMY OF SANTA FE by Paul Horgan *(Farrar)*

1976
ALL ABOARD by Phil Ault *(Dodd)*

1977
A SHEPHERD WATCHES, A SHEPHERD SINGS by Louis Irigary and Theodore Taylor *(Doubleday)*

1978
THE NO-RETURN TRAIL by Sonia Levitin *(HBJ)*

1979
No Award

1980
GETTING THERE: FRONTIER TRAVEL WITHOUT POWER by Suzanne Hilton *(Westminster)*

1981
THE LAST RUN by Mark Jonathon Harris *(Lothrop)*

1982
BEFORE THE LARK by Irene Bennett Brown *(Atheneum)*

1983
THUNDER ON THE TENNESSEE by Gary Clifton Wisler *(Lodestar)*

1984
TRAPPED IN SLICKROCK CANYON: A MOUNTAIN WEST ADVENTURE by Gloria Skurzynski *(Lothrop)*

1985
PRAIRIE SONGS by Pam Conrad *(Harper)*

1986
MAKE WAY FOR SAM HOUSTON by Jean Fritz *(Putnam)*

1987
THE ORPHAN TRAIN by Joan Lowery Nixon *(Bantam)*

1988
IN THE FACE OF DANGER by Joan Lowery Nixon *(Bantam)*
1989
MY DANIEL by Pam Conrad *(Harper)*
1990
HONEY GIRL by Madge Harrah *(Avon)*
1991
RESCUE JOSH MCGUIRE by Ben Mikaelsen *(Hyperion)*

Laura Ingalls Wilder Award 🕭

First awarded in 1954, this medal was given every five years
from 1960 through 1980. As of 1983, the award has been given
at three-year intervals. The award honors an author or illustrator
whose books, published in the U.S., have made, over a period of
years, a substantial and lasting contribution to literature for
children. Administered by the Association for Library Service to
Children, a division of the American Library Association (50 E.
Huron St., Chicago, IL 60611). (Bronze medal)

1954 Laura Ingalls Wilder
1960 Clara Ingram Judson
1965 Ruth Sawyer
1970 E.B. White
1975 Beverly Cleary
1980 Theodor S. Geisel (Dr. Seuss)
1983 Maurice Sendak
1986 Jean Fritz
1989 Elizabeth George Speare
1992 Marcia Brown

Carter G. Woodson Book Awards 🕭

The National Council for the Social Studies (3501 Newark St.,
NW, Washington, DC 20016) established the Woodson Awards to
honor trade books that provide "a multicultural or multiethnic
perspective." The awards are named for a distinguished Harvard
University Professor of History who is often termed the "father of
American black history." As of 1989 there have been Elementary
(E) and Secondary *(S)* Awards. (Plaque)

1974
ROSA PARKS by Eloise Greenfield *(Crowell)*

1975
MAKE A JOYFUL NOISE UNTO THE LORD: THE LIFE OF MAHALIA JACKSON, QUEEN OF THE GOSPEL SINGERS by Jesse Jackson *(Crowell)*

1976
DRAGONWINGS by Laurence Yep *(Harper)*

1977
THE TROUBLE THEY SEEN by Dorothy Sterling *(Doubleday)*

1978
THE BIOGRAPHY OF DANIEL INOUYE by Jane Goodsell *(Crowell)*

1979
NATIVE AMERICAN TESTIMONY: AN ANTHOLOGY OF INDIAN AND WHITE RELATIONS edited by Peter Nabokov *(Crowell)*

1980
WAR CRY ON A PRAYER FEATHER: PROSE AND POETRY OF THE UTE INDIANS by Nancy Wood *(Doubleday)*

1981
THE CHINESE AMERICANS by Milton Meltzer *(Crowell)*

1982
COMING TO NORTH AMERICA FROM MEXICO, CUBA AND PUERTO RICO by Susan Garver and Paula McGuire *(Delacorte)*

1983
MORNING STAR, BLACK SUN by Brent Ashabranner *(Dodd)*

1984
MEXICO AND THE UNITED STATES by E. B. Fincher *(Crowell)*

1985
TO LIVE IN TWO WORLDS: AMERICAN INDIAN YOUTH TODAY by Brent Ashabranner *(Dodd)*

1986
DARK HARVEST: MIGRANT FARMWORKERS IN AMERICA by Brent Ashabranner *(Dodd)*

1987
HAPPILY MAY I WALK: AMERICAN INDIANS AND ALASKA NATIVES TODAY by Arlene Hirschfelder *(Scribner)*

1988
BLACK MUSIC IN AMERICA: A HISTORY THROUGH ITS PEOPLE by James Haskins *(Harper)*

1989
E: WALKING THE ROAD TO FREEDOM by Jeri Ferris *(Carolrhoda)*
S: MARIAN ANDERSON by Charles Patterson *(Watts)*

1990

E: IN TWO WORLDS: A YUP'IK ESKIMO FAMILY by Aylette Jenness and Alice Rivers *(Houghton)*

S: PAUL ROBESON by Rebecca Larsen *(Watts)*

1991

E: SHIRLEY CHISHOLM: TEACHER AND CONGRESSWOMAN by Catherine Scheader *(Enslow)*

S: SORROW'S KITCHEN: ZORA HURSTON by Mary Lyon *(Scribner)*

PART II

United States Awards
Selected by Young Readers

ALABAMA
Emphasis on Reading:
A Children's Choice Book
Award Program 🍂

The Emphasis on Reading awards aim "to insure that children get to read some of the best literature written for their age or stage before they get beyond it." The program is sponsored by the Alabama Reading Incentive Council, an umbrella organization that includes several professional associations. Representatives of at least ten of them constitute a Nominating Committee that meets annually to assemble a nominee list of eight titles in—as of 1992—three reading categories: Grades *K-2, 3-5,* and *6-8.* An attempt is made to include titles by Alabama authors, or about Alabama, when appropriate. So there is ample time for participating schools and libraries to acquire nominated titles and for children to read them, children's votes are tabulated eighteen months after the nominee list is announced. The program is managed by the Alabama State Department of Education (50 North Ripley St., Gordon Persons Bldg. #3345, Montgomery, AL 36130-3901). (Certificate)

1980-81
K-1: KATY NO-POCKET by Emmy Payne *(Houghton)*
2-3: CHARLOTTE'S WEB by E. B. White *(Harper)*
4-6: THE BEST CHRISTMAS PAGEANT EVER by Barbara Robinson *(Harper)*
7-9: THE HOBBIT by J.R.R. Tolkien *(Houghton)*
10-12: THE ACORN PEOPLE by Ron Jones *(Abingdon)*
1981-82
K-1: THE RUNAWAY BUNNY by Margaret Wise Brown, ill. by Clement Hurd *(Harper)*
2-3: GRANNY AND THE INDIANS by Peggy Parrish, ill. by Brinton Turkle *(Macmillan)*
4-6: BUNNICULA: A RABBIT TALE OF MYSTERY by Deborah and James Howe *(Atheneum)*
7-9: MAYDAY! MAYDAY! by Hilary H. Milton *(Watts)*
10-12: CHRISTY by Catherine Marshall *(McGraw-Hill)*
1982-83
K-1: SYLVESTER AND THE MAGIC PEBBLE by William Steig *(Windmill/Simon & Schuster)*

2-3: CHOCOLATE CHIP MYSTERY by John McInnes, ill. by Paul Frame *(Garrard)*
4-6: STUART LITTLE by E. B. White *(Harper)*
7-9: KILLING MR. GRIFFIN by Lois Duncan *(Little, Brown)*
10-12: SUNSHINE by Norma Klein *(Holt)*

1983-84

K-1: THE BIG ORANGE SPLOT by Daniel Manus Pinkwater *(Hastings)*
2-3: RALPH S. MOUSE by Beverly Cleary, ill. by Paul O. Zelinsky *(Morrow)*
4-6: NOTHING'S FAIR IN FIFTH GRADE by Barthe DeClements *(Viking)*
7-9: UNICORNS IN THE RAIN by Barbara Cohen *(Atheneum)*
10-12: CAGES OF GLASS, FLOWERS OF TIME by Charlotte Culin *(Bradbury)*

1984-85

K-1: A POCKET FOR CORDUROY by Don Freeman *(Viking)*
2-3: THE GREAT GREEN TURKEY CREEK MONSTER by James Flora *(McElderry)*
4-6: THE BOXCAR CHILDREN by Gertrude Warner *(Whitman)*
7-9: A TANGLE OF ROOTS by Barbara Girion *(Scribner)*
10-12: GRENDEL by John Gardner *(Knopf)*

1985-86

K-1: THE PAIN AND THE GREAT ONE by Judy Blume, ill. by Irene Trivas *(Bradbury)*
2-3: THE ADVENTURES OF ALBERT, THE RUNNING BEAR by Barbara Isenberg and Susan Wolf, ill. by Dick Gackenbach *(Clarion)*
4-6: SUPERFUDGE by Judy Blume *(Dutton)*
7-9: DIVORCE EXPRESS by Paula Danziger *(Delacorte)*
10-12: HIM SHE LOVES? by M. E. Kerr *(Harper)*

1986-87

K-1: IF YOU GIVE A MOUSE A COOKIE by Laura Numeroff, ill. by Felicia Bond *(Harper)*
2-3: THE NEW KID ON THE BLOCK by Jack Prelutsky, ill. by James Stevenson *(Greenwillow)*
4-6: STONE FOX by John Reynolds Gardiner *(Crowell)*
7-9: YOU NEVER CAN TELL by Ellen Conford *(Little, Brown)*
10-12: YEAGER, AN AUTOBIOGRAPHY by Chuck Yeager and Leo Janos *(Bantam)*

1987-88

K-1: MY TEACHER SLEEPS IN SCHOOL by Leatie Weiss, ill. by Ellen Weiss *(Viking)*
2-3: MY MOTHER NEVER LISTENS TO ME by Marjorie Sharmat, ill. by Lynn Munsinger *(Whitman)*
4-6: THE DOLLHOUSE MURDERS by Betty Ren Wright *(Holiday House)*

7-9: REVENGE OF THE NERD by John McNamara *(Delacorte)*

10-12: WART, SON OF TOAD by Alden R. Carter *(Pacer/Putnam)*

1988-89

K-2: NO JUMPING ON THE BED! by Tedd Arnold *(Dial)*

3-5: THE WAR WITH GRANDPA by Robert K. Smith *(Delacorte)*

6-8: NO SWIMMING IN THE DARK POND AND OTHER CHILLING TALES by Judith Gorog *(Putnam)*

9-12: THE PRINCESS BRIDE by William Goldman *(Ballantine)*

1989-90

K-2: THE LITTLE OLD MAN WHO COULD NOT READ by Irma S. Black *(Whitman)*

3-5: IN TROUBLE AGAIN, ZELDA HAMMERSMITH? by Lynn Hall *(HBJ)*

6-8: MAD, MAD, MONDAY by Herma Silverstein *(Lodestar)*

9-12: No Award (no ballots submitted)

1990-91

K-2: SOCK SNATCHERS by Lorna Balian *(Abingdon)*

3-5: MORE SCARY STORIES TO TELL IN THE DARK by Alvin Schwartz *(Lippincott)*

6-8: THE GLORY GIRL by Betsy Byars *(Viking)*

9-12: WALKING ACROSS EGYPT by Clyde Edgerton *(Algonquin)*

ARIZONA
Arizona Young Readers Award 🍂

The purpose of this award "is to stimulate the interest of young readers in outstanding literature written primarily for them. The common concern of librarians, parents, administrators and teachers to assure interaction between readers and books is a major ingredient in the concept of allowing them to vote for their favorite book and identify it for others to enjoy." An additional aim of the award "is to encourage cooperation among administrators, librarians, and teachers in broadening the reading programs at all levels." Participating schools, themselves, nominate the twenty titles—ten picture books and ten chapter books—that appear on two lists that are voted on biennially by schoolchildren throughout the state. Several organizations cooperate with the sponsors and administrators, Arizona State Library Association (13832 N. 32nd St., #C1-7, Phoenix, AZ 85032, Attn.: Children's Services Roundtable). (Plaque)

1977
TALES OF A FOURTH GRADE NOTHING by Judy Blume
(Dutton)
1979
HOW TO EAT FRIED WORMS by Thomas Rockwell *(Watts)*
1981
MISS NELSON IS MISSING! by Harry Allard, ill. by James
Marshall *(Houghton)*
1983
SUPERFUDGE by Judy Blume *(Dutton)*
1985
THE STUPIDS DIE by Harry Allard, ill. by James Marshall
(Houghton)
1987
SCARY STORIES TO TELL IN THE DARK by Alvin Schwartz
(Lippincott)
1989
THE INDIAN IN THE CUPBOARD by Lynne Reid Banks
(Doubleday)
1991
WHERE'S WALDO? by Martin Handford *(Little, Brown)*

ARKANSAS
Charlie May Simon Children's Book Award ೫

Presented annually by the Elementary School Council (Dept. of
Education, State Education Bldg., 4 Capitol Mall, Little Rock,
AR 72201), and sixteen cooperating educational agencies, the
award honors Charlie May Simon (1897-1977), Arkansas author
of over twenty-seven books that include many "children's books
based on her knowledge and love of Arkansas." Arkansas
schoolchildren in grades 4-6 vote in the spring from a master list
of titles selected by representatives from sponsoring groups.
(Medallion)

1971
STRIPED ICE CREAM by Joan M. Lexau *(Lippincott)*
1972
BIG BEN by David Walker *(Houghton)*
1973
RUNAWAY RALPH by Beverly Cleary *(Morrow)*

1974
THE RUNT OF ROGERS SCHOOL by Harold Keith
(Lippincott)
1975
TALES OF A FOURTH GRADE NOTHING by Judy Blume
(Dutton)
1976
BIGFOOT by Hal Evarts *(Scribner)*
1977
THE GHOST ON SATURDAY NIGHT by Sid Fleischman
(Atlantic-Little, Brown)
1978
SHOESHINE GIRL by Clyde Robert Bulla *(Crowell)*
1979
ALVIN'S SWAP SHOP by Clifford B. Hicks *(Scholastic)*
1980
THE PINBALLS by Betsy Byars *(Viking)*
1981
BANANA TWIST by Florence Parry Heide *(Holiday House)*
1981-82
ALL THE MONEY IN THE WORLD by Bill Brittain *(Harper)*
1982-83
DO BANANAS CHEW GUM? by Jamie Gilson *(Lothrop)*
1983-84
RAMONA QUIMBY, AGE 8 by Beverly Cleary *(Morrow)*
1984-85
BE A PERFECT PERSON IN JUST THREE DAYS! by Stephen
Manes *(Clarion)*
1985-86
MY HORRIBLE SECRET by Stephen Roos *(Delacorte)*
1986-87
THE COMPUTER NUT by Betsy Byars *(Viking)*
1987-88
SARAH, PLAIN AND TALL by Patricia MacLachlan *(Harper)*
1988-89
THE WHIPPING BOY by Sid Fleischman *(Greenwillow)*
1989-90
THERE'S A BOY IN THE GIRLS' BATHROOM by Louis
Sachar *(Knopf)*
1990-91
ALL ABOUT SAM by Lois Lowry *(Houghton)*

CALIFORNIA
California Young Reader Medals 🦢

The purpose of this awards program is "to encourage California children to become better acquainted with good literature" and "to honor a favorite book and its author." Jointly sponsored by the California Reading Association (3400 Irvine Ave., Suite 118, Newport Beach, CA 92660), California Library Association (717 K St., Sacramento, CA 95814), California Media & Library Educators Association (1575 Old Bayshore Hwy., Burlingame, CA 94010) and California Association of Teachers of English (Box 4427, Whittier, CA 90607), participating schools and libraries submit preliminary nominations from children and young adults. A Young Reader Medal Committee determines the titles receiving the most support and prepares a list of final nominees from which young Californians vote for winners. Since 1983, each year there have been four categories: Primary *(P)*, with five final nominees; Intermediate *(I)*, three nominees; Junior High *(JH)*, three; and High School *(HS)*, three. Readers must have read *all* the nominated titles for the category in which they vote; they may vote for only one title in that category; they may vote in more than one category. In recent years, over 500,000 votes have been cast and counted annually. (Medals)

1975
I: HOW TO EAT FRIED WORMS by Thomas Rockwell *(Watts)*
1976
P: HOW DROOFUS THE DRAGON LOST HIS HEAD by Bill Peet *(Houghton)*
1977
I: FREAKY FRIDAY by Mary Rodgers *(Harper)*
HS: WATERSHIP DOWN by Richard Adams *(Macmillan)*
1978
P: LITTLE RABBIT'S LOOSE TOOTH by Lucy Bate *(Crown)*
1979
I: DANNY, THE CHAMPION OF THE WORLD by Roald Dahl *(Knopf)*
HS: THE LATE GREAT ME by Sandra Scoppettone *(Putnam)*
1980
P: BIG BAD BRUCE by Bill Peet *(Houghton)*
JH: THE PINBALLS by Betsy Byars *(Harper)*
1981
I: SUMMER OF THE MONKEYS by Wilson Rawls *(Doubleday)*
HS: A SUMMER TO DIE by Lois Lowry *(Houghton)*

1982
P: MISS NELSON IS MISSING! by Harry Allard, ill. by James Marshall *(Houghton)*
JH: HAIL, HAIL CAMP TIMBERWOOD by Ellen Conford *(Little, Brown)*

1983
P: LIZA LOU AND THE YELLER BELLY SWAMP by Mercer Mayer *(Four Winds)*
I: SUPERFUDGE by Judy Blume *(Dutton)*
JH: TIGER EYES by Judy Blume *(Bradbury)*
HS: SUMMER OF FEAR by Lois Duncan *(Little, Brown)*

1984
P: BAGDAD ATE IT by Phyllis Green, ill. by Joel Schick *(Watts)*
I: THE TROUBLE WITH TUCK by Theodore Taylor *(Doubleday)*
JH: THERE'S A BAT IN BUNK FIVE by Paula Danziger *(Delacorte)*
HS: STRANGER WITH MY FACE by Lois Duncan *(Little, Brown)*

1985
P: HERBIE'S TROUBLES by Carol Chapman, ill. by Kelly Oechsli *(Dutton)*
I: THE INDIAN IN THE CUPBOARD by Lynn Reid Banks *(Doubleday)*
JH: TAKING TERRI MUELLER by Norma Fox Mazer *(Avon)*
HS: THE TRUTH TRAP by Frances A. Miller *(Dutton)*

1986
P: SPACE CASE by Edward Marshall, ill. by James Marshall *(Dial)*
I: NOTHING'S FAIR IN FIFTH GRADE by Barthe DeClements *(Viking)*
JH: THE GIRL WITH THE SILVER EYES by Willo Davis Roberts *(Atheneum)*
HS: THE DARKANGEL by Meredith Ann Pierce *(Atlantic-Little, Brown)*

1987
P: THE NAPPING HOUSE by Audrey Wood, ill. by Don Wood *(HBJ)*
I: THE DOLLHOUSE MURDERS by Betty Ren Wright *(Holiday House)*
JH: YOU SHOULDN'T HAVE TO SAY GOOD-BYE by Patricia Hermes *(HBJ)*
HS: PURSUIT by Michael French *(Delacorte)*

1988
P: IF YOU GIVE A MOUSE A COOKIE by Laura Numeroff, ill. by Felicia Bond *(Harper)*
I: BE A PERFECT PERSON IN JUST THREE DAYS! by Stephen Manes *(Clarion)*
JH: THE ROOT CELLAR by Janet Lunn *(Scribner)*

HS: INTERSTELLAR PIG by William Sleater *(Dutton)*
1989
P: WHAT HAPPENED TO PATRICK'S DINOSAURS? by Carol Carrick, ill. by Donald Carrick *(Clarion)*
I: CASTLE IN THE ATTIC by Elizabeth Winthrop *(Holiday House)*
JH: THE STALKER by Joan Lowery Nixon *(Delacorte)*
HS: FACE AT THE EDGE OF THE WORLD by Eve Bunting *(Clarion)*
1990
P: EYES OF THE DRAGON by Margaret Leaf, ill. by Ed Young *(Lothrop)*
I: THE WAR WITH GRANDPA by Robert Kimmel Smith *(Delacorte)*
JH: THE OTHER SIDE OF DARK by Joan Lowery Nixon *(Delacorte)*
HS: IZZY WILLY NILLY by Cynthia Voigt *(Atheneum)*
1991
P: TACKY THE PENGUIN by Helen Lester, ill. by Lynn Munsinger *(Houghton)*
I: HARRY'S MAD by Dick King-Smith *(Crown)*
JH: DECEMBER STILLNESS by Mary Downing Hahn *(Clarion)*
HS: NIGHT KITES by M. E. Kerr *(Harper)*
1992
P: NEVER SPIT ON YOUR SHOES by Denys Cazet *(Orchard)*
I: ALL ABOUT SAM by Lois Lowry *(Houghton)*
JH: THE SNIPER by Theodore Taylor *(Harcourt)*
HS: A SUDDEN SILENCE by Eve Bunting *(Harcourt)*

COLORADO

Blue Spruce Colorado Young Adult Book Award 🪶

Established "to encourage young adults' active involvement with books and reading," this awards program invites cooperating schools, libraries, etc., to submit the top ten titles suggested by readers in grades 7-12 each year as the nominees for the following year's program. From a list of up to thirty nominees, one title is voted as the favorite. Voters must have read at least three of the nominees; they have only one vote. Nominated titles must be in print, and published within ten years of the award year. Nominees can be either fiction or nonfiction; they need not have been written exclusively for young adult readers; they must not have appeared first as a movie or a TV show. The program is co-sponsored by Colorado Council of the International Reading Association, Colorado Language Arts Society, Colorado Educational Media Association, and Colorado Library Association. (Blue Spruce Award, P.O. Box 27072, Denver, CO 80227) (Bronze medallion if author of nominated title accepts award in person; plaque if author is unable to attend annual convention of one of co-sponsors)

1985
TIGER EYES by Judy Blume *(Bradbury)*
1986
BRIDGE TO TERABITHIA by Katherine Paterson *(Crowell)*
1987
THE THIRD EYE by Lois Duncan *(Little, Brown)*
1988
THE OTHER SIDE OF DARK by Joan Lowry Nixon *(Delacorte)*
1989
THE EYES OF THE DRAGON by Stephen King *(Viking)*
1990
THE CRADLE WILL FALL by Mary Higgins Clark *(Dial)*

COLORADO
Colorado Children's Book Award ❧

Established "to encourage children's active involvement with books and reading," this awards program is sponsored by the Colorado Children's Book Award Committee of the Colorado Council of the International Reading Association (c/o M. Halvorsen, 1824 Cannes Court, Fort Collins, CO 80524). The committee is composed of teachers and librarians. Young readers in participating schools and libraries throughout the state nominate titles for the award. Based entirely on a tabulation of the nominations, a list of twenty most-nominated books is compiled by the committee. Thereafter, young Colorado readers vote for their favorite book from the committee's list. The book must be by a living American and have been published within a five-year period before the award year. (Certificate)

1976
HOW DROOFUS THE DRAGON LOST HIS HEAD by Bill Peet *(Houghton)*

1977
A DAY NO PIGS WOULD DIE by Robert Newton Peck *(Knopf)*
1978
THE SWEET TOUCH by Lorna Balian *(Abingdon)*
1979
THE GREAT GREEN TURKEY CREEK MONSTER by James Flora *(McElderry)*
1980
CLOUDY WITH A CHANCE OF MEATBALLS by Judith Barrett, ill. by Ron Barrett *(Atheneum)*
1981
CROSS-COUNTRY CAT by Mary Calhoun, ill. by Erick Ingraham *(Morrow)*
1982
SUPERFUDGE by Judy Blume *(Dutton)*
1983
SPACE CASE by Edward Marshall, ill. by James Marshall *(Dial)*
1984
THE UNICORN AND THE LAKE by Marianna Mayer, ill. by Michael Hague *(Dial)*
1985
MISS NELSON IS BACK by Harry Allard, ill. by James Marshall *(Houghton)*
1986
IN A DARK, DARK ROOM AND OTHER SCARY STORIES by Alvin Schwartz, ill. by Dirk Zimmer *(Harper)*
1987
KING BIDGOOD'S IN THE BATHTUB by Audrey Wood, ill. by Don Wood *(HBJ)*
1988
IF YOU GIVE A MOUSE A COOKIE by Laura Numeroff, ill. by Felicia Bond *(Harper)*
1989
THE MAGIC SCHOOLBUS AT THE WATERWORKS by Joanna Cole, ill. by Bruce Degen *(Scholastic)*
1990
TACKY THE PENGUIN by Helen Lester, ill. by Lynn Munsinger *(Houghton)*
1991
THE TALKING EGGS by Robert San Souci, ill. by Jerry Pinkney *(Dial)*

FLORIDA
Sunshine State Young Reader's Award 🌀

Co-sponsored by the School Library Media Services Office, Florida Dept. of Education, and the Florida Association for Media in Education (FAME), this annual award is for a work of fiction by an author living in the U.S. and published within five years before the award year. Students in participating schools and libraries are welcome to suggest titles for consideration in this program through cooperating teachers and librarians. Others affiliated with the activity are also a part of the nominating process. The ultimate responsibility for selecting titles for, and handling other aspects of, the competition rests with the Young Reader's Award Selection Committee, appointed by the President of FAME and the Florida Dept. of Education. A list of twenty titles is compiled by the committee and voted on by Florida readers in grades 3-5 and 6-8. Among its several purposes, the program aims "to encourage students to read for personal satisfaction...to help students become discriminating readers in their personal selection of books...[and] to give recognition to those who write books for children and young people." (Library Media Services, Florida Dept. of Education, Knott Building, Tallahassee FL 32399). (Engraved bookends featuring award logo)

1984
BUNNICULA: A RABBIT TALE OF MYSTERY by Deborah and James Howe *(Atheneum)*

1985
SUPERFUDGE by Judy Blume *(Dutton)*

1986
BE A PERFECT PERSON IN JUST THREE DAYS! by Stephen Manes *(Clarion)*

1987
THIRTEEN WAYS TO SINK A SUB by Jamie Gilson *(Lothrop)*

1988
3-5: SIXTH GRADE CAN REALLY KILL YOU by Barthe DeClements *(Viking)*
6-8: same title

1989
3-5: SIXTH-GRADE SLEEPOVER by Eve Bunting *(HBJ)*
6-8: same title

1990
3-5: CLASS CLOWN by Johanna Hurwitz *(Morrow)*

6-8: TRAPPED IN DEATH CAVE by Bill Wallace *(Holiday House)*
1991
3-5: THERE'S A BOY IN THE GIRLS' BATHROOM by Louis Sachar *(Knopf)*
6-8: same title

GEORGIA
Georgia Children's Book Awards 🍂

This awards program has two categories. The Georgia Children's Book Award *(GCBA)* is chosen by young readers in grades 4-8; as of 1977, a second category, the Georgia Children's Picture Storybook Award *(GCPSA),* has been chosen by children in grades K-3. In the first year of the program, approximately 5,000 children from thirty-nine schools participated; currently, approximately 185,000 children from more than 1,250 schools throughout the state participate. The award is sponsored by the university's College of Education (125 Aderhold, University of Georgia, Athens, GA 30602). For each award, a committee assembled by the sponsor selects a nominees list of twenty books by living American authors, and published within a five-year period before the award year. Children vote for books on these two lists. (Plaque)

1969
SKINNY by Robert Burch *(Viking)*
1970
RAMONA THE PEST by Beverly Cleary *(Morrow)*
1971
QUEENIE PEAVY by Robert Burch *(Viking)*
1972
J.T. by Jane Wagner *(Van Nostrand)*
1973
HEY, WHAT'S WRONG WITH THIS ONE? by Maia Wojciechowska *(Harper)*
1974
DOODLE AND THE GO-CART by Robert Burch *(Viking)*
1975
A TASTE OF BLACKBERRIES by Doris Buchanan Smith *(Crowell)*

1976
THE BEST CHRISTMAS PAGEANT EVER by Barbara
Robinson *(Harper)*

1977
GCBA: TALES OF A FOURTH GRADE NOTHING by Judy
Blume *(Dutton)*
GCPSA: ALEXANDER AND THE TERRIBLE, HORRIBLE,
NO GOOD, VERY BAD DAY by Judith Viorst, ill. by Ray
Cruz *(Atheneum)*

1978
GCBA: FREAKY FRIDAY by Mary Rodgers *(Harper)*
GCPSA: THE SWEET TOUCH by Lorna Balian *(Abingdon)*

1979
GCBA: THE PINBALLS by Betsy Byars *(Harper)*
GCPSA: BIG BAD BRUCE by Bill Peet *(Houghton)*

1980
GCBA: THE GREAT BRAIN DOES IT AGAIN by John D.
Fitzgerald *(Dial)*
GCPSA: MISS NELSON IS MISSING! by Harry Allard, ill. by
James Marshall *(Houghton)*

1981
GCBA: THE GREAT GILLY HOPKINS by Katherine Paterson
(Crowell)
GCPSA: THE TAILYPO by Joanna Galdone, ill. by Paul
Galdone *(Clarion)*

1982
GCBA: DON'T HURT LAURIE! by Willo Davis Roberts
(Atheneum)
GCPSA: PINKERTON, BEHAVE! by Steven Kellogg *(Dial)*

1983
GCBA: SUPERFUDGE by Judy Blume *(Dutton)*
GCPSA: HERBIE'S TROUBLES by Carol Chapman, ill. by Kelly
Oechsli *(Dutton)*

1984
GCBA: NOTHING'S FAIR IN FIFTH GRADE by Barthe
DeClements *(Viking)*
GCPSA: CLOUDY WITH A CHANCE OF MEATBALLS by
Judith Barrett, ill. by Ron Barrett *(Atheneum)*

1985
GCBA: SKINNYBONES by Barbara Park *(Knopf)*
GCPSA: DOCTOR DE SOTO by William Steig *(Farrar)*

1986
GCBA: THE SECRET LIFE OF THE UNDERWEAR CHAMP
by Betty Miles *(Knopf)*
GCPSA: THE UNICORN AND THE LAKE by Marianna
Mayer, ill. by Michael Hague *(Dial)*

1987
GCBA: BE A PERFECT PERSON IN JUST THREE DAYS! by
Stephen Manes *(Clarion)*
GCPSA: MY TEACHER SLEEPS IN SCHOOL by Leatie Weiss,
ill. by Ellen Weiss *(Warne)*
1988
GCBA: CHRISTINA'S GHOST by Betty Ren Wright *(Holiday
House)*
GCPSA: IF YOU GIVE A MOUSE A COOKIE by Laura
Numeroff, ill. by Felicia Bond *(Harper)*
1989
*GCBA:*THE WAR WITH GRANDPA by Robert Kimmel Smith
(Delacorte)
GCPSA: MAX, THE BAD-TALKING PARROT by Patricia
Demuth *(Putnam)*
1990
*GCBA:*THERE'S A BOY IN THE GIRLS' BATHROOM by
Louis Sachar *(Knopf)*
GCPSA: NO JUMPING ON THE BED! by Tedd Arnold *(Dial)*
1991
GCBA: HATCHET by Gary Paulsen *(Bradbury)*
GCPSA: WE'RE BACK: A DINOSAUR'S STORY by Hudson
Talbott *(Crown)*

HAWAII
Nene Award 🐦

The purposes of this awards program, sponsored by the Hawaii
Association of School Librarians and the Children's and Youth
Section, Hawaii Library Association, are to help the children of
Hawaii to "become acquainted with the best contemporary
writers of fiction for children, become aware of the qualities that
make a good book, and to choose the best rather than the
mediocre." The program also honors "an author whose book has
been enjoyed by the children of Hawaii." Children in grades 4-6
choose the winner, a book by a living author published within a
six-year period before the award year. (The Nene, for whom the
award is named, is a near-extinct native Hawaiian goose, now
being bred in captivity and released into its natural Hawaiian
habitat at a young age. Hawaiian children selected the name of
the award, voting for Nene, the State bird, over the Hibiscus, the
State flower.) (Plaque)
1964
ISLAND OF THE BLUE DOLPHINS by Scott O'Dell
(Houghton)

1965
MARY POPPINS by Pamela L. Travers *(HBJ)*

1966
OLD YELLER by Fred Gipson *(Harper)*

1967
No Award

1968
RIBSY by Beverly Cleary *(Morrow)*

1969
THE MOUSE AND THE MOTORCYCLE by Beverly Cleary *(Morrow)*

1970
HENRY REED'S BABY-SITTING SERVICE by Keith Robertson *(Viking)*

1971
RAMONA THE PEST by Beverly Cleary *(Morrow)*

1972
RUNAWAY RALPH by Beverly Cleary *(Morrow)*

1973
SOUNDER by William H. Armstrong *(Harper)*

1974
JONATHAN LIVINGSTON SEAGULL by Richard Bach *(Macmillan)*

1975
ARE YOU THERE, GOD? IT'S ME, MARGARET by Judy Blume *(Bradbury)*

1976
HOW TO EAT FRIED WORMS by Thomas Rockwell *(Watts)*

1977
FREAKY FRIDAY by Mary Rodgers *(Harper)*

1978
CHARLIE AND THE GREAT GLASS ELEVATOR by Roald Dahl *(Knopf)*

1979
RAMONA AND HER FATHER by Beverly Cleary *(Morrow)*

1980
THE CAT ATE MY GYMSUIT by Paula Danziger *(Delacorte)*

1981
MY ROBOT BUDDY by Alfred Slote *(Lippincott)*

1982
SUPERFUDGE by Judy Blume *(Dutton)*

1983
BUNNICULA: A RABBIT TALE OF MYSTERY by Deborah and James Howe *(Atheneum)*

1984
NOTHING'S FAIR IN FIFTH GRADE by Barthe DeClements
(Viking)
1985
JELLY BELLY by Robert Kimmel Smith (Delacorte)
1986
BE A PERFECT PERSON IN JUST THREE DAYS! by Stephen
Manes (Clarion)
1987
KAREN KEPPLEWHITE IS THE WORLD'S BEST KISSER by
Eve Bunting (Clarion)
1988
YOU SHOULDN'T HAVE TO SAY GOOD-BYE by Patricia
Hermes (HBJ)
1989
DEAR MR. HENSHAW by Beverly Cleary (Morrow)
1990
FUDGE by Charlotte T. Graeber (Lothrop)
1991
THERE'S A BOY IN THE GIRLS' BATHROOM by Louis
Sachar (Knopf)

ILLINOIS
Rebecca Caudill
Young Readers' Book Award

"I was born in the Appalachian Mountains of eastern Kentucky
and spent my first five years of life there. During most of my
school years before college, I lived on a farm in the hill country
of middle Tennessee. The rest of my life I have lived in cities,
but it is Appalachia that is in my blood, and it is Appalachia that
furnishes the background for most of my books," wrote Rebecca
Caudill (1899-1985) for a brochure about her distributed by her
publisher in the late 1960s. After extensive world travels as a
young professional woman, Rebecca Caudill married, settled in
Urbana, Illinois, and began to write the more than twenty books
that made her famous. She wrote in a direct, unsentimental way
about subjects with strong emotional appeal. Respected on
account of her books, Rebecca Caudill's generous nature inspired
deep bonds between herself and children's book colleagues in
Illinois, and elsewhere. The children's book award in her name
aims "to encourage children and young adults to read for
personal satisfaction; to develop a statewide awareness of
outstanding literature for children and young people and promote

a desire for literacy; and to encourage cooperation among Illinois agencies providing educational and library service to young people." It is co-sponsored by the Illinois Association for Media in Education, the Public Library Section (both Illinois Library Association), Illinois Reading Council, Illinois Association of Teachers of English, and Department of Curriculum and Instruction of Northern Illinois University. An Award Committee seeks nominations of eligible titles from a wide range of individuals, including students, statewide. A master list of twenty titles is distributed to participating institutions no later than November 30 each year; votes are tabulated by the administrator in early March, with all participants notified of the results shortly afterwards. Participating institutions pay a very modest fee to receive an Award Packet (available in late spring) that includes the essential information and forms for conducting a successful awards program. Books eligible for consideration may be fiction, nonfiction, or poetry, published within a five-year period before the master list is prepared. (Rebecca Caudill Young Readers' Book Award, c/o Department of Curriculum and Instruction, Northern Illinois University, DeKalb, IL 60115) (Plaque)

1988
THE INDIAN IN THE CUPBOARD by Lynne Reid Banks *(Doubleday)*
1989
THE DOLLHOUSE MURDERS by Betty Ren Wright *(Holiday House)*
1990
WAIT TILL HELEN COMES: A GHOST STORY by Mary Downing Hahn *(Clarion)*
1991
MATILDA by Roald Dahl *(Viking)*
1992
NUMBER THE STARS by Lois Lowry *(Houghton)*

INDIANA
Young Hoosier Book Awards

Sponsored by the Association for Indiana Media Educators (YHBA Committee, c/o School of Education, Indiana State University, Terre Haute, IN 47809), this award program was "launched to encourage boys and girls to read and enjoy good books." Indiana schoolchildren in grades 4-8 vote for their favorite book from a list of twenty works of fiction by authors who reside in the U.S. and whose books were published in a five year period before the award year. A committee appointed by the sponsor selects the titles that appear on the nominee list. As of the 1986 award year, two awards have been chosen, one selected by readers in grades 4-6, and a second by grades 6-8. As of 1992, a Young Hoosier Picture Book Award selected by children in grades K-3 will be given. (Plaque)

1975
THE TRUMPET OF THE SWAN by E.B. White *(Harper)*
1976
ARE YOU THERE, GOD? IT'S ME, MARGARET by Judy Blume *(Bradbury)*
1977
HOW TO EAT FRIED WORMS by Thomas Rockwell *(Watts)*
1978
THE BEST CHRISTMAS PAGEANT EVER by Barbara Robinson *(Harper)*
1979
THE GHOST ON SATURDAY NIGHT by Sid Fleischman *(Atlantic-Little, Brown)*
1980
DON'T HURT LAURIE! by Willo Davis Roberts *(Atheneum)*
1981
THE GOOF THAT WON THE PENNANT by Jonah Kalb *(Houghton)*
1982
HELP! I'M A PRISONER IN THE LIBRARY by Eth Clifford *(Houghton)*
1983
SUPERFUDGE by Judy Blume *(Dutton)*
1984
JELLY BELLY by Robert Kimmel Smith *(Delacorte)*
1985
OPERATION: DUMP THE CHUMP by Barbara Park *(Knopf)*
1986
4-6: WHEN THE BOYS RAN THE HOUSE by Joan Carris *(Lippincott)*
6-8: STRANGER WITH MY FACE by Lois Duncan *(Little, Brown)*
1987
4-6: THE WAR WITH GRANDPA by Robert Kimmel Smith *(Delacorte)*
6-8: THE THIRD EYE by Lois Duncan *(Little, Brown)*
1988
4-6: BABY-SITTING IS A DANGEROUS JOB by Willo Davis Roberts *(Atheneum)*

6-8: A DEADLY GAME OF MAGIC by Joan Lowery Nixon *(HBJ)*

1989
4-6: CHRISTINA'S GHOST by Betty Ren Wright *(Holiday House)*
6-8: WAIT TILL HELEN COMES: A GHOST STORY by Mary Downing Hahn *(Clarion)*

1990
4-6: FUDGE by Charlotte Graeber *(Lothrop)*
6-8: THE DARK AND DEADLY POOL by Joan Lowery Nixon *(Delacorte)*

1991
4-6: TEN KIDS, NO PETS by Ann M. Martin *(Holiday House)*
6-8: HATCHET by Gary Paulsen *(Bradbury)*

IOWA

Iowa Children's Choice Award and Iowa Teen Award ❧

The Iowa Children's Choice Award *(ICCA)* and the Iowa Teen Award *(ITA)* programs are sponsored by the Iowa Educational Media Association *(ICCA* Committee, c/o Beth Elshoff, 9 Coventry Lane, Muscatine, IA 52761; *ITA* Committee, c/o Twylla Kerr, 2412 Littell, Des Moines, IA 50321). Among the purposes of both awards, one is "to provide an avenue for positive dialogue between teacher, parent and children (students) about books and authors." Young readers are invited to suggest titles, fiction or nonfiction, that are appropriate for grades 3-6 *(ICCA)* and grades 6-9 *(ITA).* In each instance, the selection of 20-25 titles as nominees for the awards is ultimately the responsibility of the members of the respective awards committees. In the case of the *ICCA,* authors must be Americans and their nominated books published within five years of the award year; for the *ITA,* the nationality of the author is not a consideration, and the nominated books must have been published within six years of the award year. *(ICCA:* engraved bronze school bell; *ITA:* engraved brass apple)

1980
ICCA: HOW TO EAT FRIED WORMS by Thomas Rockwell *(Watts)*

1981
ICCA: THE GREAT GILLY HOPKINS by Katherine Paterson *(Crowell)*

1982
ICCA: BUNNICULA: A RABBIT TALE OF MYSTERY by
Deborah and James Howe *(Atheneum)*
1983
ICCA: SUPERFUDGE by Judy Blume *(Dutton)*
1984
ICCA: NOTHING'S FAIR IN FIFTH GRADE by Barthe
DeClements *(Viking)*
1985
ICCA: RALPH S. MOUSE by Beverly Cleary *(Morrow)*
ITA: TIGER EYES by Judy Blume *(Bradbury)*
1986
ICCA: WHEN THE BOYS RAN THE HOUSE by Joan Carris
(Lippincott)
ITA: WHEN WE FIRST MET by Norma Fox Mazer *(Scholastic)*
1987
ICCA: RAMONA FOREVER by Beverly Cleary *(Morrow)*
ITA: YOU SHOULDN'T HAVE TO SAY GOOD-BYE by
Patricia Hermes *(HBJ)*
1988
ICCA: THE DOLLHOUSE MURDERS by Betty Ren Wright
(Holiday House)
ITA: ABBY, MY LOVE by Hadley Irwin *(McElderry)*
1989
ICCA: NIGHT OF THE TWISTERS by Ivy Ruckman *(Crowell)*
ITA: THE OTHER SIDE OF DARK by Joan Lowery Nixon
(Delacorte)
1990
ICCA: WAIT TILL HELEN COMES: A GHOST STORY by
Mary Downing Hahn *(Clarion)*
ITA: HATCHET by Gary Paulsen *(Bradbury)*
1991
ICCA: THERE'S A BOY IN THE GIRLS' BATHROOM by
Louis Sachar *(Knopf)*
ITA: SILVER by Norma Fox Mazer *(Morrow)*

KANSAS
William Allen White Children's Book Award

Named in honor of the famous Kansas newspaper editor and
internationally renowned journalist William Allen White
(1868-1944), this second-in-terms-of-longevity of the U.S.

reader's choice awards programs was founded in 1952 by Ruth Garver Gagliardo, an eminent Kansas children's literature and reading promotion specialist. The purpose of the annual award has been to encourage "the boys and girls of Kansas to read and enjoy good books." The White Award Program is directed by Emporia State University (William Allen White Library, 1200 Commercial St., Emporia, KS 66801) and is supported in part by the Trusler Foundation. Each year a master list of books, including fiction, nonfiction and poetry titles, is compiled by the award's selection committee, representing educational and professional organizations as well as institutions in Kansas. Schoolchildren—currently more than 54,000—in grades 4-8 vote for the winner. (Bronze medal)

1953
AMOS FORTUNE, FREE MAN by Elizabeth Yates *(Dutton)*
1954
LITTLE VIC by Doris Gates *(Viking)*
1955
CHEROKEE BILL: OKLAHOMA PACER by Jean Bailey
(Abingdon)
1956
BRIGHTY OF THE GRAND CANYON by Marguerite Henry
(Rand McNally)
1957
DANIEL 'COON by Phoebe Erickson *(Knopf)*
1958
WHITE FALCON by Elliott Arnold *(Knopf)*
1959
OLD YELLER by Fred Gipson *(Harper)*
1960
FLAMING ARROWS by William O. Steele *(HBJ)*
1961
HENRY REED, INC. by Keith Robertson *(Viking)*
1962
THE HELEN KELLER STORY by Catherine O. Peare *(Crowell)*
1963
ISLAND OF THE BLUE DOLPHINS by Scott O'Dell
(Houghton)
1964
THE INCREDIBLE JOURNEY by Sheila Burnford *(Atlantic-Little, Brown)*
1965
BRISTLE FACE by Zachary Ball *(Holiday House)*
1966
RASCAL by Sterling North *(Dutton)*

1967

THE GRIZZLY by Annabel and Edgar Johnson *(Harper)*

1968

THE MOUSE AND THE MOTORCYCLE by Beverly Cleary *(Morrow)*

1969

HENRY REED'S BABY-SITTING SERVICE by Keith Robertson *(Viking)*

1970

FROM THE MIXED-UP FILES OF MRS. BASIL E. FRANKWEILER by E.L. Konigsburg *(Atheneum)*

1971

KAVIK THE WOLF DOG by Walt Morey *(Dutton)*

1972

SASHA, MY FRIEND by Barbara Corcoran *(Atheneum)*

1973

THE TRUMPET OF THE SWAN by E.B. White *(Harper)*

1974

Posthumous citation: MRS. FRISBY AND THE RATS OF NIMH by Robert C. O'Brien *(Atheneum)*
THE HEADLESS CUPID by Zilpha Keatley Snyder *(Atheneum)*

1975

DOMINIC by William Steig *(Farrar)*

1976

SOCKS by Beverly Cleary *(Morrow)*

1977

HARRY CAT'S PET PUPPY by George Selden *(Farrar)*

1978

THE GREAT CHRISTMAS KIDNAPPING CAPER by Jean Van Leeuwen *(Dial)*

1979

THE SUMMER OF THE MONKEYS by Wilson Rawls *(Doubleday)*

1980

THE PINBALLS by Betsy Byars *(Harper)*

1981

THE GREAT GILLY HOPKINS by Katherine Paterson *(Crowell)*

1982

THE MAGIC OF THE GLITS by C.S. Adler *(Macmillan)*

1983

PEPPERMINTS IN THE PARLOR by Barbara Brooks Wallace *(Atheneum)*

1984

A LIGHT IN THE ATTIC by Shel Silverstein *(Harper)*

1985
THE LAND I LOST: ADVENTURES OF A BOY IN
VIETNAM by Huynh Quang Nhuong *(Harper)*
1986
DAPHNE'S BOOK by Mary Downing Hahn *(Clarion)*
1987
THE WAR WITH GRANDPA by Robert Kimmel Smith
(Delacorte)
1988
CRACKER JACKSON by Betty Byars *(Viking)*
1989
ON MY HONOR by Marion Dane Bauer *(Clarion)*
1990
HATCHET by Gary Paulsen *(Bradbury)*
1991
BEAUTY by Bill Wallace *(Holiday House)*

KENTUCKY
Kentucky Bluegrass Awards

This annual voluntary reading program is designed "to encourage
Kentucky children to read and enjoy a variety of books and select
their favorites" from two lists of recently published books. As of
1987-88, the two divisions of the awards program consisted of
K-3, including picture books, beginning readers, etc., and 4-8,
including "junior novels, lengthy picture books, etc." Between
15-25 titles are selected by librarians and teachers from across
the state for the master reading lists for each division. The lists
are distributed to participating schools and libraries in the spring,
though it is not a requirement that participants have all titles on
the list in order to be a part of the program. Ballots are
tabulated as of early March each year, with the winning titles
announced in April at the sponsoring institution (Learning
Resource Center, BEP-268, Northern Kentucky University,
Highland Heights, KY 41076). "Kentucky bluegrass" is a
Mississippi valley grass, used for pasturage and hay. The state—
known for its horse farms and horse racing—is often referred to
as "the Bluegrass State." (Plaques)

1983
JUMANJI by Chris Van Allsburg *(Houghton)*
1984
MOVE OVER, TWERP by Martha Alexander *(Dial)*

1985
ANGELINA BALLERINA by Katharine Holabird, ill. by Helen Craig *(Clarkson Potter)*
1986
BADGER'S PARTING GIFTS by Susan Varley *(Lothrop)*
1987
THE POLAR EXPRESS by Chris Van Allsburg *(Houghton)*
1988
K-3: HEY, AL by Arthur Yorinks, ill. by Richard Egielski *(Farrar)*
4-8: WHO NEEDS A BRATTY BROTHER? by Linda Gondosch *(Lodestar)*
1989
K-3: THE WOLF'S CHICKEN STEW by Keiko Kasza *(Putnam)*
4-8: CLASS CLOWN by Johanna Hurwitz *(Morrow)*
1990
K-3: THE LADY WITH THE ALLIGATOR PURSE adapted and ill. by Nadine Bernard Westcott *(Joy Street/Little, Brown)*
4-8: THE STRANGER by Chris Van Allsburg *(Houghton)*
1991
K-3: CHICKA CHICKA BOOM BOOM by Bill Martin, Jr. and John Archambault, ill. by Lois Ehlert *(Simon & Schuster)*
4-8: THE BUTTERFLY JAR by Jeffrey Moss, ill. by Chris Demarest *(Bantam)*
1992
K-3: BASKET by George Ella Lyon, ill. by Mary Szilagyi *(Orchard)*
4-8: SOMETHING BIG HAS BEEN HERE by Jack Prelutsky, ill. by James Stevenson *(Greenwillow)*

MARYLAND
Maryland Children's Book Award ❧

This award is sponsored by the State of Maryland International Reading Association Council. Titles are nominated by teachers and librarians for a list of about fifteen titles, selected by an award committee annually, and voted on by young readers. The State Council does not have a permanent office to contact for information; the award is administered on a volunteer basis by a chairman and committee appointed each year. (Engraved plaque)

1988
CRACKER JACKSON by Betsy Byars *(Viking)*

1989
SWITCHAROUND by Lois Lowry *(Houghton)*
1990
THE HAUNTING OF CABIN 13 by Kristi D. Holl *(Atheneum)*
1991
THE DOLL IN THE GARDEN: A GHOST STORY by Mary
Downing Hahn *(Clarion)*

MASSACHUSETTS
Massachusetts Children's Book Award

The impetus for establishing this awards program was the
organizer's observation that, once having learned how to read,
many children lose interest in books when they reach
intermediate grades. Designed for schoolchildren in grades 4-6,
the program also included grades 7-9 from 1978 through 1983.
A committee of librarians and teachers nominates titles for the
program, and considers both literary quality and reader appeal in
selecting nominees. Until 1983, only books published in years
immediately before the award year were considered for the
award. As of 1983, and owing, in part, to the diminution of
book purchasing funds, titles published at earlier dates became
eligible for the award. Sponsored by Salem State College (c/o
Helen Constant, Education Dept., Salem, MA 01970).
(Certificate)

1976
HOW TO EAT FRIED WORMS by Thomas Rockwell *(Watts)*
1977
TALES OF A FOURTH GRADE NOTHING by Judy Blume
(Dutton)
1978
4-6: MRS. FRISBY AND THE RATS OF NIMH by Robert C.
O'Brien *(Atheneum)*
7-9: THAT WAS THEN, THIS IS NOW by S. E. Hinton
(Viking)
1979
4-6: THE CRICKET IN TIMES SQUARE by George Selden
(Farrar)
7-9: THE CAT ATE MY GYMSUIT by Paula Danziger
(Delacorte)

1980
4-6: CHOCOLATE FEVER by Robert Kimmel Smith *(Dell)*
7-9: SUMMER OF MY GERMAN SOLDIER by Bette Greene *(Dial)*

1981
4-6: THE GREAT GILLY HOPKINS by Katherine Paterson *(Crowell)*
7-9: A SUMMER TO DIE by Lois Lowry *(Houghton)*

1982
4-6: JAMES AND THE GIANT PEACH by Roald Dahl *(Knopf)*
7-9: KILLING MR. GRIFFIN by Lois Duncan *(Little, Brown)*

1983
4-6: TALES OF A FOURTH GRADE NOTHING by Judy Blume *(Dutton)*
7-9: STRANGER WITH MY FACE by Lois Duncan *(Little, Brown)*

1984
CHARLOTTE'S WEB by E. B. White *(Harper)*

1985
NOTHING'S FAIR IN FIFTH GRADE by Barthe DeClements *(Viking)*

1986
DEAR MR. HENSHAW by Beverly Cleary *(Morrow)*

1987
WHERE THE RED FERN GROWS by Wilson Rawly *(Doubleday)*

1988
THE INDIAN IN THE CUPBOARD by Lynn Reid Banks *(Doubleday)*

1989
THE CHOCOLATE TOUCH by Patrick Catling *(Morrow)*

1990
No Award (administrator on sabbatical)

1991
THERE'S A BOY IN THE GIRLS' BATHROOM by Louis Sachar *(Knopf)*

MINNESOTA
Maud Hart Lovelace Book Award ❧

Named for the author of the warmly appreciated *Betsy-Tacy* stories about growing up at the turn of the century in "Deep

Valley" (Mankato), Minnesota, this award program is sponsored by Minnesota Youth Reading Awards, Inc. (MYRA, Box 185, Mankato, MN 56002), whose chief members are the Minnesota Educational Media Organization, the Minnesota Library Association, and the Minnesota Reading Association, with additional financial support from Baker & Taylor, Bookmen, Covercraft, Econoclad, Mackin Book, and Perma-Bound. Children in grades 3-8 vote for their favorite book from a list of fifteen nominated titles, at least three of which must have been read before a participant is eligible to vote. The sponsors sell a kit relating to the nominees so that local organizers can participate in the program effectively. The winner is announced each year on April 25, the anniversary of the birthday of Maud Hart Lovelace. (Plaque)

1980
SUMMER OF THE MONKEYS by Wilson Rawls *(Doubleday)*
1981
THE PINBALLS by Betsy Byars *(Harper)*
1982
THE BEST CHRISTMAS PAGEANT EVER by Barbara Robinson *(Harper)*
1983
IT CAN'T HURT FOREVER by Marilyn Singer *(Harper)*
1984
NOTHING'S FAIR IN FIFTH GRADE by Barthe DeClements *(Viking)*
1985
SKINNYBONES by Barbara Park *(Knopf)*
1986
ZUCCHINI by Barbara Dana *(Harper)*
1987
STONE FOX by John Reynolds Gardiner *(Crowell)*
1988
NIGHT OF THE TWISTERS by Ivy Ruckman *(Crowell)*
1989
EATING ICE CREAM WITH A WEREWOLF by Phyllis Green *(Harper)*
1990
WAIT TILL HELEN COMES: A GHOST STORY by Mary Downing Hahn *(Clarion)*
1991
HATCHET by Gary Paulsen *(Bradbury)*

MISSISSIPPI
Mississippi Children's Book Award 🙊

Administered by the de Grummond Children's Literature Research Collection of the University of Southern Mississippi, with the financial assistance of the Mississippi Power Foundation and the University of Southern Mississippi, this award program was discontinued after its second year as a result of budget cutbacks. Participating schools and libraries became "sponsors" of the award. Approximately 20-25 books by American authors "honored by the American Library Association and *School Library Journal*" were selected as nominees for the award, which was determined by the votes of children in grades 4-6. (Announcement, and ceremony at annual Mississippi Library Association Convention)

1990
CLASS CLOWN by Johanna Hurwitz *(Morrow)*
1991
ALL ABOUT SAM by Lois Lowry *(Houghton)*

MISSOURI
Mark Twain Award 🙊

"The Mark Twain Award was initiated to provide children of Missouri with their very own source to enrich their lives through reading and to find the joys that lie in being able to read. Mark Twain, a native of Hannibal, Missouri, and the best-loved author the world over is the obvious Missouri author to have such an award named for him...." Sponsored by the Missouri Association of School Librarians (P. O. Box 22476, Kansas City, MO 64113), the awards program now has twelve statewide participating organizations. Twenty titles are selected for a master list by a committee representing organizations interested in children and reading. The administrators are able to supply at a modest cost many useful items to help participating institutions organize an effective program. They include a color sound filmstrip to introduce books on the master list, an annotated booklet of titles on the master lists from the beginning of the program through the current year, seals for winning titles and spine labels for nominees, recognition certificates for participating readers, and also posters and bookmarks for both current nominees and past winners. The voters are in grades 4-8. (Bronze bust of Mark Twain)

1972
SOUNDER by William H. Armstrong *(Harper)*
1973
MRS. FRISBY AND THE RATS OF NIMH by Robert C. O'Brien *(Atheneum)*
1974
IT'S A MILE FROM HERE TO GLORY by Robert C. Lee *(Little, Brown)*
1975
HOW TO EAT FRIED WORMS by Thomas Rockwell *(Watts)*
1976 THE HOME RUN TRICK by Scott Corbett *(Atlantic-Little, Brown)*
1977
THE GHOST ON SATURDAY NIGHT by Sid Fleischman *(Atlantic-Little, Brown)*
1978
RAMONA THE BRAVE by Beverly Cleary *(Morrow)*
1979
THE CHAMPION OF MERRIMACK COUNTY by Roger W. Drury *(Little, Brown)*
1980
THE PINBALLS by Betsy Byars *(Harper)*
1981
SOUP FOR PRESIDENT by Robert Newton Peck *(Knopf)*
1982
THE BOY WHO SAW BIGFOOT by Marian T. Place *(Dodd)*
1983
THE GIRL WITH THE SILVER EYES by Willo Davis Roberts *(Atheneum)*
1984
THE SECRET LIFE OF THE UNDERWEAR CHAMP by Betty Miles *(Knopf)*
1985
A BUNDLE OF STICKS by Pat Rhoads Mauser *(Atheneum)*
1986
THE DOLLHOUSE MURDERS by Betty Ren Wright *(Holiday House)*
1987
THE WAR WITH GRANDPA by Robert Kimmel Smith *(Delacorte)*
1988
BABY-SITTING IS A DANGEROUS JOB by Willo Davis Roberts *(Atheneum)*

1989
SIXTH-GRADE SLEEPOVER by Eve Bunting *(HBJ)*
1990
THERE'S A BOY IN THE GIRLS' BATHROOM by Louis
Sachar *(Knopf)*
1991
ALL ABOUT SAM by Lois Lowry *(Houghton)*

MONTANA
Treasure State Award 🐌

During the first year of this award program—1991—children in
Montana were invited to select the award name; the winning
suggestion came from a third-grader in Helena. The winner is
selected from a list of five titles, with children in grades K-3
eligible to vote. While the award is initially administered from
the Missoula Public Library and School District One in Missoula,
information about it is available from the Montana State Library
(1515 E. 6th Ave., Helena, MT 59620). This program is
designed to complement the Young Reader's Choice Awards for
older readers—the first children's choice award program—selected
by readers in four Western States and two Canadian provinces.
(Announcement)

1991
THE DRAGON NANNY by C. L. Martin, ill. by Robert
Rayevsky *(Macmillan)*

NEBRASKA
Golden Sower Awards 🐌

Initiated by the Center for Curriculum and Instruction, Teachers
College, University of Nebraska, this awards program is currently
sponsored by the Nebraska Library Association (Reinert/Alumni
Memorial Library, Creighton University, California at 24th St.,
Omaha, NE 68178). The administration of the award is handled
by its chairperson, and that responsibility changes annually.
Designed to encourage Nebraska children to read widely in
several areas of picture books (grades K-3 and fiction (grades
4-6), two lists of fifteen titles each are compiled by a committee
that considers nominations from participating institutions. A

young adult category will be included as of the 1993 program. Participants are limited to three nominations a year in each category, and are encouraged to "involve children in the nomination process as much as possible." Nominations must be of titles by people living in the U. S. at the time of nomination, and that were published in a three-year period, two years prior to the award year. The titles "should be worthy of any award from a literary and/or artistic standpoint." The administrators send a useful and informative newsletter, *The Nugget*, to participating institutions four times a year, and also offer excellent and inexpensive materials, e.g., a manual, bookmarks, stickers, to support the organization of the activity locally. The program takes its name from the monumental figure on the top of the Nebraska Capitol building in Lincoln. (Plaque)

1981
4-6: BUNNICULA: A RABBIT TALE OF MYSTERY by Deborah and James Howe *(Atheneum)*

1982
4-6: YOURS TILL NIAGARA FALLS, ABBY by Jane O'Connor *(Hastings)*

1983
K-3: CLOUDY WITH A CHANCE OF MEATBALLS by Judith Barrett, ill. by Ron Barrett *(Atheneum)*
4-6: SUPERFUDGE by Judy Blume *(Dutton)*

1984
K-3: MISS NELSON IS BACK by Harry Allard, ill. by James Marshall *(Houghton)*
4-6: NOTHING'S FAIR IN FIFTH GRADE by Barthe DeClements *(Viking)*

1985
K-3: ROUND TRIP by Ann Jonas *(Greenwillow)*
4-6: A DOG CALLED KITTY by Bill Wallace *(Holiday House)*

1986
K-3: PEABODY by Rosemary Wells *(Dial)*
4-6: NIGHT OF THE TWISTERS by Ivy Ruckman *(Crowell)*

1987
K-3: MISS NELSON HAS A FIELD DAY by Harry Allard, ill. by James Marshall *(Houghton)*
4-6: THE WAR WITH GRANDPA by Robert Kimmel Smith *(Delacorte)*

1988
K-3: DON'T TOUCH MY ROOM by Patricia Lakin, ill. by Patience Brewster *(Little, Brown)*
4-6: SIXTH GRADE CAN REALLY KILL YOU by Barthe DeClements *(Viking)*

1989
K-3: PIGGINS by Jane Yolen, ill. by Jane Dyer *(HBJ)*
4-6: FERRET IN THE BEDROOM, LIZARDS IN THE
FRIDGE by Bill Wallace *(Holiday House)*
1990
K-3: THE MAGIC SCHOOLBUS AT THE WATERWORKS by
Joanna Cole, ill. by Bruce Degen *(Scholastic)*
4-6: WAIT TILL HELEN COMES: A GHOST STORY by Mary
Downing Hahn *(Clarion)*
1991
K-3: TACKY THE PENGUIN by Helen Lester, ill. by Lynn
Munsinger *(Houghton)*
4-6: THERE'S A BOY IN THE GIRLS' BATHROOM by Louis
Sachar *(Knopf)*
1992
K-3: THE TALKING EGGS: A FOLKTALE FROM THE
AMERICAN SOUTH retold by Robert D. San Souci, ill. by
Jerry Pinkney *(Dial)*
4-6: IS ANYBODY THERE? by Eve Bunting *(HarperCollins)*

NEVADA
Nevada Young Readers Awards 🐛

This awards program now includes three categories, *K-3, 4-6,*
and Young Adult *(Y/A).* Both school and public libraries
throughout the state are encouraged to participate in the
program, organized from the office of the Library Media
Consultant, State of Nevada Department of Education (400 W.
King St., Capitol Complex, Carson City, NV 89710).
Participants receive an array of support materials, including a
Time Line for the program, a sheet detailing Selection
Procedures, a Ballot, a listing of Promotional Ideas, a
reproducible prototype for a Certificate of Merit for children
reading all the books nominated for the awards in their
categories, a Nomination Form for titles for the next year's
program, and a program Evaluation Form. An interesting feature
of the program is that institutions with the highest percentage of
reader participation from among those eligible in each category
are invited to select the (young) presenters of the awards to the
winners. (Plaques)

1988
K-3: THE POLAR EXPRESS by Chris Van Allsburg *(Houghton)*
4-6: SIXTH GRADE CAN REALLY KILL YOU by Barthe
DeClements *(Viking)*

1989
K-3: IF YOU GIVE A MOUSE A COOKIE by Laura Numeroff, ill. by Felicia Bond *(Harper)*
4-6: BABY-SITTING IS A DANGEROUS JOB by Willo Davis Roberts *(Atheneum)*
Y/A: LOCKED IN TIME by Lois Duncan *(Little, Brown)*
1990
K-3: HECKEDY PEG by Audrey Wood, ill. by Don Wood *(HBJ)*
4-6: THERE'S A BOY IN THE GIRLS' BATHROOM by Louis Sachar *(Knopf)*
Y/A: EXPERIMENT IN TERROR by Bernal C. Payne, Jr. *(Houghton)*
1991
K-3: WE'RE BACK: A DINOSAUR'S STORY by Hudson Talbott *(Crown)*
4-6: MY TEACHER IS AN ALIEN by Bruce Coville *(Simon & Schuster)*
Y/A: PRINCESS ASHLEY by Richard Peck *(Delacorte)*

NEW HAMPSHIRE
Great Stone Face Award 🐌

This award is named for a natural rock formation near Laconia that resembles a human face—the Great Stone Face, sometimes referred to as The-Old-Man-in-the-Mountains—closely identified with the State of New Hampshire. In the program's formative years, children in grades 4-6 were invited simply to vote for their favorite book on "I Love To Read Day," usually February 14. Currently, a nominee list of approximately twenty-five fiction and nonfiction titles is assembled, and children vote for the winner from that list. The sponsor is CHILIS, a Division of the New Hampshire Library Association-Children's Librarians (c/o Kathy Frasier, Concord Public Library, 45 Green St., Concord, NH 03301). (Crystal sculpture by Peppe Herman of Great Stone Face)

1980
ARE YOU THERE, GOD? IT'S ME, MARGARET by Judy Blume *(Bradbury)*
1981
SUPERFUDGE by Judy Blume *(Dutton)*
1982
TALES OF A FOURTH GRADE NOTHING by Judy Blume *(Dutton)*

1983
THE MOUSE AND THE MOTORCYCLE by Beverly Cleary
(Morrow)
1984
SUPERFUDGE by Judy Blume *(Dutton)*
1985
SUPERFUDGE by Judy Blume *(Dutton)*
1986
SUPERFUDGE by Judy Blume *(Dutton)*
1987
SUPERFUDGE by Judy Blume *(Dutton)*
1988
WHERE THE RED FERN GROWS by Wilson Rawls
(Doubleday)
1989
WHERE THE RED FERN GROWS by Wilson Rawls
(Doubleday)
1990
MATILDA by Roald Dahl *(Viking)*
1991
THE RETURN OF THE INDIAN by Lynne Reid Banks
(Doubleday)

NEW MEXICO
Land of Enchantment Book Award 🦢

Co-sponsored by the New Mexico Library Association and the
New Mexico State International Reading Association, this award
is presented annually by the Land of Enchantment Book Award
Committee (c/o Flo Starkey, Materials Center, Roswell
Independent School District, 300 Kentucky St., Roswell, NM
88201). The committee compiles a list of 25-35 titles as
nominees for the award. The winner is chosen from this list by
students in grades 4-8. The award is for a book by a U. S.
resident published during a five-year period before the award
year. Originally used by the New Mexico Highway Department,
the term "land of enchantment" has become a name by which the
state is commonly known. (Nambé—four metals combined and
polished to resemble silver, and produced only in New Mexico—
medallion with reproduction of award logo)

1981
RAMONA AND HER FATHER by Beverly Cleary *(Morrow)*

1982
BUNNICULA: A RABBIT TALE OF MYSTERY by Deborah and James Howe *(Atheneum)*
1983
SUMMER OF FEAR by Lois Duncan *(Little, Brown)*
1984
SUPERFUDGE by Judy Blume *(Dutton)*
1985
NOTHING'S FAIR IN FIFTH GRADE by Barthe DeClements *(Viking)*
1986
THIRTEEN WAYS TO SINK A SUB by Jamie Gilson *(Lothrop)*
1987
ZUCCHINI by Barbara Dana *(Harper)*
1988
THE DOLLHOUSE MURDERS by Betty Ren Wright *(Holiday House)*
1989
SIXTH GRADE CAN REALLY KILL YOU by Barthe DeClements *(Viking)*
1990
THERE'S A BOY IN THE GIRLS' BATHROOM by Louis Sachar *(Knopf)*
1991
PECOS BILL: A TALL TALE by Steven Kellogg *(Morrow)*

NORTH DAKOTA
Flicker Tale Children's Book Award ❧

Known as the Children's Choice Award through 1985, this program takes its current name from the state's nickname, the "Flickertale State"; flickertales are ground squirrels found in profusion in central regions of North Dakota. Originally, children nominated the titles for a ten-title reading list and also selected the winning title from that list. Since 1986 members of the North Dakota Library Association (520 Avenue E, Bismark, ND 58701) Children's Roundtable have selected the ten-title nominee list in two categories, Juvenile *(J)* and Picture Book *(PB)*. Nominees—known to be titles enjoyed in libraries—must have been published within a five-year period before nomination. (Plaque)

1978
J: STAR WARS by George Lucas *(Ballantine/Del Rey)*

1979
J: ARE YOU THERE, GOD? IT'S ME, MARGARET by Judy Blume *(Bradbury)*
1980
J: TALES OF A FOURTH GRADE NOTHING by Judy Blume *(Dutton)*
1981
J: WHERE THE RED FERN GROWS by Wilson Rawls *(Doubleday)*
PB: CURIOUS GEORGE by H. A. Rey *(Houghton)*
1982
J: SUPERFUDGE by Judy Blume *(Dutton)*
PB: FOX AND HOUNDS by Walt Disney Productions *(Smith)*
1983
J: BLUBBER by Judy Blume *(Bradbury)*
PB: E. T.: THE EXTRA-TERRESTRIAL STORYBOOK by William Kotzwinkle *(Putnam)*
1984
J: RETURN OF THE JEDI STORYBOOK adapted by Joan Vinge *(Random)*
PB: A SISTER FOR SAM by Evelyn Mason, ill. by Tom Cooke *(Parker Brothers)*
1985
J: CHARLIE AND THE CHOCOLATE FACTORY by Roald Dahl *(Knopf)*
PB: MISS NELSON IS MISSING! by Harry Allard, ill. by James Marshall *(Houghton)*
1986
No Awards
1987
J: SUPERFUDGE by Judy Blume *(Dutton)*
PB: THE DAY JIMMY'S BOA ATE THE WASH by Trinka Hakes Noble, ill. by Steven Kellogg *(Dial)*
1988
J: NOTHING'S FAIR IN THE FIFTH GRADE by Barthe DeClements *(Viking)*
PB: MISS NELSON HAS A FIELD DAY by Harry Allard, ill. by James Marshall *(Houghton)*
1989
J: ON MY HONOR by Marion Dane Bauer *(Clarion)*
PB: LOVE YOU FOREVER by Robert Munsch, ill. by Michael Martchenko *(Firefly)*
1990
J: HATCHET by Gary Paulsen *(Bradbury)*
PB: MEANWHILE BACK AT THE RANCH by Trinka Hakes Noble, ill. by Tony Ross *(Dial)*

1991
J: HOW TO FIGHT A GIRL by Thomas Rockwell *(Watts)*
PB: NO JUMPING ON THE BED! by Tedd Arnold *(Dial)*

OHIO
Buckeye Children's Book Awards &

"This award program was designed to encourage children to read literature critically, encourage teacher involvement in children's literature programs in their schools, and to commend authors...." Jointly sponsored by the International Reading Association Ohio Council, Ohio Council of Teachers of English Language Arts, Ohio Department of Education, Ohio Educational Library Media Association, Ohio Library Association and the State Library of Ohio, the administrative contact for the program is the State Library of Ohio (65 South Front St., Columbus, OH 43215). An Advisory Council currently prepares reading lists of not more than ten titles in three reading-level categories: grades *K-2, 3-5* and *6-8*. Titles selected for these lists are from nominations made by children at participating schools and libraries. Voting for the winners frequently takes place during Ohio Right to Read Week, the first full week in March. The award—now given biennially— is named for the State tree of Ohio, a state commonly referred to as "The Buckeye State." (Plaque)

1982
K-3: THE BERENSTAIN BEARS AND THE SPOOKY OLD TREE by Stan and Jan Berenstain *(Random)*
4-8: SUPERFUDGE by Judy Blume *(Dutton)*
1983
K-3: GRANDPA'S GHOST STORIES by James Flora *(McElderry/Atheneum)*
4-8: TIGER EYES by Judy Blume *(Bradbury)*
1984
K-3: E.T. THE EXTRA-TERRESTRIAL STORYBOOK by William Kotzwinkle *(Putnam)*
4-8: NOTHING'S FAIR IN FIFTH GRADE by Barthe DeClements *(Viking)*
1985
K-2: THE BERENSTAIN BEARS GET IN A FIGHT by Stan and Jan Berenstain *(Random)*
3-5: RAMONA QUIMBY, AGE 8 by Beverly Cleary *(Morrow)*

6-8: A LIGHT IN THE ATTIC by Shel Silverstein *(Harper)*

1987

K-2: IN A DARK, DARK ROOM AND OTHER SCARY STORIES by Alvin Schwartz *(Harper)*

3-5: SCARY STORIES TO TELL IN THE DARK by Alvin Schwartz *(Lippincott)*

6-8: THIRTEEN WAYS TO SINK A SUB by Jamie Gilson *(Lothrop)*

1989

K-2: IF YOU GIVE A MOUSE A COOKIE by Laura Numeroff, ill. by Felicia Bond *(Harper)*

3-5: MORE SCARY STORIES TO TELL IN THE DARK by Alvin Schwartz *(Lippincott)*

6-8: SIXTH GRADE CAN REALLY KILL YOU by Barthe DeClements *(Viking)*

1991

K-2: POLAR EXPRESS by Chris Van Allsburg *(Houghton)*

3-5: THERE'S A BOY IN THE GIRLS' BATHROOM by Louis Sachar *(Knopf)*

6-8: HATCHET by Gary Paulsen *(Bradbury)*

OKLAHOMA
Sequoyah Children's and Young Adult Book Awards ❧

The Sequoyah Book Awards—one for children's books and, since 1988, one designated a young adult book award—honor Sequoyah (Cherokee for "lame one") for his achievement in creating the Cherokee alphabet, the 85 symbols representing the different sounds in the Cherokee language. A statue of Sequoyah is one of the two representing the State of Oklahoma in the National Hall of Fame at the Capitol in Washington, DC. Both awards programs are projects of the Oklahoma Library Association. Committees compile Masterlists of around 20 titles for the children's book award *(C)*, and around 15 titles for the young adult book award *(YA)*. Titles on the Masterlists are deemed to be of literary excellence; all are published three years prior to the award year. A wide variety of promotional materials, both free and for sale, is available for both programs. Young readers present the awards to the winners during the annual Oklahoma Library Association Spring Conference. Information about the awards is available from the Oklahoma State Department of Education (c/o Library Resources, 2500 N. Lincoln Blvd., Oklahoma City, OK 73105). (Plaques)

1959
OLD YELLER by Fred Gipson *(Harper)*
1960
BLACK GOLD by Marguerite Henry *(Rand McNally)*
1961
HAVE SPACE SUIT WILL TRAVEL by Robert Heinlein
(Scribner)
1962
THE HELEN KELLER STORY by Catherine O. Peare *(Crowell)*
1963
THE MYSTERY OF THE HAUNTED POOL by Phyllis A.
Whitney *(Westminster)*
1964
WHERE THE PANTHER SCREAMS by William Powell
Robinson *(World)*
1965
A WRINKLE IN TIME by Madeleine L'Engle *(Farrar)*
1966
RASCAL by Sterling North *(Dutton)*
1967
HARRIET THE SPY by Louise Fitzhugh *(Harper)*
1968
GENTLE BEN by Walt Morey *(Dutton)*
1969
BLACKBEARD'S GHOST by Ben Stahl *(Houghton)*
1970
MUSTANG by Marguerite Henry *(Rand McNally)*
1971
RAMONA THE PEST by Beverly Cleary *(Morrow)*
1972
THE MAN IN THE BOX: A STORY FROM VIETNAM by
Mary Lois Dunn *(McGraw-Hill)*
1973
THE TRUMPET OF THE SWAN by E. B. White *(Harper)*
1974
FLIGHT OF THE WHITE WOLF by Mel Ellis *(Holt)*
1975
TALES OF A FOURTH GRADE NOTHING by Judy Blume
(Dutton)
1976
HOW TO EAT FRIED WORMS by Thomas Rockwell *(Watts)*
1977
THE TOOTHPASTE MILLIONAIRE by Jean Merrill
(Houghton)
1978
SHOESHINE GIRL by Clyde Robert Bulla *(Crowell)*

1979
SUMMER OF THE MONKEYS by Wilson Rawls *(Doubleday)*
1980
KID POWER by Susan Beth Pfeffer *(Watts)*
1981
THE GET-AWAY CAR by Eleanor Clymer *(Dutton)*
1982
BUNNICULA: A RABBIT TALE OF MYSTERY by Deborah and James Howe *(Atheneum)*
1983
A DOG CALLED KITTY by Bill Wallace *(Holiday House)*
1984
THE CYBIL WAR by Betsy Byars *(Viking)*
1985
THIRTEEN WAYS TO SINK A SUB by Jamie Gilson *(Lothrop)*
1986
DEAR MR. HENSHAW by Beverly Cleary *(Morrow)*
JUST TELL ME WHEN WE'RE DEAD! by Eth Clifford *(Houghton)*
1987
NIGHT OF THE TWISTERS by Ivy Ruckman *(Crowell)*
1988
C: CHRISTINA'S GHOST by Betty Ren Wright *(Holiday House)*
YA: ABBY, MY LOVE by Hadley Irwin *(McElderry)*
1989
C: SIXTH-GRADE SLEEPOVER by Eve Bunting *(HBJ)*
YA: THE OTHER SIDE OF DARK by Joan Lowery Nixon *(Delacorte)*
1990
C: FUDGE by Charlotte Towner Graeber *(Lothrop)*
YA: HATCHET by Gary Paulsen *(Bradbury)*
1991
C: BEAUTY by Bill Wallace *(Holiday House)*
YA: A SUDDEN SILENCE by Eve Bunting *(HBJ)*
1992
C: A DOLL IN THE GARDEN: A GHOST STORY by Mary Downing Hahn *(Clarion)*
YA: APPOINTMENT WITH A STRANGER by Jean Thesman *(Houghton)*

PACIFIC NORTHWEST
(Alaska; Alberta, Canada; British Columbia, Canada; Idaho; Montana; Oregon; Washington)
Young Reader's Choice Awards 🐦

This awards program has been in existence longer than any other North American program in which children choose the winning books. For the first fifty years of the program, a single award was given to a book on a nominee list of fifteen titles assembled from suggestions by librarians, teachers, and children. These were books of appeal to readers in grades 4-8. In 1991 a second award for books published for grades 9-12 was added to the program to commemorate a notable milestone in the program's history. Currently, twelve titles are on the nominee list for grades 4-8, and five on the list for 9-12, the "Senior Division." Voting takes place throughout the region in early March, with the total number of votes for each nominated title forwarded to the administrator (Graduate School of Library & Information Science, FM-30, University of Washington, Seattle, WA 98195) for tabulation. The sponsor is the Pacific Northwest Library Association (PNLA), which offers a variety of materials at very little cost to promote the award and to help local participants administer it. It also sells a videotaped slide-cassette presentation introducing and promoting the titles nominated for the award. The award is presented to the winner during the PNLA Annual Conference. (Hand-printed parchment scroll)

1940
PAUL BUNYAN SWINGS HIS AXE by Dell J. McCormick *(Caxton)*

1941
MR. POPPER'S PENGUINS by Richard and Florence Atwater *(Little, Brown)*

1942
BY THE SHORES OF SILVER LAKE by Laura Ingalls Wilder *(Harper)*

1943
LASSIE COME HOME by Eric Knight *(Holt)*

1944
THE BLACK STALLION by Walter Farley *(Random)*

1945
SNOW TREASURE by Marie McSwigan *(Dutton)*

1946
THE RETURN OF SILVER CHIEF by Jack O'Brien *(Holt)*

1947
HOMER PRICE by Robert McCloskey *(Viking)*
1948
THE BLACK STALLION RETURNS by Walter Farley
(Random)
1949
COWBOY BOOTS by Shannon Garst *(Abingdon)*
1950
McELLIGOT'S POOL by Dr. Seuss *(Random)*
1951
KING OF THE WIND by Marguerite Henry *(Rand McNally)*
1952
SEA STAR by Marguerite Henry *(Rand McNally)*
1953-1955
No Awards
1956
MISS PICKERELL GOES TO MARS by Ellen MacGregor
(McGraw-Hill)
1957
HENRY AND RIBSY by Beverly Cleary *(Morrow)*
1958
GOLDEN MARE by William Corbin *(Coward)*
1959
OLD YELLER by Fred Gipson *(Harper)*
1960
HENRY AND THE PAPER ROUTE by Beverly Cleary
(Morrow)
1961
DANNY DUNN AND THE HOMEWORK MACHINE by Jay
Williams *(McGraw-Hill)*
1962
THE SWAMP FOX OF THE REVOLUTION by Stewart
Holbrook *(Random)*
1963
DANNY DUNN ON THE OCEAN FLOOR by Jay Williams
(McGraw-Hill)
1964
THE INCREDIBLE JOURNEY by Sheila Burnford *(Atlantic-Little, Brown)*
1965
JOHN F. KENNEDY AND PT-109 by Richard Tregaskis
(Random)
1966
RASCAL by Sterling North *(Dutton)*
1967
CHITTY-CHITTY-BANG-BANG by Ian Fleming *(Random)*

1968
THE MOUSE AND THE MOTORCYCLE by Beverly Cleary *(Morrow)*

1969
HENRY REED'S BABY-SITTING SERVICE by Keith Robertson *(Viking)*

1970
SMOKE by William Corbin *(Coward)*

1971
RAMONA THE PEST by Beverly Cleary *(Morrow)*

1972
ENCYCLOPEDIA BROWN KEEPS THE PEACE by Donald J. Sobol *(Nelson)*

1973
No Award

1974
MRS. FRISBY AND THE RATS OF NIMH by Robert C. O'Brien *(Atheneum)*

1975
TALES OF A FOURTH GRADE NOTHING by Judy Blume *(Dutton)*

1976
THE GREAT BRAIN REFORMS by John D. Fitzgerald *(Dial)*

1977
BLUBBER by Judy Blume *(Bradbury)*

1978
THE GREAT BRAIN DOES IT AGAIN by John D. Fitzgerald *(Dial)*

1979
ROLL OF THUNDER, HEAR MY CRY by Mildred Taylor *(Dial)*

1980
RAMONA AND HER FATHER by Beverly Cleary *(Morrow)*

1981
HAIL, HAIL, CAMP TIMBERWOOD by Ellen Conford *(Little, Brown)*

1982
BUNNICULA: A RABBIT TALE OF MYSTERY by Deborah and James Howe *(Atheneum)*

1983
SUPERFUDGE by Judy Blume *(Dutton)*

1984
THE INDIAN IN THE CUPBOARD by Lynne Reid Banks *(Doubleday)*

1985
THIRTEEN WAYS TO SINK A SUB by Jamie Gilson *(Lothrop)*

1986
THE DOLLHOUSE MURDERS by Betty Ren Wright *(Holiday House)*
1987
THE WAR WITH GRANDPA by Robert Kimmel Smith *(Delacorte)*
1988
SIXTH GRADE CAN REALLY KILL YOU by Barthe DeClements *(Viking)*
1989
WAIT TILL HELEN COMES: A GHOST STORY by Mary Downing Hahn *(Clarion)*
1990
THERE'S A BOY IN THE GIRLS' BATHROOM by Louis Sachar *(Knopf)*
1991
4-8: TEN KIDS, NO PETS by Ann M. Martin *(Holiday House)*
9-12: SEX EDUCATION by Jenny Davis *(Orchard)*

RHODE ISLAND
Rhode Island Children's Book Award 🦆

This award program "encourages children to read." A Book Award Committee consisting of representatives of the three sponsors—Rhode Island Library Association, Rhode Island State Council of the International Reading Association, and Rhode Island Educational Media Association—prepares a nomination list of twenty fiction and nonfiction titles appropriate for grades 3-6. Children cast their votes at participating schools and libraries on February 1 each year; the site of the fall award ceremony is a school that has participated in the program. Currently, there is no permanent address for the award; the Children's Department of the Providence Public Library (225 Washington St., Providence, RI 02903) handles some aspects of the program's administration. (Presentation)

1991
SOMETHING UPSTAIRS: A TALE OF GHOSTS by Avi *(Orchard)*

SOUTH CAROLINA
South Carolina Children's and Young Adult Book Awards ❧

Sponsored by the South Carolina Association of School Librarians (P.O. Box 2442, Columbia, SC 29202) in cooperation with State Department of Education and the College of Library and Information Science, University of South Carolina, a stated purpose of the Children's Book Science Award *(C)* is to expose students in grades 4-8 to "contemporary and realistic literature concerned with a variety of subjects that relate to children's lives today...humor, sports, friendships, death, divorce, innermost problems, fantasy, survival, family relations, minority groups...." A list of twenty nominees is selected by an award committee, that cites reviews and other distinctions relating to all titles on the list when it is disseminated to cooperating schools statewide. Titles must have been published in a five-year period before the award year. The Young Adult Award *(YA)* is designed "to encourage young adults to read good contemporary literature which gives an understanding of the human experience." Students in grades 7-12 vote for the winners from a list of twenty titles compiled by an award committee. Titles must have been published in a three-year period before the award year. (Bronze medallion for each award)

1976
C: HOW TO EAT FRIED WORMS by Thomas Rockwell *(Watts)*
1977
C: TALES OF A FOURTH GRADE NOTHING by Judy Blume *(Dutton)*
1978
C: OTHERWISE KNOWN AS SHEILA THE GREAT by Judy Blume *(Dutton)*
1979
C: THE GREAT CHRISTMAS KIDNAPPING CAPER by Jean Van Leeuwen *(Dial)*
1980
C: SHOESHINE GIRL by Clyde Robert Bulla *(Crowell)*
YA: AMITYVILLE HORROR by Jay Anson *(Prentice-Hall)*
1981
C: BUNNICULA: A RABBIT TALE OF MYSTERY by Deborah and James Howe *(Atheneum)*
YA: A SHINING SEASON by William Buchanan *(Coward)*
1982
C: THE GHOST OF TILLIE CASSAWAY by Ellen Showell *(Four Winds)*

YA: THE BOY WHO DRANK TOO MUCH by Shep Greene *(Viking)*
1983
C: PRISONERS AT THE KITCHEN TABLE by Barbara Holland *(Clarion)*
YA: ABOUT DAVID by Susan Beth Pfeffer *(Delacorte)*
1984
C: JELLY BELLY by Robert Kimmel Smith *(Delacorte)*
YA: STRANGER WITH MY FACE by Lois Duncan *(Little, Brown)*
1985
C: THE MONSTER'S RING by Bruce Coville *(Pantheon)*
YA: THE DIVORCE EXPRESS by Paula Danziger *(Delacorte)*
1986
C: THE WAR WITH GRANDPA by Robert Kimmel Smith *(Delacorte)*
YA: A STRING OF CHANCES by Phyllis Reynolds Naylor *(Atheneum)*
1987
C: CRACKER JACKSON by Betsy Byars *(Viking)*
YA: IF THIS IS LOVE, I'LL TAKE SPAGHETTI by Ellen Conford *(Four Winds)*
1988
C: BABY-SITTING IS A DANGEROUS JOB by Willo Davis Roberts *(Atheneum)*
YA: LOCKED IN TIME by Lois Duncan *(Little, Brown)*
1989
C: FERRET IN THE BEDROOM, LIZARDS IN THE FRIDGE by Bill Wallace *(Holiday House)*
YA: FACE AT THE EDGE OF THE WORLD by Eve Bunting *(Clarion)*
1990
C: CLASS CLOWN by Johanna Hurwitz *(Morrow)*
YA: THE YEAR WITHOUT MICHAEL by Susan Beth Pfeffer *(Bantam)*
1991
C: IS ANYBODY THERE? by Eve Bunting *(Lippincott)*
YA: FALLEN ANGELS by Walter Dean Myers *(Scholastic)*

SOUTH DAKOTA
Prairie Pasque Award 🌸

The program is for children in grades 4-6 throughout the state. A committee of school and public librarians develops a reading list of twenty titles to be read through the school year. Children vote for the winners. Management of the award rotates at two-year intervals among volunteers. A permanent source of information about the program is the Director of Library Development, South Dakota State Library (800 Governor's Drive, Pierre, SD 57501). (Plaque)

1987
NIGHT OF THE TWISTERS by Ivy Ruckman *(Crowell)*
1988
SWITCHAROUND by Lois Lowry *(Houghton)*
1989
ROYAL PAIN by Ellen Conford *(Scholastic)*
1990
THIS ISLAND ISN'T BIG ENOUGH FOR THE FOUR OF US by Gery Greer and Bob Ruddick *(Crowell)*
1991
ALL ABOUT SAM by Lois Lowry *(Houghton)*

TENNESSEE
Volunteer State Book Awards 🖋

Begun originally as the Tennessee Children's Choice Book Award intended for students in grades 4, 5, and 6, as of the program for 1988-89, awards have been given in four divisions: *K-3, 4-6, 7-9,* and *10-12.* Committees of school and public librarians and library educators select Master Lists of twenty titles for each division. Titles on the lists are read by (and to) children during the school year, with children's votes tabulated in time for formal announcements of the winners during the annual Tennessee Library Association Spring Conference, when the following year's Master Lists are also introduced. The awards program takes its name from the state's nickname: in 1847 the governor called for three regiments of soldiers to serve in the Mexican War; thirty thousand volunteered at once. The program is administered from Department of Youth Education, Middle Tennessee State University, Murfreesboro, TN 37132. (Plaques)

1979
HOW TO EAT FRIED WORMS by Thomas Rockwell *(Watts)*
1980
RAMONA AND HER FATHER by Beverly Cleary *(Morrow)*
1981
SHADOWS by Lynn Hall *(Follett)*

1982
SUPERFUDGE by Judy Blume *(Dutton)*
1983
THE CYBIL WAR by Betsy Byars *(Viking)*
1984
HOWLIDAY INN by James Howe *(Atheneum)*
1985
WHEN THE BOYS RAN THE HOUSE by Joan Carris *(Lippincott)*
1986
OPERATION: DUMP THE CHUMP by Barbara Park *(Knopf)*
1987
SKINNYBONES by Barbara Park *(Knopf)*
1988
THE WAR WITH GRANDPA by Robert Kimmel Smith *(Delacorte)*
1989
K-3: IN A DARK, DARK ROOM AND OTHER SCARY STORIES by Alvin Schwartz, ill. by Dirk Zimmer *(Harper)*
4-6: WAIT TILL HELEN COMES: A GHOST STORY by Mary Downing Hahn *(Clarion)*
7-9: DOGSONG by Gary Paulsen *(Bradbury)*
10-12: IZZY, WILLY-NILLY by Cynthia Voigt *(Atheneum)*
1990
K-3: ABIYOYO by Pete Seeger *(Macmillan)*
4-6: CHRISTINA'S GHOST by Betty Ren Wright *(Holiday House)*
7-9: PUTTING ON AN ACT by Christi Killien *(Houghton)*
10-12: LOCKED IN TIME by Lois Duncan *(Little, Brown)*
1991
K-3: THE MAGIC SCHOOL BUS AT THE WATERWORKS by Joanna Cole, ill. by Bruce Degen *(Scholastic)*
4-6: BEETLES, LIGHTLY TOASTED by Phyllis Reynolds Naylor *(Atheneum)*
7-9: THE SHADOW CLUB by Neal Shusterman *(Little, Brown)*
10-12: SAY GOODNIGHT, GRACIE by Julie Rice Deaver *(Harper)*

TEXAS
The Texas Bluebonnet Award 🌸

In the words of a resolution adopted by the Texas House of Representatives, honoring this award program, the sponsors are commended for seeking "to encourage the children of Texas, through their school and public libraries, to explore and read with discrimination a variety of quality books; to recognize children's personal reading interests and selections; and to honor those who create children's books of superior quality." The award is sponsored by the Texas Association of School Librarians and the Children's Round Table, affiliates of the Texas Library Association (TLA) (3355 Bee Cave Road, Suite 603, Austin, TX 78746). The award is named for the State flower of Texas, a blue-flowered lupine. An award committee compiles a Master List of nominees after receiving suggestions from librarians, teachers and students across the state. The program is for children in grades 3-6, who must have read (or heard read aloud) at least five books on the list to be eligible to vote. Both fiction and nonfiction are represented on the Master Lists; authors must be alive, and U.S. citizens. The award is presented during the annual TLA Conference. (Medallion)

1981
RAMONA AND HER FATHER by Beverly Cleary *(Morrow)*
1982
SUPERFUDGE by Judy Blume *(Dutton)*
1983
A DOG CALLED KITTY by Bill Wallace *(Holiday House)*
1984
NOTHING'S FAIR IN FIFTH GRADE by Barthe DeClements *(Viking)*
1985
SKINNYBONES by Barbara Park *(Knopf)*
1986
THE DOLLHOUSE MURDERS by Betty Ren Wright *(Holiday House)*
1987
THE HOT AND COLD SUMMER by Johanna Hurwitz *(Morrow)*
1988
CHRISTINA'S GHOST by Betty Ren Wright *(Holiday House)*
1989
WAIT TILL HELEN COMES: A GHOST STORY by Mary Downing Hahn *(Clarion)*
1990
THERE'S A BOY IN THE GIRLS' BATHROOM by Louis Sachar *(Knopf)*
1991
ALIENS FOR BREAKFAST by Jonathan Etra and Stephanie Spinner *(Random)*
1992
SNOT STEW by Bill Wallace *(Holiday House)*

UTAH
Utah Children's, Informational, and Young Adults' Book Awards ❧

Sponsored by the Children's Literature Association of Utah (209 East 500 South, Salt Lake City, UT 84111), the Children's Book Award *(C)* was first presented in 1980, the Informational Book Award *(I)* in 1986, and the Young Adults' Award *(Y/A)* in 1991. The first two awards are determined by the votes of children in grades 3-6 from, in the case of the Children's Award, a nomination list of twenty titles, and, in the case of the Informational Award, a list of no more than seven titles. The Young Adults' Award is determined by readers in grades 7-12 from a list of ten nominations. Titles that have won the Newbery Medal are not eligible for any of the awards; titles that have won the Caldecott Medal are not eligible for the Children's or Informational Awards. Titles can be nominated for the awards one time only. Detailed "Eligibility & Selection Criteria for Nominations" information sheets are prepared for participating schools and libraries. (Plaques)

1980
RAMONA AND HER FATHER by Beverly Cleary *(Morrow)*
1981
EDDIE'S MENAGERIE by Carolyn Haywood *(Morrow)*
THE LETTER, THE WITCH AND THE RING by John Bellairs *(Dial)*
1982
SUPERFUDGE by Judy Blume *(Dutton)*
1983
THE CHOCOLATE TOUCH by Patrick Catling *(Morrow)*
1984
LOST IN THE DEVIL'S DESERT by Gloria Skurzynski *(Lothrop)*
1985
STONE FOX by John Reynolds Gardiner *(Crowell)*
1986
C: ME AND THE WEIRDOS by Jane Sutton *(Houghton)*
I: GREAT PAINTERS by Piero Ventura *(Putnam)*
1987
C: SKINNYBONES by Barbara Park *(Knopf)*
I: No Award (no nominations)
1988
C: WAIT TILL HELEN COMES: A GHOST STORY by Mary Downing Hahn *(Clarion)*

I: HOW MUCH IS A MILLION? by David M. Schwartz, ill. by Steven Kellogg *(Lothrop)*

1989
C: TRAPPED IN DEATH CAVE by Bill Wallace *(Holiday House)*
I: YOUR AMAZING SENSES: THIRTY-SIX GAMES, PUZZLES, & TRICKS TO SHOW HOW YOUR SENSES WORK by Ron and Atie Van Der Meer *(Aladdin)*

1990
C: THIS ISLAND ISN'T BIG ENOUGH FOR THE FOUR OF US by Gery Greer and Bob Ruddick *(Crowell)*
I: HOW TO MAKE POP-UPS by Joan Irvine, ill. by Barbara Reid *(Morrow)*

1991
C: MATILDA by Roald Dahl *(Viking)*
I: BILL PEET: AN AUTOBIOGRAPHY by Bill Peet *(Houghton)*
Y/A: THE OTHER SIDE OF DARK by Joan Lowery Nixon *(Delacorte)*

VERMONT
Dorothy Canfield Fisher Children's Book Award 🍂

Dorothy Canfield Fisher (1879-1958) was a long-time Vermont resident whose most notable book for young readers was *Understood Betsy* (1917), a novel first serialized in the magazine *St. Nicholas.* She was best known for her adult work as a member of the editorial selection board of Book-of-the-Month Club from its founding in 1926 until her death, and as a critic, short story writer and translator. The award established in her name was the third of its sort in this country, and modeled on the William Allen White Award program in Kansas, her birth state. At the time of its founding, literature about the program was as spirited as the writer it honored: "Parents and teachers in Vermont know that 'the only thing necessary for the complete triumph of evil is that good men do nothing,' and increasingly they are sending their children to libraries to read good books because they know that this is one of the best preventive medicines for the treatment of juvenile delinquency, as well as reading problems." This awards program is co-sponsored by the Vermont Department of Libraries and the Vermont Congress of Parents and Teachers, the administrator (138 Main St., Montpelier, VT 05602). Children in grades 4-8 select the winner from a master list of thirty titles published two years prior to the award year and compiled by an award committee. (Illuminated scroll)

1957
OLD BONES by Mildred M. Pace *(McGraw-Hill)*
1958
FIFTEEN by Beverly Cleary *(Morrow)*
1959
COMMANCHE OF THE SEVENTH by Margaret Leighton *(Farrar)*
1960
DOUBLE OR NOTHING by Phoebe Erickson *(Harper)*
1961
CAPTAIN GHOST by Thelma Harrington Bell *(Viking)*
1962
THE CITY UNDER THE BACK STEPS by Evelyn Lampman *(Doubleday)*
1963
THE INCREDIBLE JOURNEY by Sheila Burnford *(Atlantic-Little, Brown)*
1964
BRISTLE FACE by Zachary Ball *(Holiday House)*
1965
RASCAL by Sterling North *(Dutton)*
1966
RIBSY by Beverly Cleary *(Morrow)*
1967
THE SUMMER I WAS LOST by Phillip Viereck *(John Day)*
1968
THE TASTE OF SPRUCE GUM by Jacqueline Jackson *(Little, Brown)*
1969
TWO IN THE WILDERNESS by Mary W. Thompson *(McKay)*
1970
KAVIK THE WOLF DOG by Walt Morey *(Dutton)*
1971
GO TO THE ROOM OF THE EYES by Betty Erwin *(Little, Brown)*
1972
FLIGHT OF THE WHITE WOLF by Mel Ellis *(Holt)*
1973
NEVER STEAL A MAGIC CAT by Don and Joan Caulfield *(Doubleday)*
1974
CATCH A KILLER by George A. Woods *(Harper)*

1975
THE EIGHTEENTH EMERGENCY by Betsy Byars *(Viking)*

1976
THE TOOTHPASTE MILLIONAIRE by Jean Merrill
(Houghton)

1977
A SMART KID LIKE YOU by Stella Pevsner *(Clarion)*

1978
SUMMER OF FEAR by Lois Duncan *(Little, Brown)*

1979
KID POWER by Susan Beth Pfeffer *(Watts)*

1980
BONES ON BLACK SPRUCE MOUNTAIN by David Budbill
(Dial)

1981
BUNNICULA: A RABBIT TALE OF MYSTERY by Deborah
and James Howe *(Atheneum)*

1982
THE HAND-ME-DOWN KID by Francine Pascal *(Viking)*

1983
TIGER EYES by Judy Blume *(Bradbury)*

1984
A BUNDLE OF STICKS by Pat Rhoads Mauser *(Atheneum)*

1985
DEAR MR. HENSHAW by Beverly Cleary *(Morrow)*

1986
THE WAR WITH GRANDPA by Robert Kimmel Smith
(Delacorte)

1987
THE CASTLE IN THE ATTIC by Elizabeth Winthrop *(Holiday
House)*

1988
WAIT TILL HELEN COMES: A GHOST STORY by Mary
Downing Hahn *(Clarion)*

1989
HATCHET by Gary Paulsen *(Bradbury)*

1990
WHERE IT STOPS NOBODY KNOWS by Amy Ehrlich *(Dial)*

1991
NUMBER THE STARS by Lois Lowry *(Houghton)*

VIRGINIA
Virginia Young Readers Program 🐝

This program began to encourage reading for pleasure at the elementary *(E)* level. For the 1984 award year, the contest was at the middle school level *(M)*, and for 1985 at the high school level *(HS)*. All three of these levels were a part of the program for 1986 and 1987. From 1988, a primary level *(P)* has been incorporated, so four awards, primary through high school, are now presented annually. One of the program's objectives is "to broaden students' awareness of literature as a life-long pleasure." The sponsor is the Virginia State Reading Association (address changes with officers), which appoints Young Readers Book Selection Committees to develop nomination lists of 10-15 titles for each level. (Pewter Virginia Cups)

1982
E: ISLAND OF THE BLUE DOLPHINS by Scott O'Dell *(Houghton)*
1983
E: BRIDGE TO TERABITHIA by Katherine Paterson *(Crowell)*
1984
M: THE WESTING GAME by Ellen Raskin *(Dutton)*
1985
HS: THE OUTSIDERS by S. E. Hinton *(Viking)*
1986
E: SUPERFUDGE by Judy Blume *(Dutton)*
M: THE CAT ATE MY GYMSUIT by Paula Danziger *(Delacorte)*
HS: THE THIRD EYE by Mollie Hunter *(Harper)*
1987
E: MY FRIEND THE VAMPIRE by Angela Sommer-Bodenburg *(Dial)*
M: THE CURSE OF THE BLUE FIGURINE by John Bellairs *(Dial)*
HS: THE MAN IN THE WOODS by Rosemary Wells *(Dial)*
1988
P: IN A DARK, DARK ROOM by Alvin Schwartz; ill. by Dirk Zimmer *(Harper)*
E: THE INDIAN IN THE CUPBOARD by Lynne Reid Banks *(Doubleday)*
M: THE GHOST IN MY SOUP by Judi Miller *(Bantam)*
HS: IZZY, WILLY-NILLY by Cynthia Voigt *(Atheneum)*

1989
P: HECKEDY PEG by Audrey Wood, ill. by Don Wood *(HBJ)*
E: WAIT TILL HELEN COMES: A GHOST STORY by Mary Downing Hahn *(Clarion)*
M: THE OTHER SIDE OF DARK by Joan Lowery Nixon *(Delacorte)*
HS: THE FACE AT THE EDGE OF THE WORLD by Eve Bunting *(Clarion)*

1990
P: THE MAGIC SCHOOL BUS INSIDE THE EARTH by Joanna Cole, ill. by Bruce Degen *(Scholastic)*
E: CHRISTINA'S GHOST by Betty Ren Wright *(Holiday House)*
M: HATCHET by Gary Paulsen *(Bradbury)*
HS: WOLF RIDER: A TALE OF TERROR by Avi *(Bradbury)*

1991
P: TWO BAD ANTS by Chris Van Allsburg *(Houghton)*
E: MATILDA by Roald Dahl *(Viking)*
M: GOOD NIGHT, MR. TOM by Michelle Magorian *(Harper)*
HS: SAY GOODNIGHT, GRACIE by Julie Rice Deaver *(Harper)*

WASHINGTON
Washington Children's Choice Picture Book Award ❧

Sponsored by the Washington Library Media Association (c/o P.O. Box 1413, Bothell, WA 98011), this award is for a picture book—fiction or nonfiction—selected by children in grades K-3 from a ballot list of twenty titles compiled by an award committee. Titles on the ballot have been published in a two-year period prior to the award year. (Armatale—pewter-like—plate)

1982
CROSS-COUNTRY CAT by Mary Calhoun, ill. by Erick Ingraham *(Morrow)*

1983
SPACE CASE by Edward Marshall, ill. by James Marshall *(Dial)*

1984
JUMANJI by Chris Van Allsburg *(Houghton)*

1985
NIMBY by Jasper Tomkins *(Green Tiger)*

1986
THE UNICORN AND THE LAKE by Marianna Mayer, ill. by Michael Hague *(Dial)*

1987
IN A DARK, DARK ROOM AND OTHER SCARY STORIES
by Alvin Schwartz, ill. by Dirk Zimmer *(Harper)*
1988
KING BIDGOOD'S IN THE BATHTUB by Audrey Wood, ill.
by Don Wood *(HBJ)*
1989
THE MAGIC SCHOOL BUS AT THE WATERWORKS by
Joanna Cole, ill. by Bruce Degen *(Scholastic)*
1990
AMOS: THE STORY OF AN OLD DOG AND HIS COUCH by
Howie Schneider and Susan Seligson, ill by Howie Schneider
(Little, Brown)
1991
TWO BAD ANTS by Chris Van Allsburg *(Houghton)*

WEST VIRGINIA
West Virginia Children's Book Award 🖙

The purpose of this awards program is "to enrich the lives of
children in grades 3 through 6 by encouraging the reading of
books of literary quality. The award provides a personal
relationship and interaction between authors and readers in order
to increase children's enjoyment of books. . . [the award] is a
celebration of children, books, and authors." A master list of
titles—all fiction—is compiled by an award committee (c/o Main
Library, P.O. Box 6069, Morgantown, WV 26506) that
considers "literary excellence" and "appropriateness" in
assembling the list. Books are by living authors and have been
published in a three-year period before the award year.
Participating schools pay a modest five dollar registration fee to
help to defray postage and materials costs. (West Virginia-crafted
artifact)

1985
JUMANJI by Chris Van Allsburg *(Houghton)*
1986
MUSTARD by Charlotte Graeber *(Macmillan)*
1987
RALPH S. MOUSE by Beverly Cleary *(Morrow)*
1988
HERBIE JONES by Suzy Kline *(Putnam)*

1989
CLASS CLOWN by Johanna Hurwitz *(Morrow)*

1990
FUDGE by Charlotte Graeber *(Lothrop)*

1991
THERE'S A BOY IN THE GIRLS' BATHROOM by Louis
Sachar *(Knopf)*

WISCONSIN
Golden Archer and *Little Archer* *Awards* 🕮

In the formative years of this award program, honorees were
often writers whose recent books "impress with the power of
their characterizations, the strengths of their plots and themes,
and the author's mastery of style," and not for specific books.
The Golden Archer Award *(GA)* is determined by the votes of
readers in grades 4-8, and the Little Archer Award *(LA)* by
grades K-3. There are no nominations; children in participating
schools and libraries cast votes based entirely on independent
reading. The program takes its name in part from one of the
award founders, children's book writer Marian Fuller Archer,
and in part from the words of the archer in Longfellow's verse, "I
shot an arrow into the air,/It fell to earth, I know not where...."
The sponsor is Department of Library and Learning Resources,
University of Wisconsin-Oshkosh, Oshkosh, WI 54901.
(Medallions and certificates for each award)

1974
GA: Judy Blume

1975
GA: Thomas Rockwell

1976
GA: Florence Parry Heide
LA: THE FUNNY LITTLE WOMAN retold by Arlene Mosel,
ill. by Blair Lent *(Dutton)*

1977
GA: Beverly Cleary
LA: Bill Peet

1978
GA: Scott Corbett
LA: Peter Spier

1979
GA: Wilson Rawls
LA: Lorna Balian
1980
GA: Nat Hentoff
LA: CROSS-COUNTRY CAT by Mary Calhoun, ill. by Erick
Ingraham *(Morrow)*
1981
GA: Betsy Byars
LA: Steven Kellogg
1982
GA: Beverly Butler
LA: Eileen Christelow
1983
GA: S. E. Hinton
LA: William Steig
1984
GA: NOTHING'S FAIR IN FIFTH GRADE by Barthe
DeClements *(Viking)*
LA: THE BUTTER BATTLE BOOK by Dr. Seuss *(Random)*
1985
GA: TORNADO! by Hilary Milton *(Watts)*
LA: WHAT'S UNDER MY BED? by James Stevenson
(Greenwillow)
1986
GA: WHALESONG by Robert Siegel *(Good News)*
LA: POLAR EXPRESS by Chris Van Allsburg *(Houghton)*
1987
GA: THE WHIPPING BOY by Sid Fleischman *(Greenwillow)*
LA: KING BIDGOOD'S IN THE BATHTUB by Audrey Wood,
ill. by Don Wood *(HBJ)*
1988
GA: ON MY HONOR by Marion Dane Bauer *(Clarion)*
LA: HEY, AL by Arthur Yorinks, ill. by Richard Egielski
(Farrar)
1989
GA: HATCHET by Gary Paulsen *(Bradbury)*
LA: UNDERWEAR! by Mary Monsell, ill. by Lynn Munsinger
(Whitman)
1990
GA: NUMBER THE STARS by Lois Lowry *(Houghton)*
LA: THE TUB PEOPLE by Pam Conrad, ill. by Richard Egielski
(Harper)

WYOMING
Indian Paintbrush Book Award ❧

Twenty titles constitute the candidates for this award each year.
Selection of the nominees is entirely by children in grades 4-6;
the books must be fiction and have been published within a five
year period before being nominated. The sponsor is the Wyoming
Library Association (c/o Executive Secretary, P. O. Box 1387,
Cheyenne, WY 82003). (Plaque)

1986
NAYA NUKI: THE GIRL WHO RAN by Ken Thomasma
(Baker Book House)
1987
THE HOT AND COLD SUMMER by Johanna Hurwitz
(Morrow)
1988
THE DOLLHOUSE MURDERS by Betty Ren Wright *(Holiday House)*
1989
THE RETURN OF THE INDIAN by Lynne Reid Banks
(Doubleday)
1990
THERE'S A BOY IN THE GIRLS' BATHROOM by Louis
Sachar *(Knopf)*
1991
MATILDA by Roald Dahl *(Viking)*

WYOMING
Soaring Eagle Awards ❧

Young readers suggest the nominees for these two awards given
by voters in grades 7-9 and 10-12. An adult committee verifies
that the fifteen nominations have received at least two positive
reviews. The sponsors are the Wyoming Educational Media
Association and the Wyoming Council for the International
Reading Association. Administrative responsibilities are managed
by Library Services, Natrona County School District #1 (970 N.
Glenn Rd., Casper, WY 82601). (Bookends with stained glass
depiction of soaring eagle)

1989
7-9: SUPERFUDGE by Judy Blume *(Dutton)*
1990
7-9: SOMEONE IS HIDING ON ALCATRAZ ISLAND by Eve Bunting *(Clarion)*
10-12: OF LOVE AND SHADOWS by Isabel Allende *(Knopf)*
1991
7-9: TRAPPED IN DEATH CAVE by Bill Wallace *(Holiday House)*
10-12: PRINCESS ASHLEY by Richard Peck *(Delacorte)*

PART III

Australian, Canadian, New Zealand, and United Kingdom (UK) Awards

AUSTRALIA
Australian Book Publishers Association Book Design Awards ❧
ASHTON SCHOLASTIC AWARD

As of 1987, the Australian Book Publishers Association (ABPA) Book Design Awards program—which had until then judged children's books annually with all other books as a group—established a series of sponsored book design awards in several categories, one of them for the "best designed illustrated children's book," sponsored by the publisher Ashton Scholastic. ABPA is at Suite 60, Level 3, 89 Jones St. Ultimo, Sydney, N. S. W. 2007, Australia. The listing below is the publication year; the awards are decided on in the following year. (Exhibition and illustrated catalog)

1986
KOJURO AND THE BEARS by Junko Morimoto, designed by Deborah Brash *(Collins/Angus & Robertson)*
1987
DEREK THE DINOSAUR by Mary Blackwood, ill. and designed by Kerry Argent *(Omnibus)*
1988
ROSIE SIPS SPIDERS by Alison Lester, designed by Alison Lester *(Oxford)*
1989
THE STORY OF A FALLING STAR by Elsie Jones, ill. by Doug Jones, designed by Karin Donaldson and Maureen MacKenzie *(Aboriginal Studies Press)*
1990
MAGIC BEACH by Alison Lester, designed by Alison Lester and Sandra Nobes *(Allen & Unwin/Little Ark Books)*

Australian Multicultural Children's Literature Awards ઠ

Inaugurated in 1991 by the Office of Multicultural Affairs (Department of the Prime Minister and Cabinet, Barton, A. C. T. 2600), this annual award is for books with "a multicultural theme which focuses on aspects and values of a multicultural society, for example, cultural diversity, community relations and social harmony, or social justice." Awards are given in three categories: senior fiction, junior fiction, and picture books. For 1991, only a picture book was honored. ($5,000 in each category; if illustrator is not the author in the picture book category, an additional $5,000 to illustrator)

1991
THE RAINBOW SERPENT by Elaine Sharpe, ill. by Jennifer Inkamala *(Yipirinya School Council)*

Books I Love Best Yearly (BILBY) Awards ઠ

"The aim of the BILBY Awards is to promote books for young people to read and to give publicity to the books that appeal to young people." The bilby is a rare species of bandicoot, a small marsupial with long floppy ears as on a rabbit. Established by the Queensland Branch of The Children's Book Council of Australia (P. O. Box 484, Moorooka, Queensland 4105), awards—chosen by children—are in three categories: Read Alone (Primary), *P*; Read Alone (Secondary), *S*; and Read Aloud (P-12), *P-12*. (Apologies for not naming publishers; information not available to CBC.) (Certificates and honoraria)

1990
P: SUPERFUDGE by Judy Blume
S: THE SECRET DIARY OF ADRIAN MOLE AGED 13 3/4 by Sue Townsend
P-12: MATILDA by Roald Dahl
1991
P: THE B. F. G. by Roald Dahl
S: THE OUTSIDERS by S. E. Hinton
P-12: THE B. F. G. by Roald Dahl

Children's Books of the Year Awards ᡒ᠕

This awards program for Australian children's books began in 1946. It was administered by a number of agencies until the Children's Book Council of Australia became responsible for it in 1959. The Council is composed of branches in Australian states and the Australia Capitol Territory, with its administrative functions handled among the states on a biennial basis. There is no permanent administrative address. Awards are currently given in three categories. Publishers make nominations of titles by Australians or persons resident in Australia. A short list of finalists (including the winners, chosen but not announced) is issued by the judges in March. Children's book enthusiasts and the public speculate about winners, and they are announced at the beginning of Children's Book Week in July or August. Judges have the right not to give awards if in their opinion no books deserve them. (Currently sponsored by Myer/Grace Bros., the prominent Australian retail business, honorees receive various stipends and medals previously contributed by Australian cultural, literary, and visual arts agencies)

BOOK OF THE YEAR: OLDER READERS

1946
THE STORY OF KARRAWINGI THE EMU by Leslie Rees (*Sands*)

1947
No Award

1948
SHACKLETON'S ARGONAUTS by Frank Hurley (*Angus & Robertson*)

1949
No Competition

1950
WHALERS OF THE MIDNIGHT SUN by Alan Villiers (*Angus & Robertson*)

1951
VERITY OF SYDNEY TOWN by Ruth Williams (*Angus & Robertson*)

1952
THE AUSTRALIA BOOK by Eve Pownall (*Sands*)

1953
AIRCRAFT OF TODAY & TOMORROW by J.H. and W.D. Martin (*Angus & Robertson*)

GOOD LUCK TO THE RIDER by Joan Phipson *(Angus & Robertson)*

1954
AUSTRALIAN LEGENDARY TALES by K.L. Parker *(Angus & Robertson)*

1955
THE FIRST WALKABOUT by H.A. Lindsay and N.B. Tindale *(Kestrel)*

1956
THE CROOKED SNAKE by Patricia Wrightson *(Angus & Robertson)*

1957
THE BOOMERANG BOOK OF LEGENDARY TALES by Enid Moodie-Heddle *(Kestrel)*

1958
TIGER IN THE BUSH by Nan Chauncy *(Oxford)*

1959
DEVIL'S HILL by Nan Chauncy *(Oxford)*
SEA MENACE by John Gunn *(Constable)*

1960
ALL THE PROUD TRIBESMEN by Kylie Tennant *(Macmillan)*

1961
TANGARA by Nan Chauncy *(Oxford)*

1962
THE RACKETTY STREET GANG by H.L. Evers *(Hodder & Stoughton)*
RAFFERTY RIDES A WINNER by Joan Woodbery *(Parrish)*

1963
THE FAMILY CONSPIRACY by Joan Phipson *(Angus & Robertson)*

1964
THE GREEN LAUREL by Eleanor Spence *(Oxford)*

1965
PASTURES OF THE BLUE CRANE by Hesba F. Brinsmead *(Oxford)*

1966
ASH ROAD by Ivan Southall *(Angus & Robertson)*

1967
THE MIN MIN by Mavis Thorpe Clark *(Landsdowne)*

1968
TO THE WILD SKY by Ivan Southall *(Angus & Robertson)*

1969
WHEN JAYS FLY TO BARBMO by Margaret Balderson *(Oxford)*

1970
UHU by Annette Macarthur-Onslow *(Ure Smith)*
1971
BREAD AND HONEY by Ivan Southall *(Angus & Robertson)*
1972
LONGTIME PASSING by Hesba F. Brinsmead *(Angus & Robertson)*
1973
FAMILY AT THE LOOKOUT by Noreen Shelly *(Oxford)*
1974
THE NARGUN AND THE STARS by Patricia Wrightson *(Hutchinson)*
1975
No Award
1976
FLY WEST by Ivan Southall *(Angus & Robertson)*
1977
THE OCTOBER CHILD by Eleanor Spence *(Oxford)*
1978
THE ICE IS COMING by Patricia Wrightson *(Hutchinson)*
1979
THE PLUM-RAIN SCROLL by Ruth Manley *(Hodder & Stoughton)*
1980
DISPLACED PERSON by Lee Harding *(Hyland House)*
1981
PLAYING BEATIE BOW by Ruth Park *(Nelson)*
1982
THE VALLEY BETWEEN by Colin Thiele *(Rigby)*
1983
MASTER OF THE GROVE by Victor Kelleher *(Penguin)*
1984
A LITTLE FEAR by Patricia Wrightson *(Hutchinson)*
1985
THE TRUE STORY OF LILLI STUBECK by James Aldridge *(Hyland House)*
1986
THE GREEN WIND by Thurley Fowler *(Rigby)*
1987
ALL WE KNOW by Simon French *(Angus & Robertson)*
1988
SO MUCH TO TELL YOU by John Marsden *(Walter McVitty)*
1989
BEYOND THE LABYRINTH by Gillian Rubinstein *(Hyland House)*

1990
CAME BACK TO SHOW YOU I COULD FLY by Robin Klein *(Viking Kestrel)*
1991
STRANGE OBJECTS by Gary Crew *(Heinemann)*

BOOK OF THE YEAR: YOUNGER READERS
1982
RUMMAGE by Christobel Mattingley, ill. by Patricia Mullins *(Angus & Robertson)*
1983
THING by Robin Klein, ill. by Alison Lester *(Oxford)*
1984
BERNICE KNOWS BEST by Max Dann, ill. by Ann James *(Oxford)*
1985
SOMETHING SPECIAL by Emily Rodda, ill. by Noela Young *(Angus & Robertson)*
1986
ARKWRIGHT by Mary Steele *(Hyland House)*
1987
PIGS MIGHT FLY by Emily Rodda, ill. by Noela Young *(Angus & Robertson)*
1988
MY PLACE by Nadia Wheatley, ill by Donna Rawlins *(Collins Dove)*
1989
THE BEST-KEPT SECRET by Emily Rodda *(Angus & Robertson)*
1990
PIGS AND HONEY by Jeanie Adams *(Omnibus)*
1991
FINDERS KEEPERS by Emily Rodda *(Omnibus)*

PICTURE BOOK OF THE YEAR
1956
WISH AND THE MAGIC NUT by Peggy Barnard, ill. by Sheila Hawkins *(Sands)*
1957
No Award
1958
PICCANINNY WALKABOUT by Axel Poignant *(Angus & Robertson)*
1959-1964
No Awards

1965
HUGO'S ZOO by Elisabeth MacIntyre *(Angus & Robertson)*

1966-1968
No Awards

1969
SLY OLD WARDROBE by Ivan Southall, ill. by Ted Greenwood *(Cheshire)*

1970
No Award

1971
WALTZING MATILDA by A.B. Paterson, ill. by Desmond Digby *(Collins)*

1972-1973
No Awards

1974
THE BUNYIP OF BERKELEY'S CREEK by Jenny Wagner, ill. by Ron Brooks *(Kestrel)*

1975
THE MAN FROM IRONBARK by A.B. Paterson, ill. by Quentin Hole *(Collins)*

1976
THE RAINBOW SERPENT by Dick Roughsey *(Collins)*

1977
No Award

1978
JOHN BROWN, ROSE AND THE MIDNIGHT CAT by Jenny Wagner, ill. by Ron Brooks *(Kestrel)*

1979
THE QUINKINS written and ill. by Percy Trezise and Dick Roughsey *(Collins)*

1980
ONE DRAGON'S DREAM by Peter Pavey *(Nelson)*

1981
No Award

1982
SUNSHINE by Jan Ormerod *(Kestrel)*

1983
WHO SANK THE BOAT? by Pamela Allen *(Nelson)*

1984
BERTIE AND THE BEAR by Pamela Allen *(Nelson)*

1985
No Award

1986
FELIX & ALEXANDER by Terry Denton *(Oxford)*

1987
KOJURO AND THE BEARS adapted by Helen Smith, ill. by Junko Morimoto *(Collins)*
1988
CRUSHER IS COMING by Bob Graham *(Lothian)*
1989
DRAC AND THE GREMLIN by Allan Baillie, ill by Jane Tanner *(Viking Kestrel)*
THE ELEVENTH HOUR by Graeme Base *(Viking Kestrel)*
1990
THE VERY BEST OF FRIENDS by Margaret Wild, ill. by Julie Vivas *(Margaret Hamilton)*
1991
GREETINGS FROM SANDY BEACH by Bob Graham *(Lothian)*

Children's Peace Literature Award

The award program is for authors who are Australian or normally resident in Australia, and whose books considered for the award promote the peaceful resolution of conflict. The sponsor, Psychologists for the Prevention of War (4 Blyth St., Glen Osmond, South Australia 5064), a special interest group of the Australian Psychological Society, states, "We believe that literature has a significant influence on children's attitudes and behaviour...we wish to support and encourage authors whose work promotes peace and the understanding of others." The award is given biennially; a short list of under a dozen worthwhile titles is disseminated before a winner is selected. ($1,000)

1987
SPACE DEMONS by Gillian Rubenstein *(Omnibus)*
1989
THE MAKERS by Victor Kelleher *(Viking Kestrel)*
1991
DODGER by Libby Gleeson *(Turton & Chambers)*

Crichton Award

The award is for achievement in an illustrator's first major published work for children. It is sponsored by the Victorian

Branch of the Children's Council (P. O. Box 310, Heidelberg 3084, Vic., Australia). (Certificate and $500)

1988
PHEASANT AND KINGFISHER by Catherine Berndt, ill. by Raymond Meeks *(Martin Educational)*
1989
AUSTRALIAN DINOSAURS by Marilyn Pride *(Collins)*
1990
PIGS AND HONEY by Jeanie Adams *(Omnibus)*
1991
BIP: THE SNAPPING BUNGAROO by Narelle McRobbie, ill. by Grace Fielding *(Magabala)*
1992
THE MAGNIFICENT NOSE AND OTHER MARVELS by Anna Fienberg, ill. by Kim Ganmble (Allen & Unwin)

Family Award 🐾

The award is for a book that contains a "realistic and balanced depiction of family life according to what are known to be the characteristics of a healthy family." "Healthy" refers to emotional and psychological health. The year in the listing is the book's publication year; the award is presented during Children's Book Week of the following year. (New South Wales Family Therapy Association, P. O. Box 27, Rozelle, N. S. W. 2039, Australia) ($1,000)

1987
DEEZLE BOY by Eleanor Spence *(Collins Dove)*
1988
YOU TAKE THE HIGH ROAD by Mary K. Pershall *(Penguin)*
1989
THE BLUE CHAMELEON by Katherine Scholes *(Hill of Content)*
1990
TWO WEEKS WITH THE QUEEN by Morris Gleitzman *(Pan)*

Kids Own Australian Literature Awards (KOALA) 🐾

Each year children in the State of New South Wales (N. S. W.) have the opportunity to nominate their favorite Australian books—fiction, poetry, plays, picture books, or myths and legends—for the KOALA Awards. Two shortlists of about thirty titles each in Primary *(P)* and Secondary *(S)* categories are distributed to participating institutions throughout the state, and children vote for the winners from those lists. The program is administered by an all-volunteer KOALA Council that does not have a permanent mailing address. The award was initiated as a joint undertaking of N. S. W. branches of the Schools and Children's Sections of the Library Association, Children's Book Council, Australian Reading Association, English Teachers Association, Primary English Teachers Association, School Library Association, and Australian Book Publishers Association. (Certificate)

1987
P: POSSUM MAGIC by Mem Fox, ill. by Julie Vivas *(Omnibus)*
S: HATING ALISON ASHLEY by Robin Klein *(Puffin)*

1988
P: SISTER MADGE'S BOOK OF NUNS by Doug McLeod, ill. by Craig Smith *(Omnibus)*
S: ANIMALIA by Graeme Base *(Viking Kestrel)*
One-time only Bicentennial Award: THE COMPLETE ADVENTURES OF SNUGGLEPOT AND CUDDLEPIE by May Gibbs *(Angus & Robertson)*

1989
P: THE ELEVENTH HOUR by Graeme Base *(Viking Kestrel)*
S: SO MUCH TO TELL YOU by John Marsden *(Walter McVitty)*

1990
P: WHERE THE FOREST MEETS THE SEA by Jeannie Baker *(Julia MacRae)*
S: UNREAL! EIGHT SURPRISING STORIES by Paul Jennings *(Puffin)*

National Children's Literature Award

The National Children's Literature Award is part of the biennial Festival Awards for Literature given since 1986 to Australian authors, or authors resident in Australia, in six categories: Fiction, Poetry, Children's Literature, Nonfiction, Playwrighting, and the Carclew Fellowship to assist a writer in developing her or his skills. Independent panels of three judges select the winners, with award presentations made during Writers Week of the Adelaide Festival. The program is administered by the

Awards Secretariat, Department for the Arts and Cultural Heritage (GPO Box 2308, Adelaide, S. A. 5001). ($16,000)

1986
THE LONG NIGHT WATCH by Ivan Southall *(Methuen)*
1988
SPACE DEMONS by Gillian Rubinstein *(Omnibus/Puffin)*
1990
BEYOND THE LABYRINTH by Gillian Rubinstein *(Hyland House)*

New South Wales State Literary Awards

CHILDREN'S BOOK AWARD

Sponsored by The Ministry for the Arts (Box R105, Royal Exchange Post Office, Sydney, N. S. W. 2000, Australia) the State Literary Awards are given in several categories and also include various Prizes. The Children's Book Award "is offered for a work of fiction or nonfiction. Works may be nominated by writers, their agents or publishers. In the case of books containing original illustrations, the judging committee may determine that the award be shared by the writer and illustrator." ($5,000 and medallion)

1979
JOHN BROWN, ROSE AND THE MIDNIGHT CAT by Jenny Wagner *(Kestrel)*
1980
MR. ARCHIMEDES BATH by Pamela Allen *(Collins)*
1981
WHEN THE WIND CHANGED by Ruth Park and Deborah Niland *(Collins)*
1982
WHISTLE UP THE CHIMNEY by Nan Hunt and Craig Smith *(Collins)*
1983
WHO SANK THE BOAT? by Pamela Allen *(Nelson)*
1984
POSSUM MAGIC by Mem Fox and Julie Vivas *(Omnibus)*
1985
THE HOUSE THAT WAS EUREKA by Nadia Wheatley *(Viking Kestrel)*

1986
THE TRUE STORY OF SPIT MACPHEE by James Aldridge
(*Viking/Penguin*)
1987
A RABBIT NAMED HARRIS by Nan Hunt and Betina Ogden
(*Collins*)
1988
ANSWERS TO BRUT by Gillian Rubinstein (*Omnibus*)
1989
YOU TAKE THE HIGH ROAD by Mary Pershall (*Penguin*)
1990
THE BLUE CHAMELEON by Katherine Scholes (*Hill of Content*)
1991
STRANGE OBJECTS by Gary Crew (*Heinemann*)

Victorian Premier's Literary Awards 🍎

ALAN MARSHALL PRIZE FOR CHILDREN'S LITERATURE

The Victorian Ministry for the Arts (Private Bag No. 1, City Road Post Office, Victoria 3205, Australia) Literary Awards program honors Australian writers, and includes a prize for children's literature. Fiction, poetry, and nonfiction are eligible; literary merit is the most important factor in determining the winner. ($7,500)

1988
SO MUCH TO TELL YOU by John Marsden (*Walter McVitty*)
1989
THE LAKE AT THE END OF THE WORLD by Caroline McDonald (*Viking/Kestrel*)
1990
ONION TEARS by Diana Kidd (*Collins/Angus & Robertson*)
1991
STRANGE OBJECTS by Gary Crew (*Heinemann*)

West Australian Young Readers' Book Awards (WAYRBA) 🐌

This is Australia's first statewide children's choice book award. According to the sponsors (School Libraries Section, West Australian Group, P. O. Box 251, Mundaring, W. A. 6073, Australia), while the program is modeled on the Georgia Book Awards in the U. S., it has been modified for use in West Australia. Its aims include promoting "the reading of quality fiction." Selections from a preselected listing of high quality titles nominated by young readers in two categories—Upper Primary (P) and Lower Secondary (S)—are read by children throughout the state to choose the winners each year. (Apologies for not including publishers; information not available to CBC). (Trophies made of Western Australian jarrah wood in the form of a book)

1980
P: TALES OF A FOURTH GRADE NOTHING by Judy Blume
S: MY DARLING VILLAIN by Lynne Reid Banks

1981
P: SADAKO AND THE THOUSAND PAPER CRANES by Eleanor Coerr
S: DON'T HURT LAURIE by Willow Roberts

1982
P: SUPERFUDGE by Judy Blume
S: FORBIDDEN PATHS OF THUAL by Victor Kelleher

1983
P: SAMANTHA ON STAGE by Susan Farrar
S: GOOD NIGHT, MR. TOM by Michelle Magorian

1984
P: GEORGE'S MARVELLOUS MEDICINE by Roald Dahl
S: DID YOU HEAR WHAT HAPPENED TO ANDREA? by Gloria Miklowitz

1985
P: THE BFG by Roald Dahl
S: THE SECRET DIARY OF ADRIAN MOLE, AGED 13¾ by Sue Townsend

1986
P: THE WITCHES by Roald Dahl
S: THE GROWING PAINS OF ADRIAN MOLE by Sue Townsend

1987
P: SELBY'S SECRET by Duncan Ball

S: THE EYES OF KAREN CONNORS by Lois Duncan
BACK HOME by Michelle Magorian
1988
P: GRANDMA CADBURY'S TRUCKING TALES by Dianne
Bates
S: DEAD BIRDS SINGING by Marc Talbert
1989
P: MATILDA by Roald Dahl
S: WHEN THE PHONE RANG by Harry Mazer
1990
P: SELBY SPEAKS by Duncan Ball
S: REDWALL by Brian Jacques

Whitley Awards ❧

Named in honor of Gilbert Whitley, a prominent member of the
Royal Zoological Society of New South Wales, who was an
eminent ichthyologist and historian of Australia's zoology, this
program presents annual awards to books in several categories in
the field of Australian zoology. Children's books are honored in
categories that vary from year to year. The only category on our
list is Best Children's Book. The year dates are award years. The
sponsor is the Royal Zoological Society (P. O. Box 20, Mosman,
N. S. W. 2088, Australia). (Certificate)

1980
THE GOULD LEAGUE BOOK OF AUSTRALIAN BIRDS by
Don Goodsir, ill. by Tony Oliver *(Golden)*
1981
FEATHERS, FUR AND FRILLS by Kilmeny Niland *(Hodder &
Stoughton)*
1982
THE FRIENDS OF BURRAMYS by June Epstein *(Oxford)*
1983
THE GOULD LEAGUE BOOK OF AUSTRALIAN MAMMALS
by Don Goodsir, ill. by Tony Oliver *(Golden)*
1984
AUSTRALIAN ANIMALS by Peter Sloan, ill. by Ross Lathan
(Methuen)
1985
AUSTRALIA'S PREHISTORIC ANIMALS by Peter Murray
(Methuen)
1986
SEBASTIAN LIVES IN A HAT by Thelma Catterwall, ill. by K.
Argent *(Omnibus)*

1987
THE ARROW BOOK OF BACKYARD CREATURES by Brian Macness *(Ashton Scholastic)*
1988
ANIMAL TRACKS by Carson Creagh, ill. by Kathie Atkinson *(Methuen)*
1989
ALDITA AND THE FOREST by Thelma Catterwall, ill. by Derek Stone *(Dent)*
1990
AUSTRALIAN JUNIOR FIELD GUIDES (entire series) by Eleanor Stodart *(Weldon)*
1991
TOM'S FRIEND by Pat Reynolds *(Allen and Unwin)*

Young Australians Best Book Awards (YABBA) 🐌

This program is sponsored by the YABBA Council (P. O. Box 238, Kew 3101, Vic., Australia), an organization of volunteers from Victorian groups interested in Australian children's literature and children's reading. Young readers in the State of Victoria in grades 1-9 vote for awards for Australian fiction in three categories—Picture Story *(P)*, Junior *(J)*, and Older *(O)*. "Australian" means written in Australia, written by an Australian, or about Australia. Voting lists are compiled from children's nominations. Year dates in our listing refer to award years. (Citations)

1986
P: WHEN THE WIND CHANGED by Ruth Park, ill. by Deborah Niland *(Collins)*
J: THE TWENTY-SEVENTH ANNUAL AFRICAN HIPPOPOTAMUS RACE by Morris Lurie *(Penguin)*
0: HATING ALISON ASHLEY by Robin Klein *(Viking Kestrel)*
1987
P: ANIMALIA by Graeme Base *(Viking Kestrel)*
J: SISTER MADGE'S BOOK OF NUNS by Doug Macleod, ill. by Craig Smith *(Omnibus)*
0: UNREAL by Paul Jennings *(Penguin)*
1988
P: WHERE THE FOREST MEETS THE SEA by Jeannie Baker *(Julia MacRae)*
J: MY PLACE by Nadia Wheatley, ill. by Donna Rawlins *(Collins/Dove)*

0: UNBELIEVABLE by Paul Jennings *(Penguin)*
1989
P: THE ELEVENTH HOUR by Graeme Base *(Viking Kestrel)*
J: THE CABBAGE PATCH FIB by Paul Jennings *(Penguin)*
0: UNCANNY! by Paul Jennings *(Penguin)*
1990
P: THE MONSTER WHO ATE AUSTRALIA by Michael
Salmon *(Lamont)*
J: PAW THING by Paul Jennings *(Penguin)*
0: SPACE DEMONS by Gillian Rubinstein *(Penguin)*

CANADA

(Note that the Pacific Northwest Young Reader's Choice Award
in Part II of this work includes the votes of young Canadian
readers in the provinces of Alberta and British Columbia.)

Alcuin Society Citations 🐌

The Alcuin Society (P. O. Box 3216, Vancouver, BC V6B 3X8,
Canada) promotes awareness of excellence in the book arts. Its
awards program honors Canadian publishers and designers of
general trade books, limited editions, texts and reference
works, and juveniles. We list the children's book winners,
which were published in the year before being honored.
(Citation)

1984
CAPTAIN CARP SAVES THE SEA by John Larsen, designed
by John Larsen *(Annick)*
1985
DINNER AT AUNTIE ROSE'S by Janet Munsil, ill. by Scot
Ritchie, designed by Blair Kerrigan *(Annick)*
1986
THE SORCERER'S APPRENTICE by Robin Muller, designed
by Michael Solomon *(Kids Can Press)*
1987
THE SEA SERPENT OF GRENADIER POND by David
Peacock, designed by David Peacock *(Hounslow)*
1988
No first prize
1989
THE WILDLIFE ABC: A NATURE ALPHABET by Jan
Thornhill, designed by Wycliffe Smith *(Greey de Pencier)*

1990
THE TIME BEFORE DREAMS by Stefan Czernecki and
Timothy Rhodes, ill. by Stefan Czernecki, designed by Arlene
Osen *(Hyperion)*
1991
THE SIGN OF THE SCALES by Marianne Brandis, designed by
Tim Inkster *(Porcupine's Quill)*

Prix Alvine-Bélisle 🐚

This award is for the author or illustrator of the best children's
book by a Canadian national published in French in Canada each
year. It is administered by the Association pour l'avancement des
sciences et des techniques de la documentation (A.S.T.E.D., 1030
rue Cherrier, Bur. 505, Montréal, Que. H2L 1H9, Canada). (An
art object or $500)

1975
JEANNE, FILLE DU ROY by Suzanne Martel *(Fides)*
1976
LES SAISONS DE LA MER by Monique Corriveau *(Fides)*
1977
ÉMILIE, LA BAIGNOIRE À PATTES by Bernadette Renaud
(Héritage)
1978
L'ÉVANGILE EN PAPIER by Henriette Major *(Fides)*
1979
LA PETITE FILLE AUX YEUX ROUGES by Gabrielle
Grandbois-Paquin *(Fides)*
1980
LES QUATRE SAISONS DE PIQUOT by Gilles Vigneault
(Editions de l'Arc)
1981
LE VISITEUR DU SOIR by Robert Soulières *(Fides)*
1982
LE VOYAGE À LA RECHERCHE DU TEMPS by Lucie
Ledoux, ill. by Philippe Béha *(Mondia)*
(Both author and illustrator received awards.)
1983
DORS PETIT OURS, J'AIME CLAIRE, MES CHEVEUX and
PIPI LE POT by Sylvie Assathiany and Louise Pelletier, ill. by
Philippe Béha *(Ovale)*
(Both authors and illustrator received awards.)

1984
LA SOEUR DE ROBERT by Marie-Louise Gay *(La courte échelle)*
1985
ZUNIK by Bertrand Gauthier *(La courte échelle)*
1986
LE COMPLOT by Christine Brouillet *(La courte échelle)*
1987
ALLER-RETOUR by Yves Beauchesne *(Schinkel)*
1988
VENIR AU MONDE by Marie-France Hébert, ill. by Darcia Labrosse *(La courte échelle)*
1989
NE TOUCHES PAS A MA BABOUCHE by Gilles Gauthier *(La courte échelle)*
1990
SAUVETAGES by Sonia Sarfati *(Québec-Amérique)*
1991
LA VRAIE HISTOIRE DU CHIEN DE CLARA VIC by Christine Duchesne *(Québec-Amérique)*

Geoffrey Bilson Award for Historical Fiction for Young People ❧

Named for a respected author and historian, whose three children's books were published by Kids Can Press. Awarded annually for an outstanding work of historical fiction for young people written by a Canadian author. Administered by the Canadian Children's Book Centre (35 Spadina St., Toronto, Ont. M5R 2S9, Canada). Our listing is of the year in which the award was presented; books were published the year before. ($1,000, contributed by children's book publishers and booksellers)

1988
LISA by Carol Matas *(Lester & Orpen Dennys)*
1989
MYSTERY IN THE FROZEN LANDS by Martyn Godfrey *(Lorimer)*
RACHEL'S REVOLUTION by Dorothy Perkyns *(Lancelot)*
1990
THE SKY IS FALLING by Kit Pearson *(Penguin)*

1991
THE SIGN OF THE SCALES by Marianne Brandis *(Porcupine's Quill)*

Ann Connor Brimer Award 🐌

Named for a woman who was a dedicated supporter and promoter of Canadian children's literature, and who opened Nova Scotia's first children's bookstore, this annual award for a resident of Atlantic Canada is for a book published in Canada that has made an outstanding contribution to children's literature. The sponsor is the Nova Scotia Library Association (c/o Halifax County Regional Library, 32 Glendale Ave., Lower Sackville, NS B4C 3M1). ($500)

1991
PIT PONY by Joyce Barkhouse *(Gage)*

Canadian Library Association Book of the Year for Children Award 🐌

Given annually since 1947 by the Canadian Library Association (200 Elgin St., Suite 602, Ottawa, Ont. K2P 1L5, Canada) to outstanding children's books, one in English, and from 1954 through 1973, one in French, published during the preceding year and written by a Canadian citizen. (Medals)

1947
STARBUCK VALLEY WINTER by Roderick Haig-Brown *(Collins)*
1948
No Award
1949
KRISTLI'S TREES by Mabel Dunham *(McClelland & Stewart)*
1950
FRANKLIN OF THE ARCTIC by Richard S. Lambert *(McClelland & Stewart)*
1951
No Award

1952
THE SUN HORSE by Catherine Anthony Clark *(Macmillan)*
1953
No Award
1954
No English Award
LE VÉNÉRABLE FRANÇOIS DE MONTMORENCY-LAVAL
by Emile Gervais *(Comité des Fondateurs de l'Eglise canadienne)*
1955
No Awards
1956
TRAIN FOR TIGER LILY by Louise Riley *(Macmillan)*
No French Award
1957
GLOOSKAP'S COUNTRY by Cyrus Macmillan *(Oxford)*
No French Award
1958
LOST IN THE BARRENS by Farley Mowat *(Little, Brown)*
CHEVALIER DU ROI by Beatrice Clément *(Atelier)*
1959
THE DANGEROUS COVE by John F. Hayes *(Copp Clark)*
UN DRÔLE DE PETIT CHEVAL by Hélène Flamme *(Leméac)*
1960
THE GOLDEN PHOENIX by Marius Barbeau, retold by
Michael Hornyansky *(Oxford)*
L'ÉTÉ ENCHANTÉ by Paule Daveluy *(Atelier)*
1961
THE ST. LAWRENCE by William Toye *(Oxford)*
PLANTES VAGABONDES by Marcelle Gauvreau *(Centre de
Psychologie et de Pédagogie)*
1962
No English Award
LES ÎLES DU ROI MAHA MAHA II by Claude Aubry *(Pélican)*
1963
THE INCREDIBLE JOURNEY by Sheila Burnford *(Little,
Brown)*
DRÔLE D'AUTOMNE by Paule Daveluy *(Pélican)*
1964
THE WHALE PEOPLE by Roderick Haig-Brown *(Collins)*
FÉRIE by Cécile Chabot *(Beauchemin)*
1965
TALES OF NANABOZHO by Dorothy Reid *(Oxford)*
LE LOUP DE NÖEL by Claude Aubry *(Centre de Psychologie et
de Pédagogie)*
1966
TIKTÁ LIKTAK by James Houston *(Longmans)* (Published 1964)

THE DOUBLE KNIGHTS by James McNeil *(Oxford)* (Published 1965)

LE CHÊNE DES TEMPÊTES by Andrée Maillet-Hobden *(Fides)* (Published 1964)

LE WAPITI by Monique Corriveau *(Jeunesse)* (Published 1965)

1967
RAVEN'S CRY by Christie Harris *(McClelland & Stewart)*
No French Award

1968
THE WHITE ARCHER by James Houston *(Academic)*
LÉGENDES INDIENNES DU CANADA by Claude Mélancon *(Editions du Jour)*

1969
AND TOMORROW THE STARS by Kay Hill *(Dodd)*
No French Award

1970
SALLY GO ROUND THE SUN by Edith Fowke *(McClelland & Stewart)*
LA MERVEILLEUSE HISTOIRE DE LA NAISSANCE by Lionel Gendron *(Les Editions de l'Homme)*

1971
CARTIER DISCOVERS THE ST. LAWRENCE by William Toye *(Oxford)*
LA SURPRISE DE DAME CHENILLE by Henriette Major *(Centre de Psychologie et de Pédagogie)*

1972
MARY OF MILE 18 by Ann Blades *(Tundra)*
No French Award

1973
THE MARROW OF THE WORLD by Ruth Nichols *(Macmillan)*
LA PETIT SAPIN QUI A POUSSÉ SUR UNE ÉTOILE by Simone Bussières *(Laurentiennes)*

1974
THE MIRACULOUS HIND by Elizabeth Cleaver *(Holt)*

1975
ALLIGATOR PIE by Dennis Lee *(Macmillan)*

1976
JACOB TWO-TWO MEETS THE HOODED FANG by Mordecai Richler *(McClelland & Stewart)*

1977
MOUSE WOMAN AND THE VANISHED PRINCESSES by Christie Harris *(McClelland & Stewart)*

1978
GARBAGE DELIGHT by Dennis Lee *(Macmillan)*

1979
HOLD FAST by Kevin Major *(Clarke, Irwin)*
1980
RIVER RUNNERS by James Houston *(McClelland & Stewart)*
1981
THE VIOLIN MAKER'S GIFT by Donn Kushner *(Macmillan)*
1982
THE ROOT CELLAR by Janet Lunn *(Lester & Orpen Dennys)*
1983
UP TO LOW by Brian Doyle *(Groundwood/Douglas & McIntyre)*
1984
SWEETGRASS by Jan Hudson *(Tree Frog Press)*
1985
MAMA'S GOING TO BUY YOU A MOCKINGBIRD by Jean Little *(Penguin)*
1986
JULIE by Cora Taylor *(Western Producer Prairie Books)*
1987
SHADOW IN HAWTHORN BAY by Janet Lunn *(Lester & Orpen Dennys)*
1988
A HANDFUL OF TIME by Kit Pearson *(Penguin)*
1989
EASY AVENUE by Brian Doyle *(Groundwood/Douglas & McIntyre)*
1990
THE SKY IS FALLING by Kit Pearson *(Penguin)*
1991
REDWORK by Michael Bedard *(Lester & Orpen Dennys)*
1992
EATING BETWEEN THE LINES by Kevin Major *(Doubleday Canada)*

Children's Literature Roundtables of Canada Information Book Award ❧

"The purpose of the Roundtable Information Book Award is to recognize an outstanding information book for children (5-12 years) that captures the imagination, arouses interest, stimulates curiosity, and fosters concern for the world around us. The award's aim is to foster excellence in Canadian publishing." Sponsored by the Children's Literature Roundtables of Canada (c/o Dept. of Language Education, 2034 Lower Mall, University of British Columbia, Vancouver, BC V67 1Z5), each Roundtable in Canada participates by nominating five titles submitted to an award committee, and then votes on a national list of five titles compiled by that committee. (Certificate and $500 honorarium)

1988
LET'S CELEBRATE by Caroline Parry *(Kids Can Press)*
1989
EXPLORING THE SKY BY DAY by Terence Dickinson *(Camden House)*
1990
WOLF ISLAND by Celia Godkin *(Fitzhenry & Whiteside)*
1991
HANDS ON, THUMBS UP by Camilla Gryski *(Kids Can Press)*

Max and Greta Ebel Memorial Award 🐝

This awards program, sponsored by the Canadian Society of Children's Authors, Illustrators and Performers (CANSCAIP), was for a Canadian author of a young readers' book honored for its contribution to understanding people of different backgrounds, cultures, or generations. The award was discontinued after 1990. ($100)

1986
WINNERS by Mary-Ellen Lang Collura *(Western Producer Prairie Books)*
1987
LAST CHANCE SUMMER by Diana Wieler *(Western Producer Prairie Books)*
1988
FALSE FACE by Welwyn Wilton Katz *(Groundwood/Douglas & McIntyre)*
1989
WHITEOUT by James Houston *(Greey de Pencier)*
1990
WINDWARD ISLAND by Karleen Bradford *(Kids Can Press)*

Sheila A. Egoff Children's Prize 🔊

The B. C. Book Prizes celebrate the achievements of British Columbia writers in several categories annually. The program was established in 1985, and included children's books as of 1987. The children's book prize is named for a distinguished former professor at the University of British Columbia, who is also an author of works on children's literature and a prominent critic. The prize is awarded for the best book for children sixteen years and younger by an author and/or illustrator who have lived in B. C. for three of the most recent five years. The winner is selected from a shortlist of books, which may have been published anywhere in the world. ($1,500)

1987
THE BABY PROJECT by Sarah Ellis *(Groundwood/Douglas & McIntyre)*
1988
PRIDE OF LIONS by Nicola Morgan *(Fitzhenry & Whiteside)*
1989
SUNNY by Mary-Ellen Lang Collura *(Irwin)*
1990
TALES FROM GOLD MOUNTAIN by Paul Yee *(Groundwood/Douglas & McIntyre)*
1991
I HEARD MY MOTHER CALL MY NAME by Nancy Hundal *(HarperCollins)*

Governor General's Literary Awards Children's Literature Categories 🔊

The former Canada Council Children's Literature Prizes became Governor General's Awards as of prizes awarded for 1986 titles. Currently, the Governor General's Awards are for the best English-language and the best French-language work in seven categories, including Children's Literature (text) *(T)* and Children's Literature (illustration) *(I)*. Submissions are by publishers only; they must be trade books written or illustrated by Canadian citizens or permanent residents of Canada; the books may have been published in Canada or abroad. English-

language and French-language juries review submissions
independently of each other. The administrator is the Writing
and Publishing Section of The Canada Council (99 Metcalfe St.,
P. O. Box 1047, Ottawa, Ontario KlP 5V8, Canada). ($10,000
each)

1975
SHANTYMEN OF CACHE LAKE by Bill Freeman *(Lorimer)*
RAMINAGRADU: HISTOIRES ORDINAIRES POUR
ENFANTS EXTRAORDINAIRES by Louise Aylwin *(Editions du
Jour)*

1976
THE WOODEN PEOPLE by Myra Paperny *(Little, Brown)*
ÉMILIE, LA BAIGNOIRE À PATTES by Bernadette Renaud
(Héritage)

1977
LISTEN FOR THE SINGING by Jean Little *(Clarke, Irwin)*
LUNE DE NEIGE by Denise Houle *(Maheux)*
L'ÉVANGILE EN PAPIER by Henriette Major, ill. by Claude
Lafortune *(Fides)*

1978
HOLD FAST by Kevin Major *(Clarke, Irwin)*
A SALMON FOR SIMON by Betty Waterton, ill. by Ann Blades
(Douglas & McIntyre)
LA CHICANE by Ginette Anfousse *(La courte échelle)*
LA VARICELLE by Ginette Anfousse *(La courte échelle)*

1979
T: DAYS OF TERROR by Barbara Smucker *(Clarke, Irwin)*
I: THE TWELVE DANCING PRINCESSES retold by Janet
Lunn, ill. by Laszlo Gal *(Methuen)*
T: COURTE-QUEUE by Gabrielle Roy *(Stanké)*
I: UNE FENÊTRE DANS MA TÊTE by Raymond Plante, ill. by
Roger Paré *(La courte échelle)*

1980
T: THE TROUBLE WITH PRINCESSES by Christie Harris
(McClelland & Stewart)
I: PETROUCHKA retold and ill. by Elizabeth Cleaver
(Macmillan)
T: HÉBERT LUÉE by Bertrand Gauthier *(La courte échelle)*
I: LES GENS DE MON PAYS by Gilles Vigneault, ill. by
Miyuki Tanobe *(La courte échelle)*

1981
T: THE GUARDIAN OF ISIS by Monica Hughes *(Hamish
Hamilton)*
I: YTEK AND THE ARCTIC ORCHID: AN INUIT LEGEND
by Garnet Hewitt, ill. by Heather Woodall *(Douglas &
McIntyre)*

T: NOS AMIS ROBOTS by Suzanne Martel *(Héritage)*
I: LES PAPINACHOIS by Michel Noël, ill. by Joanne Ouellet *(Hurtubise HMH)*

1982

T: HUNTER IN THE DARK by Monica Hughes *(Clarke, Irwin)*
I: ABC, 123, THE CANADIAN ALPHABET AND COUNTING BOOK by Vlasta van Kampen *(Hurtig)*
T: FABIEN 1 and FABIEN 2 by Ginette Anfousse *(Leméac)*
I: AGNÈS ET LE SINGULIER BESTIAIRE by Marie José Théricault, ill. by Darcia LaBrosse *(Pierre Tisseyre)*

1983

T: THE GHOST HORSE OF THE MOUNTIES by Sean Ohuigin *(Black Moss Press)*
I: THE LITTLE MERMAID retold by Margaret Crawford Maloney, ill. by Laszlo Gal *(Methuen)*
T: HOCKE YEURS CYBERNÉTIQUES by Denis Côté *(Paulines)*
I: GRAND-MANAN, MON BÉBÉ-SOEUR, OÙ EST MA TÉTINE and QUAND ÇA VA MAL by Sylvie Assathiany and Louise Pelletier, ill. by Philippe Béha *(Ovale)*

1984

T: SWEETGRASS by Jan Hudson *(Tree Frog Press)*
I: LIZZY'S LION by Dennis Lee, ill. by Marie-Louise Gay *(Stoddart)*
T: LE CERCLE VIOLET by Daniel Sernine *(Pierre Tisseyre)*
I: DRÔLE D'ÉCOLE by Marie-Louise Gay *(Ovale)*

1985

T: JULIE by Cora Taylor *(Western Producer Prairie Books)*
I: MURDO'S STORY by Murdo Scribe, ill. by Terry Gallagher *(Pemmican)*
T: CASSE-TÊTE CHINOIS by Robert Soulières *(Pierre Tisseyre)*
I: L'ALPHABET by Roger Pare *(La courte échelle)*

1986

T: SHADOW IN HAWTHORN BAY by Janet Lunn *(Lester & Orpen Dennys)*
I: HAVE YOU SEEN BIRDS? by Joanne Oppenheim, ill. by Barbara Reid *(Scholastic-TAB)*
T: LE DERNIER DES RAISINS by Raymond Plante *(Québec-Amérique)*
I: ALBUM DE FAMILLE *(Michel Quintin)* and AS-TU VU JOSÉPHINE? *(Tundra)*, both by Stéphane Poulin

1987

T: GALAHAD SCHWARTZ AND THE COCKROACH ARMY by Morgan Nyberg *(Groundwood/Douglas & McIntyre)*
I: RAINY DAY MAGIC by Marie-Louise Gay *(Stoddart)*
T: LE DON by David Schinkel and Ives Beauchesne *(Cercle du livre de France)*

I: VENIR AU MONDE by Dorcia Labrosse *(La courte échelle)*
1988
T: THE THIRD MAGIC by Welwyn Wilton Katz
(Groundwood/Douglas & McIntyre)
I: AMOS'S SWEATER by Janet Lunn, ill. by Kim LaFave
(Groundwood/Douglas & McIntyre)
T: CASSIOPÉE OU L'ÉTÉ POLONAIS by Michele Marineau
(Québec-Amérique)
I: LES JEUX DE PIC-MOTS by Marie-Antoinette Delolme, ill.
by Philippe Beha *(Graficor)*
1989
T: BAD BOY by Diana Wieler *(Groundwood/Douglas &
McIntyre)*
I: THE MAGIC PAINTBRUSH by Robin Muller *(Doubleday)*
T: TEMPS MORT by Charles Montpetit *(Paulines)*
I: BENJAMIN ET LE SAGA DES OREILLERS by Stéphane
Poulin *(Annick)*
1990
T: REDWORK by Michael Bedard *(Lester & Orpen Dennys)*
I: THE ORPHAN BOY by Tololwa Mollel, ill. by Paul Morin
(Oxford)
T: LA VRAIE HISTOIRE DU CHIEN DE CLARA VIC by
Christiane Duchesne *(Québec-Amérique)*
I: LES FANTAISIES DE L'ONCLE HENRI by Bénédicte
Froissart, ill. by Pierre Pratt *(Annick)*
1991
T: PICK-UP STICKS by Sarah Ellis *(Groundwood)*
I: DOCTOR KISS SAYS YES by Teddy Jam, ill. by Joanne
Fitzgerald *(Groundwood)*
T: DEUX HEURES ET DEMIE AVANT JASMINE by François
Gravel *(Éditions du Boréal)*
I: UN CHAMPION by Roch Carrier, ill. by Sheldon Cohen
(Tundra)

Amelia Frances Howard-Gibbon Medal ❧

Given annually in June since 1971 by the Canadian Library
Association (200 Elgin St., Suite 602, Ottawa, Ont. K2P 1L5,
Canada) for outstanding illustrations in a children's book
published in Canada. Illustrator must be a native or resident of
Canada. (Medal)

1971
THE WIND HAS WINGS edited by Mary Alice Downie and
Barbara Robertson, ill. by Elizabeth Cleaver *(Oxford)*
1972
A CHILD IN PRISON CAMP by Shizuye Takashima *(Tundra)*
1973
AU DELA DU SOLEIL/BEYOND THE SUN by Jacques de
Roussan *(Tundra)*
1974
A PRAIRIE BOY'S WINTER by William Kurelek *(Tundra)*
1975
THE SLEIGHS OF MY CHILDHOOD/LES TRAÎNEAUX DE
MON ENFANCE by Carlo Italiano *(Tundra)*
1976
A PRAIRIE BOY'S SUMMER by William Kurelek *(Tundra)*
1977
DOWN BY JIM LONG'S STAGE: RHYMES FOR CHILDREN
AND YOUNG FISH by Al Pittman, ill. by Pam Hall
(Breakwater)
1978
THE LOON'S NECKLACE by William Toye, ill. by Elizabeth
Cleaver *(Oxford)*
1979
A SALMON FOR SIMON by Betty Waterton, ill. by Ann Blades
(Douglas & McIntyre)
1980
THE TWELVE DANCING PRINCESSES retold by Janet Lunn,
ill. by Laszlo Gal *(Methuen)*
1981
THE TROUBLE WITH PRINCESSES by Christie Harris, ill. by
Douglas Tait *(McClelland & Stewart)*
1982
YTEK AND THE ARCTIC ORCHID: AN INUIT LEGEND by
Garnet Hewitt, ill. by Heather Woodall *(Douglas & McIntyre)*
1983
CHESTER'S BARN by Lindee Climo *(Tundra)*
1984
ZOOM AT SEA by Tim Wynne-Jones, ill. by Ken Nutt
(Groundwood/Douglas & McIntyre)
1985
CHIN CHIANG AND THE DRAGON'S DANCE by Ian
Wallace *(Groundwood/Douglas & McIntyre)*
1986
ZOOM AWAY by Tim Wynne-Jones, ill. by Ken Nutt
(Groundwood/Douglas & McIntyre)

1987
MOONBEAM ON A CAT'S EAR by Marie-Louise Gay
(Stoddart)

1988
RAINY DAY MAGIC by Marie-Louise Gay *(Stoddart)*

1989
AMOS'S SWEATER by Janet Lunn, ill. by Kim LaFave
(Groundwood/Douglas & McIntyre)

1990
TIL ALL THE STARS HAVE FALLEN: CANADIAN POEMS
FOR CHILDREN selected by David Booth, ill. by Kady
MacDonald Denton *(Kids Can Press)*

1991
THE ORPHAN BOY by Tololwa Mollel, ill. by Paul Morin
(Oxford)

1992
WAITING FOR THE WHALES by Sheryl McFarlane, ill. by
Ron Lightburn *(Orca Books)*

IODE (National Chapter of Canada) ❧

VIOLET DOWNEY BOOK AWARD

A project of the National Chapter of Canada Imperial Order of
the Daughters of the Empire (IODE) (40 Orchard View Blvd.,
Toronto, Ont. M4R 1B9, Canada), this award is for the best
English-language book, with at least 500 words and preferably
with Canadian content, for children 13 and under. The book
must have been written by a Canadian citizen, and have been
published in Canada in the year before receiving the award. A
panel of five judges—three affiliated with IODE and two
"recognized specialists in the field of children's literature" select
the honorees. The award is named for a benefactor of the IODE
National Chapter of Canada. (Up to $3,000)

1985
WINNERS by Mary-Ellen Lang Collura *(Western Producer
Prairie Books)*

1986
THE QUARTER-PIE WINDOW by Marianne Brandis
(Porcupine's Quill)

1987
SHADOW IN HAWTHORN BAY by Janet Lunn *(Lester &
Orpen Dennys)*

1988
A BOOK DRAGON by Donn Kushner *(Macmillan)*
1989
No Award
1990
TALES FROM GOLD MOUNTAIN by Paul Yee
(Groundwood/Douglas & McIntyre)
1991
INCREDIBLE JUMBO by Barbara Smucker *(Viking)*
REDWORK by Michael Bedard *(Lester & Orpen Dennys)*

IODE *(Toronto)* 🐛
BOOK AWARD

The Toronto Municipal Chapter of the Imperial Order of the Daughters of the Empire (IODE) (40 St. Clair Ave. East, Toronto, Ont. M4T 1M9, Canada) has given an award annually since 1975 to a Toronto-area author or illustrator of an outstanding Canadian-published children's book. A committee from the Toronto Public Library Board and IODE-Toronto selects the award recipients. In our listing and in IODE's, the award year is the publication year. ($1,000)

1974
Dennis Lee, for ALLIGATOR PIE *(Macmillan)*
1975
William Kurelek, for A PRAIRIE BOY'S SUMMER *(Tundra)*
1976
Aviva Layton, for HOW THE KOOKABURRA GOT HIS LAUGH *(McClelland & Stewart)*
1977
William Toye, for THE LOON'S NECKLACE *(Oxford)*
1978
Laszlo Gal, for illustrations in MY NAME IS NOT ODESSA YARKER by Marian Engel *(Kids Can Press)*, THE SHIRT OF THE HAPPY MAN by Mariella Bertelli *(Kids Can Press)* and WHY THE MAN IN THE MOON IS HAPPY by Ronald Melzak *(McClelland & Stewart)*
1979
Janet Lunn, for THE TWELVE DANCING PRINCESSES *(Methuen)*
1980
Olena Kassian, for illustrations in AFRAID OF THE DARK by Barry Dickson *(Lorimer)* and THE HUNGRY TIME by Selwyn Dewdney *(Lorimer)*

1981
Bernice Thurman Hunter, for THAT SCATTERBRAIN BOOKY *(Scholastic-TAB)*
1982
Kathy Stinson, for RED IS BEST *(Annick)*
1983
Tim Wynne-Jones, for ZOOM AT SEA *(Groundwood/Douglas & McIntyre)*
1984
Ian Wallace, for CHIN CHIANG AND THE DRAGON'S DANCE *(Groundwood/Douglas & McIntyre)*
1985
Robin Muller, for THE SORCERER'S APPRENTICE *(Kids Can Press)*
1986
Barbara Reid, for illustrations in HAVE YOU SEEN BIRDS? by Joanne Oppenheim *(Scholastic-TAB)*
1987
Caroline Parry, for LET'S CELEBRATE! CANADA'S SPECIAL DAYS *(Kids Can Press)*
1988
Eric Beddows, for illustrations in NIGHT CARS by Teddy Jam *(Groundwood/Douglas & McIntyre)*
1989
Brenda Clark, for illustrations in LITTLE FINGERLING by Monica Hughes *(Kids Can Press)*
1990
David Booth, selector, for VOICES ON THE WIND: POEMS FOR ALL SEASONS *(Kids Can Press)*

Vicky Metcalf Award ❧

Presented by the Canadian Authors Association (275 Slater St., Suite 500, Ottawa, Ont. K1P 5H9, Canada) to a Canadian writer — citizen or landed immigrant — who has produced a body of work with appeal for children age 7-17. (As of 1991, $10,000)

1963   Kerry Wood
1964   John F. Hayes
1965   Roderick Haig-Brown
1966   Fred Swayze
1967   John Patrick Gillese
1968   Lorrie McLaughlin

1969 Audrey McKim
1970 Farley Mowat
1971 Kay Hill
1972 William E. Toye
1973 Christie Harris
1974 Jean Little
1975 Lyn Harrington
1976 Suzanne Martel
1977 James Houston
1978 Lyn Cook
1979 Cliff Faulknor
1980 John Craig
1981 Monica Hughes
1982 Janet Lunn
1983 Claire MacKay
1984 Bill Freeman
1985 Edith Fowke
1986 Dennis Lee
1987 Robert Munsch
1988 Barbara Smucker
1989 Stéphane Poulin
1990 Bernice Thurman Hunter
1991 Brian Doyle

Mr. Christie's Book Awards™ ๛

Sponsored by Christie Brown & Co., a division of Nabisco Brands Ltd., a manufacturer of cookies and crackers, this awards program is designed to honor high quality in children's books and to stimulate children to read. The Canadian Children's Book Centre and Communication Jeunesse compile lists of eligible titles, which must have been written or illustrated by Canadians and be for readers ages 12 and under. English-language and French-language panels of children's book specialists select short lists of honorees for English text and illustration *(ET, EI)* and French text and illustration *(FT, FI)*. The panels that create the short lists also select the winners. The program is administered by Mr. Christie's Book Awards™ Information Centre (2150 Lakeshore Blvd. West, Toronto, Ont. M8V 1A3, Canada). ($7,500 to each winner, and a seal)

1990
ET: THE SKY IS FALLING by Kit Pearson *(Penguin)*
EI: THE NAME OF THE TREE: A BANTU TALE by Celia
Lottridge, ill. by Ian Wallace *(Groundwood/Douglas &*
McIntyre)
FT: ROSALIE S'EN VA-T-EN GUERRE by Ginette Anfousse
(La courte échelle)
FI: MAIS QUE FONT LES FÉES AVEC TOUTES CES
DENTS? by Philippe Béha *(Raton-Laveur)*
1991
ET: COVERED BRIDGE by Brian Doyle *(Groundwood/Douglas*
& McIntyre)
EI: THE STORY OF LITTLE QUACK by Kady MacDonald
Denton *(Kids Can Press)*
FT: ZAMBONI by Francois Gravel *(Boréal)*
FI: LES FANTAISIES DE L'ONCLE HENRI by Bénédicte
Froissart, ill. by Pierre Pratt *(Annick)*

Elizabeth Mrazik-Cleaver
Canadian Picture Book Award ❧

This award honors a Canadian illustrator whose widely praised
books were published under the name Elizabeth Cleaver before
her early death in 1985. It is for a Canadian illustrator's work in
a distinguished children's picture book. Sponsored by the
Canadian National Section of the International Board on Books
for Young People (IBBY), the award is administered from the
Children's Literature Service (National Library of Canada, 395
Wellington St., Ottawa, Ont. K1A ON4, Canada). ($1,000 and
certificate)

1986
BY THE SEA: AN ALPHABET BOOK by Ann Blades *(Kids Can*
Press)
1987
HAVE YOU SEEN BIRDS? by Joanne Oppenheimer, ill. by
Barbara Reid *(Scholastic-TAB)*
1988
CAN YOU CATCH JOSEPHINE? by Stéphane Poulin *(Tundra)*
1989
NIGHT CARS by Ken Nutt *(Groundwood/Douglas & McIntyre)*
1990
THE NAME OF THE TREE: A BANTU TALE by Celia

Lottridge, ill. by Ian Wallace *(Groundwood/Douglas & McIntyre)*

1991
THE ORPHAN BOY by Tololwa M. Mollel, ill. by Paul Morin *(Oxford)*

Prix Québec Wallonie-Bruxelles du Livre de la Jeunesse ❧

This award is for a Québec or Belgian author or illustrator for either a body of work or a book. The award alternates between the two communities. When the award is for a book, its publisher also receives a grant to enable it to distribute the title in the other market. The award hopes to encourage the development and distribution of French-language children's books in Québec and Belgium and to make the works of each community known to the other. The Canadian sponsor and administrator is the Gouvernement du Québec, Ministère des Affaires Internationales (1225 place George-V Est, Québec, Québec G1R 4Z7, Canada). ($3,500)

1981
Body of work of Belgian illustrator Françoise Souply-Clabots

1982
Body of work of Québec author Raymond Plante

1983
No Award

1984
ANIMAUX SAUVAGES D'EUROPE ET D'AMÉRIQUE DU NORD by René Hausman *(Éditions Jean Dupuis, Belgium)*

1985
ZUNIK by Bertrand Gauthier, ill. by Daniel Sylvestre *(La courte échelle, Québec)*

1986
No award

1987
Body of work of Belgian author Marie-Josée Sacré

1988
LES CATASTROPHES DE ROSALIE by Ginette Anfousse *(La courte échelle, Québec)*

1989
LÉONIE DÉVORE LES LIVRES by Frédéric du Bus *(Casterman, Belgium)*

1990
ALBUM DE FAMILLE by Stéphane Poulin *(Michel Quintin, Québec)*
1991
MAGRITTE by Lillo Canta *(Duculot, Belgium)*

Ruth Schwartz Foundation Award for Excellence in Children's Literature

The award is for an outstanding work of children's literature published in Canada by an author or illustrator of Canadian citizenship. The award honors the late Ruth Schwartz, for many years the proprietor of a Toronto Bookstore. The program is a joint activity of the Canadian Booksellers Association (CBA) and the Ontario Arts Council (151 Bloor Street West, Toronto, Ont. M5S 1T6, Canada). CBA members select a short list of nominees, which is submitted to a panel of six judges, who are children in a different Ontario community each year and are selected by the Arts Council. ($2,000)

1976
JACOB TWO-TWO MEETS THE HOODED FANG by Mordecai Richler *(McClelland & Stewart)*
1977
THE VIOLIN by Robert Thomas Allen *(McGraw-Hill)*
1978
GARBAGE DELIGHT by Dennis Lee *(Macmillan)*
1979
HOLD FAST by Kevin Major *(Clarke, Irwin)*
1980
DAYS OF TERROR by Barbara Smucker *(Clarke, Irwin)*
1981
THE KING'S DAUGHTER by Suzanne Martel *(Douglas & McIntyre)*
1982
ONE PROUD SUMMER by Claire MacKay and Marsha Hewitt *(Women's Press)*
1983
JASMIN by Jan Truss *(Douglas & McIntyre)*
1984
ZOOM AT SEA by Tim Wynne-Jones, ill. by Ken Nutt *(Groundwood/Douglas & McIntyre)*

1985
MAMA'S GOING TO BUY YOU A MOCKINGBIRD by Jean Little *(Penguin)*
1986
THOMAS' SNOWSUIT by Robert Munsch, ill. by Michael Martchenko *(Annick)*
1987
HAVE YOU SEEN BIRDS? by Joanne Oppenheim, ill. by Barbara Reid *(Scholastic-TAB)*
1988
THE DOLL by Cora Taylor *(Western Producer Prairie Books)*
1989
AMOS'S SWEATER by Janet Lunn, ill. by Kim LaFave *(Groundwood/Douglas & McIntyre)*
1990
BAD BOY by Diana Wieler *(Groundwood/Douglas & McIntyre)*
1991
FORBIDDEN CITY by William Bell *(Doubleday)*

Writers Guild of Alberta Awards for Excellence 🐝

R. ROSS ANNETT AWARD
FOR CHILDREN'S LITERATURE

This award is for books by authors who have been recent residents of Alberta, though their works may have been published anywhere in the world. (Leather-bound copies of book, extensive promotion, i.e., bookmarks, poster, etc., and $500 honorarium)

1982
HUNTER IN THE DARK by Monica Hughes *(Clarke, Irwin)*
1983
SPACE TRAP by Monica Hughes *(Douglas & McIntyre)*
1984
IN THE CITY OF THE KING by William Pasnak *(Douglas & McIntyre)*
1985
JULIE by Cora Taylor *(Western Producer Prairie Books)*
1986
BLAINE'S WAY by Monica Hughes *(Irwin)*
1987
NOBODY SAID IT WOULD BE EASY by Marilyn Halvorson *(Irwin)*

1988
UNDER THE EAGLE'S CLAW by William Pasnak *(Douglas & McIntyre)*
1989
DOG RUNNER by Don Meredith *(Western Producer Prairie Books)*
1990
DAWN RIDER by Jan Hudson *(HarperCollins)*

Young Adult Canadian Book Award

Begun by the Young Adult Caucus of the Saskatchewan Library Association, as of 1989 the award sponsor became the Young Adult Services Interest Group of the Canadian Library Association (200 Elgin St., Suite 602, Ottawa, Ont. K2P 1L5, Canada). The purpose of the award was, and remains, to "recognize the author of an outstanding English-language Canadian book which appeals to young adults between the ages of 13 and 18." Designed to promote Canadian authors and publishing companies, "the title must be a Canadian publication in either hardcover or paperback, and the author must be a Canadian citizen or landed immigrant." We list the award year below; winners were published in the preceding year. (Seal, designed by a young adult from Regina, and leatherbound copy of book)

1981
FAR FROM SHORE by Kevin Major *(Clarke, Irwin)*
1982
SUPER BIKE! by Jamie Brown *(Clarke, Irwin)*
1983
HUNTER IN THE DARK by Monica Hughes *(Clarke, Irwin)*
1984
THE DRUID'S TUNE by O.R. Melling *(Penguin)*
1985
WINNERS by Mary-Ellen Lang Collura *(Western Producer Prairie Books)*
1986
THE QUARTER-PIE WINDOW by Marianne Brandis *(Porcupine's Quill)*
1987
SHADOW IN HAWTHORN BAY by Janet Lunn *(Lester & Orpen Dennys)*

1988
WHO IS FRANCES RAIN? by Margaret Buffie *(Kids Can Press)*
1989
JANUARY, FEBRUARY, JUNE OR JULY by Helen Fogwill
Porter *(Breakwater)*
1990
BAD BOY by Diana Wieler *(Groundwood/Douglas & McIntyre)*
1991
THE LEAVING by Budge Wilson *(Anansi)*

NEW ZEALAND
AIM Children's Book Awards ❧

Originally funded by the Government Printer to recognize authors
and illustrators of New Zealand children's books and to reward
literary excellence, this program is administered by the AIM
Children's Book Week Management Committee, representing the
Literature Program of the Queen Elizabeth II Arts Council,
Booksellers New Zealand, and the Book Publishers Association of
New Zealand. CBC does not have the address of the
administrator; information about the program is available from
National Library of New Zealand (Molesworth & Aitken Sts.,
P. O. Box 1467, Wellington 1, New Zealand) or New Zealand
Children's Book Foundation (P. O. Box 96094, Balmoral,
Aukland, New Zealand). The awards are in two categories:
Picture Book of the Year *(P)* and Book of the Year *(B)*. The
sponsor is Lever Rexona; AIM is a brand of toothpaste. (First
prizes for each: $5,000; generous second and third prizes)

1982
P: THE KUIA AND THE SPIDER by Patricia Grace, ill. by
Robyn Kahukiwa *(Longman Paul, in association with Kidarus 2,
Inc.; simultaneous Maori-language edition)* (Two awards)
B: THE SILENT ONE by Joy Cowley *(Whitcoulls)*
1983
P: MR. FOX by Gavin Bishop *(Oxford)*
B: THE HALFMEN OF O by Maurice Gee *(Oxford)*
1984
P: HAIRY MACLARY FROM DONALDSON'S DAIRY by
Lynley Dodd *(Mallinson Rendell)*
B: JACKY NOBODY by Anne de Roo *(Methuen)*
1985
P: THE FISH OF OUR FATHERS by Ron Bacon, ill. by Robert
Jahnke *(Waiatarua)*

B: VISITORS by Caroline MacDonald *(Hodder)*

1986
P: HAIRY MACLARY SCATTERCAT by Lynley Dodd *(Mallinson Rendell)*
B: No Award

1987
P: TANIWHA by Robyn Kahukiwa *(Penguin)*
B: THE KEEPER by Barry Faville *(Oxford)*

1988
P: HAIRY MACLARY'S CATERWAUL CAPER by Lynley Dodd *(Mallinson Rendell)*
B: ALEX by Tessa Duder *(Oxford)*

1989
No Awards

1990
P: ANNIE AND MOON by Miriam Smith, ill. by Lesley Moyes *(Mallinson Rendell)*
B: ALEX IN WINTER by Tessa Duder *(Oxford)*

1991
P: MY CAT MAISIE by Pamela Allen *(Hodder)*
B: ROCCO by Sheryl Jordan *(Ashton Scholastic)*

Russell Clark Award ❧

Established in 1976, the award was first given in 1978 by its administrator, the New Zealand Library Association (P. O. Box 12-212, Wellington, New Zealand). The award is "made for the most distinguished illustrations for a children's book; the illustrator must be a citizen or resident of New Zealand." The award is named for the prominent New Zealand illustrator Russell Clark (1905-1966) whose drawings of ordinary people engaged in everyday activities have proved to be, of themselves, valuable historical records. The award "is offered annually and awarded when merited." (Medal and NZ $200)

1978
THE HOUSE OF THE PEOPLE by Ron L. Bacon, ill. by Robert F. Jahnke *(Collins)*

1979
KIM by Bruce Treloar *(Collins)*

1980-1981
No Awards

1982
MRS. McGINTY AND THE BIZARRE PLANT by Gavin Bishop *(Oxford)*

1983
No Award

1984
THE TREE WITCHES by Gwenda Turner *(Penguin)*

1985
THE DUCK IN THE GUN by Joy Cowley, ill. by Robyn Belton *(Shortland Educational)*

1986
A LION IN THE NIGHT by Pamela Allen *(Hodder)*

1987
TANIWHA by Robyn Kahukiwa *(Viking Kestrel)*

1988
THE MAGPIES by Denis Glover, ill. by Dick Frizzell *(Century Hutchinson)*

1989
JOSEPH'S BOAT by Caroline Macdonald, ill. by Chris Gaskin *(Hodder)*

1990
A WALK TO THE BEACH by Chris Gaskin *(Heinemann Reed)*

1991
ARTHUR AND THE DRAGON by Pauline Cartwright, ill. by David Elliott *(Highgate)*

Esther Glen Award ☙

Established in 1945 in honor of Esther Glen, New Zealand journalist, children's book editor and author, the award is administered by The New Zealand Library Association (P. O. Box 12-212, Wellington, New Zealand). Given for the most distinguished contribution to New Zealand literature for children by an author who is a citizen or resident of New Zealand, the award "is offered annually and awarded when merited." (Medal and NZ $200)

1945
THE BOOK OF WIREMU by Stella Morice *(Angus & Robertson)*

1946
No Award

1947
MYTHS AND LEGENDS OF MAORILAND by A. W. Reed *(Reed)*

1948-1949
No Awards

1950
THE ADVENTURES OF NIMBLE, RUMBLE AND TUMBLE
by Joan Smith *(Paul's Book Arcade)*
1951-1958
No Awards
1959
FALTER TOM AND THE WATER BOY by Maurice Duggan
(Paul's Book Arcade)
1960-1963
No Awards
1964
TURI: THE STORY OF A LITTLE BOY by Leslie C. Powell
(Paul's Book Arcade)
1965-1969
No Awards
1970
A LION IN THE MEADOW by Margaret Mahy *(Dent)*
1971-1972
No Awards
1973
THE FIRST MARGARET MAHY STORY BOOK by Margaret
Mahy *(Dent)*
1974
No Award
1975
MY CAT LIKES TO HIDE IN BOXES by Eve Sutton and
Lynley Dodd *(Hamish Hamilton)*
1976-1977
No Awards
1978
THE LIGHTHOUSE KEEPER'S LUNCH by Ronda and David
Armitage *(Deutsch)*
1979
TAKE THE LONG PATH by Joan de Hamel *(Lutterworth)*
1980-1981
No Awards
1982
THE YEAR OF THE YELVERTONS by Katherine O'Brien
(Oxford)
1983
THE HAUNTING by Margaret Mahy *(Dent)*
1984
ELEPHANT ROCK by Caroline Macdonald *(Hodder)*
1985
THE CHANGEOVER: A SUPERNATURAL ROMANCE by
Margaret Mahy *(Dent)*

1986
MOTHERSTONE by Maurice Gee *(Oxford)*
1987
No Award
1988
ALEX by Tessa Duder *(Oxford)*
1989
THE MANGROVE SUMMER by Jack Lazenby *(Oxford)*
1990
ALEX IN WINTER by Tessa Duder *(Oxford)*
1991
AGNES THE SHEEP by William Taylor *(Ashton Scholastic)*

New Zealand Library Association Young People's Nonfiction Award

This annual award is for the author of the book considered by the New Zealand Library Association (P. O. Box 12-212, Wellington, New Zealand) to be the most distinguished contribution to nonfiction children's literature. (Publisher and prize information not available to CBC; apologies)

1987
GAIJAIN: FOREIGN CHILDREN OF JAPAN by Olive Hill and Ngaio Hill
1988
No Award
1989
IT'S OK TO BE YOU by Claire Patterson
1990
THE WEB by Deborah Furley

UNITED KINGDOM (UK)
Best Books for Babies Award
PARENTS MAGAZINE

Begun by the British Book Marketing Council and *Parents*, a magazine with wide readership in Britain, this program is currently administered by Book Trust (Book House, 45 East Hill, London SW18 2QZ). A panel of knowledgeable specialists selects a short list of books—usually ten titles—published for under-fours in the previous year. The list is widely publicized to parents throughout the country, to draw attention of parents to the number and variety of new books published for infants and toddlers each year. *Parents* selects a "team of ten mums and dads across the country that 'tests' the books" and chooses the top title. (£1,000)

1985
PEEPO! by Janet and Allan Ahlberg *(Viking Kestrel)*
1986
WHERE IS BOBO? by Susan Hulme, ill. with photographs by Jan Siegieda *(Methuen)*
1987
FIVE MINUTES' PEACE by Jill Murphy *(Walker)*
1988
A DAY OF RHYMES by Sarah Pooley *(Bodley Head)*
1989
WAKE UP, DAD! by Sally Grindley, ill. by Siobhan Dodds *(Simon & Schuster)*
1990
ROSIE'S BABIES by Martin Waddell, ill. by Penny Dale *(Walker)*
1991
No Award

British Book Awards ❧
CHILDREN'S BOOK CATEGORIES

This prize program, honoring books, publishing, bookselling, distributing and other aspects of the book trade is organized by *Publishing News* (43 Museum St., London WClA lLY, England). It currently includes awards in two children's book categories: Children's Author of the Year *(A)*, and Illustrated Children's Book of the Year *(I)*. Honorees are selected by booksellers, librarians, and literary agents from publishers' suggestions. ("Nibbies," polished brass trophy-size pen nibs; the illustrator of the Illustrated Children's Book of the Year also receives £1,000, contributed by Bowater Book Printing, the largest printing and packaging group in the U. K.)

1990
A: Roald Dahl

1991
A. Anne Fine
I: THE MOUSEHOLE CAT by Antonia Barber, ill. by Nicola
Bayley (Walker)

British Book Design and Production 🐾

Children's books have been included in this touring exhibition in recent years, and have been singled out as one of eleven categories honored as winners for the excellent quality of their production. The exhibition and prize-giving are organized and sponsored by the British Printing Industries Federation (11 Bedford Row, London WC1R 4DX, England), Publishers Association, and Book Trust. (Prize)

1987
IN GRANDPA'S HOUSE by Philip Sendak, ill. by Maurice Sendak, designed by Constance Fogler (Bodley Head)
1988
EACH PEACH PEAR PLUM by Janet and Allan Ahlberg, designed by Janet and Allan Ahlberg (Penguin)
1989
THE FOUR SEASONS OF BRAMBLY HEDGE by Jill Barklem, designed by Bob Hook and Ian Butterworth (Collins)
1990
ANGELINA'S BIRTHDAY by Katharine Holabird, ill. by Helen Craig, designed by Helen Craig (Aurum)
UNDER THE SUN AND OVER THE MOON by Kevin Crossley-Holland, ill. by Ian Penney (Orchard)
1991
THE MOUSEHOLE CAT by Antonia Barber, ill. by Nicola Bayley (Walker)

Carnegie Medal 🐾

Given annually since 1937 by the (British) Library Association (LA) (7 Ridgmount St., London WC1E 7AE, England) for a children's book of outstanding merit written in English and first published in the United Kingdom in the preceding year. As of the award for 1990—given in 1991—Peters Library Service makes a substantial annual grant, matched by the Business Sponsorship Incentive Scheme of the British government, to the LA to enable it to publicize both the Carnegie and Greenaway awards programs aggressively throughout Britain. The years cited in our listing are publication years. (Medal; in addition, as of the 1991 award year, the winner can select an organization to receive £750 worth of books)

1936
PIGEON POST by Arthur Ransome *(Cape)*
1937
THE FAMILY FROM ONE END STREET by Eve Garnett
(Muller)
1938
THE CIRCUS IS COMING by Noel Streatfeild *(Dent)*
1939
RADIUM WOMAN by Eleanor Doorly *(Heinemann)*
1940
VISITORS FROM LONDON by Kitty Barne *(Dent)*
1941
WE COULDN'T LEAVE DINAH by Mary Treadgold *(Penguin)*
1942
THE LITTLE GREY MEN by BB *(Eyre & Spottiswoode)*
1943
No Award
1944
THE WIND ON THE MOON by Eric Linklater *(Macmillan)*
1945
No Award
1946
THE LITTLE WHITE HORSE by Elizabeth Goudge
(Brockhampton)
1947
COLLECTED STORIES FOR CHILDREN by Walter de la Mare
(Faber)
1948
SEA CHANGE by Richard Armstrong *(Dent)*
1949
THE STORY OF YOUR HOME by Agnes Allen *(Faber)*
1950
THE LARK ON THE WING by Elfrida Vipont Foulds *(Oxford)*
1951
THE WOOL-PACK by Cynthia Harnett *(Methuen)*
1952
THE BORROWERS by Mary Norton *(Dent)*

1953
A VALLEY GROWS UP by Edward Osmond *(Oxford)*
1954
KNIGHT CRUSADER by Ronald Welch *(Oxford)*
1955
THE LITTLE BOOKROOM by Eleanor Farjeon *(Oxford)*
1956
THE LAST BATTLE by C. S. Lewis *(Bodley Head)*
1957
A GRASS ROPE by William Mayne *(Oxford)*
1958
TOM'S MIDNIGHT GARDEN by Philippa Pearce *(Oxford)*
1959
THE LANTERN BEARERS by Rosemary Sutcliff *(Oxford)*
1960
THE MAKING OF MAN by I. W. Cornwall *(Phoenix)*
1961
A STRANGER AT GREEN KNOWE by Lucy Boston *(Faber)*
1962
THE TWELVE AND THE GENII by Pauline Clarke *(Faber)*
1963
TIME OF TRIAL by Hester Burton *(Oxford)*
1964
NORDY BANK by Sheena Porter *(Oxford)*
1965
THE GRANGE AT HIGH FORCE by Philip Turner *(Oxford)*
1966
No Award
1967
THE OWL SERVICE by Alan Garner *(Collins)*
1968
THE MOON IN THE CLOUD by Rosemary Harris *(Faber)*
1969
THE EDGE OF THE CLOUD by K. M. Peyton *(Oxford)*
1970
THE GOD BENEATH THE SEA by Leon Garfield and Edward Blishen *(Longman)*
1971
JOSH by Ivan Southall *(Angus & Robertson)*
1972
WATERSHIP DOWN by Richard Adams *(Rex Collings)*
1973
THE GHOST OF THOMAS KEMPE by Penelope Lively *(Heinemann)*

1974
THE STRONGHOLD by Mollie Hunter *(Hamish Hamilton)*

1975
THE MACHINE-GUNNERS by Robert Westall *(Macmillan)*

1976
THUNDER AND LIGHTNINGS by Jan Mark *(Kestrel)*

1977
THE TURBULENT TERM OF TYKE TILER by Gene Kemp *(Faber)*

1978
THE EXETER BLITZ by David Rees *(Hamish Hamilton)*

1979
TULKU by Peter Dickinson *(Gollancz)*

1980
CITY OF GOLD by Peter Dickinson *(Gollancz)*

1981
THE SCARECROWS by Robert Westall *(Chatto)*

1982
THE HAUNTING by Margaret Mahy *(Dent)*

1983
HANDLES by Jan Mark *(Kestrel)*

1984
THE CHANGEOVER by Margaret Mahy *(Dent)*

1985
STORM by Kevin Crossley-Holland *(Heinemann)*

1986
GRANNY WAS A BUFFER GIRL by Berlie Doherty *(Methuen)*

1987
THE GHOST DRUM by Susan Price *(Faber)*

1988
A PACK OF LIES by Geraldine McCaughrean *(Oxford)*

1989
GOGGLE-EYES by Anne Fine *(Hamish Hamilton)*

1990
WOLF by Gillian Cross *(Oxford)*

Children's Book Award 🐦

Organized by the Federation of Children's Book Groups (Award Coordinator: Jenny Blanch, 30 Senneleys Park Rd., Northfield, Birmingham B31 1AL, England; National Secretary: Marianne Adey, Old Malt House, South St., Aldbourne, Marlborough,

Wiltshire SN8 2DW, England) and sponsored by Save & Prosper Educational Foundation, this program currently involves more than 10,000 children nationally in selecting the winner. Children's involvement begins when regional Federation (adult) members, reflecting children's ratings, select fifty titles as "Pick of the Year." The top ten are re-tested; six titles make up a shortlist that is ranked by children in order of preference to select the winner. Authors and illustrators sometimes share the award. (Portfolios prepared by children for all honorees on shortlist; winner holds silver and oak trophy in form of tree for one year, and silver acorn permanently)

1981
MR. MAGNOLIA by Quentin Blake *(Cape)*
1982
FAIR'S FAIR by Leon Garfield *(Macdonald)*
1983
THE BFG by Roald Dahl *(Cape)*
1984
THE SAGA OF ERIK THE VIKING by Terry Jones, ill. by Michael Foreman *(Pavilion)*
1985
BROTHER IN THE LAND by Robert Swindells *(Oxford)*
1986
ARTHUR by Amanda Graham, ill. by Donna Gynell *(Spindlewood)*
1987
THE JOLLY POSTMAN OR OTHER PEOPLE'S LETTERS by Janet and Allan Ahlberg *(Heinemann)*
1988
WINNIE THE WITCH by Valerie Thomas, ill. by Korky Paul *(Oxford)*
1989
MATILDA by Roald Dahl *(Cape)*
1990
ROOM 13 by Robert Swindells *(Doubleday)*
1991
THREADBEAR by Mick Inkpen *(Hodder & Stoughton)*

Children's Book of the Year 🌰

Organized by the Lancashire County Library (143 Corporation St., Preston PRl 2UQ, Lancashire, England) and sponsored by National Westminster Bank, this program honors original fiction for readers 11-14 years old. All secondary schools in Lancashire County are invited to participate; one school in each of the fourteen districts of the county is chosen as the participant each year. Pupils 13-14 years old participate in the voting, with student representatives attending meetings to discuss the entries, which are made by publishers. One reader from each school is on the final judging panel, which selects a shortlist and then a winner. (Engraved glass decanter and honorarium)

1987
RUBY IN THE SMOKE by Philip Pullman *(Oxford)*
1988
REDWALL by Brian Jacques *(Century Hutchinson)*
1989
GROOSHAM GRANGE by Anthony Horowitz *(Methuen)*
1990
PLAGUE '99' by Jean Ure *(Methuen)*
1991
MATTIMEO by Brian Jacques *(Random Century)*

Earthworm Award 🪱

This awards program has as its motto: The Prize for books that help children to enjoy and care for the Earth. It is designed "to promote and reward environmental awareness and sensitivity in literature for children of all ages..." and honors "books which not only highlight the threats to our natural world, but also explore and celebrate its richness, variety and beauty." It is an activity of The Arts for the Earth, Friends of the Earth (26-28 Underwood St., London N1 7JQ, England), sponsored by the investment house Save & Prosper. (£2,000 to winner; £250 for up to three other titles)

1987
THE BOY AND THE SWAN by Catherine Storr *(Deutsch)*
1988
WHERE THE FOREST MEETS THE SEA by Jeannie Baker *(Julia MacRae)*
1989
AWAITING DEVELOPMENTS by Judy Allen *(Julia MacRae)*
1990
THE YOUNG GREEN CONSUMER GUIDE by John Elkington and Julia Hailes *(Gollancz)*
1991
THE LAST RABBIT edited by Jennifer Curry *(Methuen)*

Kathleen Fidler Award 🕭

Suggested by the Edinburgh Children's Book Group, this award is a memorial to the author of over eighty books for children. It is a manuscript competition for novels for children ages 8-12; entrants have not previously had a novel published for this age group. The winning entry each year is published. While a panel of children's book professionals selects the winners, children in two schools read shortlisted entries and their views are considered when final selections are made. The program is administered by Book Trust Scotland (15a Lynedoch St., Glasgow G3 6EF, Scotland). (£1,000 cash prize; publication by Blackie Children's Books; rosewood and silver trophy held for one year)

1983
ADRIFT by Allan Baillie *(Blackie)*
1984
NO SHELTER by Elizabeth Lutzeier *(Blackie)*
1985
BARTY by Janet Collins *(Blackie)*
1986
DIAMOND by Caroline Pitcher *(Blackie)*
1987
SIMON'S CHALLENGE by Theresa Breslin *(Blackie)*
1988
FLIGHT OF THE SOLAR DUCKS by Charles Morgan *(Blackie)*
1989
MIGHTIER THAN THE SWORD by Clara Bevan *(Blackie)*
1990
MAGIC WITH EVERYTHING by Roger Burt *(Blackie)*

Kate Greenaway Medal 🕭

Given annually by the (British) Library Association (LA) (7 Ridgmount St., London WC1E 7AE, England) to the most distinguished work in the illustration of children's books first published in the United Kingdom in the preceding year. As of the award for 1990—given in 1991—Peters Library Service makes a substantial annual grant, matched by the Business Sponsorship Incentive Scheme of the British government, to the LA to enable it to publicize both the Greenaway and Carnegie awards programs aggressively throughout Britain. The years cited in our listing are publication years. (Medal; in addition, as of the 1991 award year, the winner can select an organization to receive £750 worth of books)

1955
No Award

1956
TIM ALL ALONE by Edward Ardizzone *(Oxford)*

1957
MRS. EASTER AND THE STORKS by V. H. Drummond *(Faber)*

1958
No Award

1959
KASHTANKA AND A BUNDLE OF BALLADS by William Stobbs *(Oxford)*

1960
OLD WINKLE AND THE SEAGULLS by Elizabeth Rose, ill. by Gerald Rose *(Faber)*

1961
MRS. COCKLE'S CAT by Philippa Pearce, ill. by Antony Maitland *(Longman)*

1962
BRIAN WILDSMITH'S A B C by Brian Wildsmith *(Oxford)*

1963
BORKA by John Burningham *(Cape)*

1964
SHAKESPEARE'S THEATRE by C. W. Hodges *(Oxford)*

1965
THREE POOR TAILORS by Victor Ambrus *(Hamish Hamilton)*

1966
MOTHER GOOSE TREASURY by Raymond Briggs *(Hamish Hamilton)*

1967
CHARLIE, CHARLOTTE & THE GOLDEN CANARY by Charles Keeping *(Oxford)*

1968
DICTIONARY OF CHIVALRY by Grant Uden, ill. by Pauline Baynes *(Longman)*

1969
THE QUANGLE-WANGLE'S HAT by Edward Lear, ill. by Helen Oxenbury *(Heinemann)*
DRAGON OF AN ORDINARY FAMILY by Margaret Mahy, ill. by Helen Oxenbury *(Heinemann)*

1970
MR. GUMPY'S OUTING by John Burningham *(Cape)*

1971
THE KINGDOM UNDER THE SEA by Jan Pieńkowski *(Cape)*

1972
THE WOODCUTTER'S DUCK by Krystyna Turska *(Hamish Hamilton)*
1973
FATHER CHRISTMAS by Raymond Briggs *(Hamish Hamilton)*
1974
THE WIND BLEW by Pat Hutchins *(Bodley Head)*
1975
HORSES IN BATTLE by Victor Ambrus *(Oxford)*
MISHKA by Victor Ambrus *(Oxford)*
1976
THE POST OFFICE CAT by Gail E. Haley *(Bodley Head)*
1977
DOGGER by Shirley Hughes *(Bodley Head)*
1978
EACH PEACH PEAR PLUM by Allan Ahlberg, ill. by Janet Ahlberg *(Kestrel)*
1979
THE HAUNTED HOUSE by Jan Pieńkowski *(Heinemann)*
1980
MR. MAGNOLIA by Quentin Blake *(Cape)*
1981
THE HIGHWAYMAN by Alfred Noyes, ill. by Charles Keeping *(Oxford)*
1982
LONG NECK AND THUNDER FOOT by Helen Piers, ill. by Michael Foreman *(Kestrel)*
SLEEPING BEAUTY AND OTHER FAVOURITE FAIRY TALES chosen by Angela Carter, ill. by Michael Foreman *(Gollancz)*
1983
GORILLA by Anthony Browne *(Julia MacRae)*
1984
HIAWATHA'S CHILDHOOD by Errol Le Cain *(Faber)*
1985
SIR GAWAIN AND THE LOATHLY LADY by Selina Hastings, ill. by Juan Wijngaard *(Walker)*
1986
SNOW WHITE IN NEW YORK by Fiona French *(Oxford)*
1987
CRAFTY CHAMELEON by Mwenye Hadithi, ill. by Adrienne Kennaway *(Hodder & Stoughton)*
1988
CAN'T YOU SLEEP, LITTLE BEAR? by Martin Waddell, ill. by Barbara Firth *(Walker)*

1989
WAR BOY by Michael Foreman *(Pavilion)*
1990
THE WHALE'S SONG by Dyan Sheldon, ill. by Gary Blythe
(Hutchinson)

Guardian Award for Children's Fiction 📖

Given annually by *The Guardian* (119 Farringdon Road, London
EC1R 3ER, England), for an outstanding work of fiction for
children by a British or Commonwealth author, which was first
published in the United Kingdom during the preceding year. The
award is chosen by a panel of authors and *The Guardian*'s
children's books review editor. Picture books and previous
winners are excluded from consideration. In the listing below, the
year cited is the year in which the award was made. (£500)

1967
DEVIL-IN-THE-FOG by Leon Garfield *(Longman)*
1968
THE OWL SERVICE by Alan Garner *(Collins)*
1969
THE WHISPERING MOUNTAIN by Joan Aiken *(Cape)*
1970
FLAMBARDS (The Trilogy) by K. M. Peyton *(Oxford)*
1971
THE GUARDIANS by John Christopher *(Hamish Hamilton)*
1972
A LIKELY LAD by Gillian Avery *(Collins)*
1973
WATERSHIP DOWN by Richard Adams *(Rex Collings)*
1974
THE IRON LILY by Barbara Willard *(Longman)*
1975
GRAN AT COALGATE by Winifred Cawley *(Oxford)*
1976
THE PEPPERMINT PIG by Nina Bawden *(Gollancz)*
1977
THE BLUE HAWK by Peter Dickinson *(Gollancz)*
1978
A CHARMED LIFE by Diana Wynne Jones *(Macmillan)*

1979
CONRAD'S WAR by Andrew Davies *(Blackie)*
1980
THE VANDAL by Ann Schlee *(Macmillan)*
1981
THE SENTINELS by Peter Carter *(Oxford)*
1982
GOODNIGHT MISTER TOM by Michelle Magorian *(Kestrel)*
1983
THE VILLAGE BY THE SEA by Anita Desai *(Heinemann)*
1984
THE SHEEP-PIG by Dick King-Smith *(Gollancz)*
1985
WHAT IS THE TRUTH? by Ted Hughes *(Faber)*
1986
HENRY'S LEG by Ann Pilling *(Viking Kestrel)*
1987
THE TRUE STORY OF SPIT MacPHEE by James Aldridge
(Viking Kestrel)
1988
THE RUNAWAYS by Ruth Thomas *(Hutchinson)*
1989
A PACK OF LIES by Geraldine McCaughrean *(Oxford)*
1990
GOGGLE-EYES by Anne Fine *(Hamish Hamilton)*
1991
THE KINGDOM BY THE SEA by Robert Westall *(Methuen)*

Mary Vaughn Jones Award ✿

Mary Vaughn Jones was an outstanding contributor to Welsh
children's literature, and the author of nearly forty books. In
addition, her Welsh-language reading textbook *Sali Mali*
introduced the language to thousands of very young children,
selling nearly 40,000 copies in the last twenty years, a record for
a minority language book. She also translated English-language
books into Welsh, such as Tamasin Cole's *Fourteen Rats and a
Rat Catcher* and Pat Hutchins' *Rosie's Walk*. The award
honoring her is presented every three years to "a person who has
made an outstanding contribution to children's literature in the
Welsh language over a considerable period of time." The sponsor
is the Welsh National Centre for Children's Literature (Castell

Brychan, Heol y Bryn, Aberystwyth, Dyfed, Wales SY23 2JB).
(Silver trophy depicting characters from Mary Vaughn Jones'
books)

1985   Ifor Owen
1988   Emily Huws
1991   T. Llew Jones

Macmillan Prize
for a Children's Picture Book ❧

The object of this competition, sponsored by Pan Macmillan
Children's Books (Cavaye Place, London SW10 9PG, England) is
"to stimulate new work from young illustrators in art schools and
to help them start their professional lives." Working to a length
of 24 or 32 pages, art students in higher education establishments
in the UK submit portfolios that are judged by a distinguished
panel of illustrators and the Publishing Director of Macmillan's
Children's Books. Cash prizes for the winner and those placing
second and third in the competition are made; Macmillan
Children's Books has an option—not always exercised—to
publish any of the prize winners. (£750 for the first-place winner;
lesser amounts to other winners)

1986
SHH! IT'S THE SECRET CLUB by John Watson *(Macmillan)*
1987
BUSH VARK'S FIRST DAY OUT by Charles Fuge *(Macmillan)*
1988
ALPHABET CITY by Mark Hudson *(Macmillan)*
1989
A CLOSE CALL by Amanda Harvey *(Macmillan)*
1990
No first-place winner
1991
MY GRANDPA HAS BIG POCKETS by Selina Young
(Macmillan, 1993)

Kurt Maschler 'Emil' Award ❧

The award is for "a work of imagination in the children's field in
which text and illustration are of excellence and so presented that
each enhances yet balances the other." The award was established

by the founder of Atrium Press in Zurich, which published banned German writers in the 1930s. It honors Erich Kästner's *Emil und die Detektive*, illustrated by Walter Trier, and is administered by Book Trust (Book House, 45 East Hill, London SW18 2QZ, England). (£1,000 and bronze statuette of 'Emil')

1982
SLEEPING BEAUTY & OTHER FAVOURITE FAIRY TALES chosen by Angela Carter, ill. by Michael Foreman *(Gollancz)*
1983
GORILLA by Anthony Browne *(Julia MacRae)*
1984
GRANPA by John Burningham *(Cape)*
1985
THE IRON MAN by Ted Hughes, ill. by Andrew Davidson *(Faber)*
1986
THE JOLLY POSTMAN by Janet and Allan Ahlberg *(Heinemann)*
1987
JACK THE TREACLE EATER by Charles Causley, ill. by Charles Keeping *(Macmillan)*
1988
ALICE'S ADVENTURES IN WONDERLAND by Lewis Carroll, ill. by Anthony Browne *(Julia MacRae)*
1989
THE PARK IN THE DARK by Martin Waddell, ill. by Barbara Firth *(Walker)*
1990
ALL JOIN IN by Quentin Blake *(Cape)*
1991
HAVE YOU SEEN WHO'S JUST MOVED IN NEXT DOOR TO US? by Colin McNaughton *(Walker)*

Mother Goose Award ❧

Established in 1979 by bookseller Clodagh Corcoran, this award is presented in the spring to "the most exciting newcomer to British children's book illustration." Its sponsor and administrator is Books for Children (Whiteway Court, The Whiteway, Cirencester, Glos. GL7 2AN, England). Recipients are selected by a panel of illustrators and children's book specialists. (£1,000 and bronze egg)

1979
PIPPIN AND POD by Michelle Cartlidge *(Heinemann)*

1980
MR. POTTER'S PIGEON by Patrick Kinmouth, ill. by Reg Cartwright *(Hutchinson)*

1981
GREEN FINGER HOUSE by Rosemary Harris, ill. by Juan Wijngaard *(Eel Pie)*

1982
SUNSHINE by Jan Ormerod *(Kestrel)*

1983
ANGRY ARTHUR by Satoshi Kitamura *(Andersen)*

1984
THE HOB STORIES by William Mayne, ill. by Patrick Benson *(Walker)*

1985
BADGER'S PARTING GIFTS by Susan Varley *(Andersen)*

1986
No Award

1987
A BAG OF MOONSHINE selected by Alan Garner, ill. by Patrick James Lynch *(Collins)*

1988
LISTEN TO THIS compiled by Laura Cecil, ill. by Emma Chichester-Clark *(Bodley Head)*

1989
BUSH VARK'S FIRST DAY OUT by Charles Fuge *(Macmillan)*

1990
STRAT AND CHATTO by Jan Mark, ill. by David Hughes *(Walker)*

1991
A CLOSE CALL by Amanda Harvey *(Macmillan)*

Nottinghamshire Children's Book Awards 🌰

Organized by the Nottingham County Library Service (Education Library South, Glaisdale Parkway, Nottingham NG8 4GP, England) and the Dillons Bookstores, these awards aim to promote the enjoyment of reading. A shortlist of eight titles is selected by the County Children's Librarians; the list is widely publicized and voted on by "children, parents, teachers, librarians—in fact anyone who has an interest in children's books." Titles may be borrowed from libraries throughout the county, or purchased at Dillons. The Acorn Award *(A)* is for books for children up to 7; the Oak Tree Award *(O)* is for titles for readers 8-12. (£250 for each award, shared between the author and illustrator if they are not the same person)

1989
A: SIDNEY THE MONSTER by David Wood, ill. by Clive Scruton (Walker)
O: MATILDA by Roald Dahl (Cape)
1990
A: KNICKERLESS NICOLA by Kara May, ill. by Duffy Weir (Macmillan)
O: BILL'S NEW FROCK by Anne Fine (Methuen)
1991
A: THREADBEAR by Mick Inkpen (Hodder & Stoughton)
O: THE AFTERDARK PRINCESS by Annie Dalton (Methuen)

Other Award 🦢

This awards program, an activity begun by the Children's Rights Workshop, honored books of literary merit that children enjoy and that are progressive in their treatment of ethnic minorities, sex roles, and social differences. The award was discontinued after 1987. (Commendation)

1975
HAL by Jean MacGibbon (Heinemann)
JOE AND TIMOTHY TOGETHER by Dorothy Edwards (Methuen)
TWOPENCE A TUB by Susan Price (Faber)
1976
HELPERS by Shirley Hughes (Bodley Head)
NOBODY'S FAMILY IS GOING TO CHANGE by Louise Fitzhugh (Gollancz)
THE TROUBLE WITH DONOVAN CROFT by Bernard Ashley (Oxford)
1977
EAST END AT YOUR FEET by Farrukh Dhondy (Macmillan)
RAILWAYWORKER, HOSPITALWORKER, BUILDINGWORKER, and TEXTILEWORKER by Sarah Cox and Robert Golden (Kestrel)
THE TURBULENT TERM OF TYKE TILER by Gene Kemp (Faber)
1978
DISCOVERING AFRICA'S PAST by Basil Davidson (Longmans)
THE GOALKEEPER'S REVENGE by Bill Naughton (Puffin)
GYPSY FAMILY by Mary Waterson and Lance Brown (A. & C. Black)

SONG FOR A DARK QUEEN by Rosemary Sutcliff *(Pelham)*

1979
COME TO MECCA by Farrukh Dhondy *(Collins)*
A COMPREHENSIVE EDUCATION by Roger Mills *(Centerprise)*
OLD DOG, NEW TRICKS by Dick Cate *(Hamish Hamilton)*
TWO VICTORIAN FAMILIES by Sue Wagstaff *(A. & C. Black)*

1980
ABORIGINES by Virginia Luling *(Macdonald)*
THE GREEN BOUGH OF LIBERTY by David Rees *(Dobson)*
THE MACHINE BREAKERS by Angela Bull *(Collins)*
MRS. PLUG THE PLUMBER by Allan Ahlberg, ill. by Joe Wright *(Kestrel)*

1981
HAVE YOU STARTED YET? by Ruth Thomson *(Heinemann)*
A STRONG AND WILLING GIRL by Dorothy Edwards *(Methuen)*
THE TERRACED HOUSE BOOKS: SET D by Peter Heaslip and Anne Griffiths *(Methuen Educ.)*
WHAT IS A UNION? by Althea *(Dinosaur)*

1982
BLACK LIVES WHITE WORLDS by Keith Ajebo *(Cambridge)*
GIRLS ARE POWERFUL edited by Susan Hemmings *(Sheba)*
INTO THE PAST 1-4 by Sallie Purkis and Elizabeth Merson *(Longmans)*
WELCOME HOME, JELLYBEAN by Marlene Fanta Shyer *(Granada)*
WHEN THE WIND BLOWS by Raymond Briggs *(Hamish Hamilton)*

1983
EVERYBODY HERE! compiled by Michael Rosen *(Bodley Head)*
NOWHERE TO PLAY by Karusa *(A. & C. Black)*
TALKING IN WHISPERS by James Watson *(Gollancz)*
WILL OF IRON by Gerard Melia *(Longmans)*

1984
BROTHER IN THE LAND by Robert Swindells *(Oxford)*
A CHAIR FOR MY MOTHER by Vera B. Williams *(Julia MacRae)*
WHEEL AROUND THE WORLD edited by Chris Searle *(Macdonald)*
WHO LIES INSIDE by Timothy Ireland *(Gay Men's Press)*

1985
COALMINING WOMEN by Angela V. John *(Cambridge Educ.)*
COMFORT HERSELF by Geraldine Kaye *(Deutsch)*
JOURNEY TO JO'BURG by Beverley Naidoo *(Longman)*
MOTHERLAND by Elyse Dodgson *(Heinemann Educ.)*
OUR KIDS by Peckham Publishing Project *(community project)*
VILA by Sarah Baylis *(Brilliance)*

1986
THE BUS DRIVER by Anne Stewart, photog. by Chris Fairclough *(Hamish Hamilton)*
THE PEOPLE COULD FLY by Virginia Hamilton, ill. by Leo and Diane Dillon *(Walker)*
SAY IT AGAIN, GRANNY by John Agard, ill. by Susanna Gretz *(Bodley Head)*
STARRY NIGHT by Catherine Sefton *(Hamish Hamilton)*
1987
GRANDMA'S FAVOURITE, WHICH TEAM WINS?, WOK'S COOKING and CHAPATIS NOT CHIPS by Peter Heaslip *(Methuen)*
THE PALESTINIANS by David McDowall *(Watts)*
PUSH ME PULL ME by Sandra Chick *(Women's Press)*
Rosa Guy, for Overall Contribution to Literature for Teenagers

Quest for a Kelpie Competition ❧

This biennial manuscript competition "aims to encourage new children's writers who live in Scotland or those of Scottish birth residing elsewhere." Texts of 30,000-60,000 words for readers 8-12 years are eligible for consideration. A shortlist is submitted to a panel of six judges that selects the winning story, which is published and serialized by BBC Radio Scotland. The sponsors are BBC Scotland, Scottish Library Association, and Canongate Press (14 Frederick St., Edinburgh EH2 2HB, Scotland). (£1,000 advance against royalties on paperback edition of book)

1987
QUEST FOR A KELPIE by Frances Mary Hendry *(Canongate)*
1989
THE DARK SHADOW by Mary Rhind *(Canongate)*
1991
THE BAILIE'S DAUGHTER by Donald Lightwood *(Canongate)*

Science Book Prizes ❧

This program honors authors of popular nonfiction science and technology books written in English and first published in the United Kingdom "which are judged to contribute most to the public understanding of science." It is a joint project of the (British) Science Museum (The National Museum of Science & Industry) and the Committee on the Public Understanding of Science (COPUS), which administers the prize from The Royal Society (6 Carlton House Terrace, London SW1Y 5AG,

England). One prize is for a book for a general reading audience; another prize—listed below—is for "books aimed primarily at young people, i.e., under-14 year olds" (under-16 in 1989); while a third Discretionary Prize (DP) for books for readers under-8 may be given. (£10,000 as of 1991, with the sponsorship of the chemical company Rhône-Poulenc; a lesser amount for the Discretionary Prize)

1989
THE WAY THINGS WORK by David Macaulay *(Dorling Kindersley)*
1990
THE STARTING POINT SERIES (WHAT MAKES A FLOWER GROW?, WHAT MAKES IT RAIN?, WHAT'S UNDER THE GROUND?, and WHERE DOES ELECTRICITY COME FROM?) by Susan Mayes *(Usborne)*
DP: THE GIANT BOOK OF SPACE by Ian Ridpath *(Hamlyn)*
1991
CELLS ARE US and CELL WARS by Fran Balkwill and Mic Rolph *(HarperCollins)*

Signal Poetry Award ❧

Intended to honor excellence in a variety of areas associated with poetry for children, the award has been presented to single-poet collections published for children, and to poetry anthologies published for children. The award is given for work published in the preceding year in Britain, regardless of the original country of publication. The sponsor is the journal *Signal: Approaches to Children's Books* (The Thimble Press, Lockwood, Station Road, South Woodchester, Stroud, Glos. GL5 5EQ, England). In its May issue each year, *Signal* includes lively reports from its award's judges; the pieces—even in a year when the award is not given—constitute a first-class critical retrospective of the year in poetry for children in Britain. (£100 and Certificate)

1979
MOON-BELLS AND OTHER POEMS by Ted Hughes *(Chatto)*
1980-1991
No Awards
1982
YOU CAN'T CATCH ME! by Michael Rosen, ill. by Quentin Blake *(Deutsch)*
(Poet and illustrator shared the award.)
1983
THE RATTLE BAG edited by Seamus Heaney and Ted Hughes *(Faber)*

1984
SKY IN THE PIE by Roger McGough *(Kestrel)*
1985
WHAT IS THE TRUTH? by Ted Hughes *(Faber)*
1986
SONG OF THE CITY by Gareth Owen *(Fontana)*
1987
EARLY IN THE MORNING by Charles Causley *(Viking Kestrel)*
1988
BOO TO A GOOSE by John Mole *(Peterloo Poets)*
1989
WHEN I DANCE by James Berry *(Hamish Hamilton)*
1990
HEARD IT IN THE PLAYGROUND by Allan Ahlberg *(Viking Kestrel)*
1991
THIS POEM DOESN'T RHYME edited by Gerald Benson *(Viking)*

Smarties Book Prize ❧

The Smarties Book Prize is designed to encourage high standards and stimulate interest in children's books. Prizes are given in three categories; one of the three category winners receives a Grand Prize. Winners are selected from a shortlist of 15 titles, 5 in each category. A knowledgeable panel—currently numbering five persons—selects titles for a shortlist widely publicized throughout the UK. The panel is assisted by ten students—"Young Judges"—in selecting the winners. The prize is administered by Book Trust (Book House, 45 East Hill, London SW18 2QZ, England) and sponsored by Rowntree Mackintosh Confectionery Ltd., manufacturers of numerous taste treats for children, including "Smarties," multicolored chocolate beans that are described as the "number one confectionery line in the UK." (£8,000 to Grand Prize winner; £1,000 to winners in other two categories)

1985
Grand Prize + over 7's: GAFFER SAMSON'S LUCK by Jill Paton Walsh *(Viking Kestrel)*
7's and under: IT'S YOUR TURN, ROGER! by Susanna Gretz *(Bodley Head)*
Innovation: WATCH IT WORK! THE PLANE by Ray Marshall and John Bradley *(Viking Kestrel)*

1986

Grand Prize + 7's to 11's: THE SNOW SPIDER by Jenny
Nimmo *(Methuen)*

6's and under: THE GOOSE THAT LAID THE GOLDEN EGG
retold and ill. by Geoffrey Patterson *(Deutsch)*

Innovation (joint winner): THE MIRRORSTONE by Michael
Palin, Alan Lee and Richard Seymour *(Cape)*

Innovation (joint winner): VILLAGE HERITAGE by Miss Pinnell
and the Children of Sapperton School *(Alan Sutton)*

1987

Grand Prize + 9's to 11's: A THIEF IN THE VILLAGE by
James Berry *(Hamish Hamilton)*

5's and under: THE ANGEL AND THE SOLDIER BOY by
Peter Collington *(Methuen)*

6's to 8's: TANGLE AND THE FIRESTICKS by Benedict
Blathwayt *(Julia MacRae)*

1988

Grand Prize + 5's and under: CAN'T YOU SLEEP LITTLE
BEAR? by Martin Waddell, ill. by Barbara Firth *(Walker)*

6's to 8's: CAN IT BE TRUE? by Susan Hill, ill. by Angela
Barrett *(Hamish Hamilton)*

9's to 11's: RUSHAVENN TIME by Theresa Whistler
(Brixworth Primary School)

1989

Grand Prize + 5's and under: WE'RE GOING ON A BEAR
HUNT by Michael Rosen, ill. by Helen Oxenbury *(Walker)*

6's to 8's: BILL'S NEW FROCK by Anne Fine *(Methuen)*

9's to 11's: BLITZCAT by Robert Westall *(Macmillan)*

1990

Grand Prize + 9's to 11's: MIDNIGHT BLUE by Pauline Fisk
(Lion)

5's and under: SIX DINNER SID by Inga Moore *(Simon &*
Schuster)

6's to 8's: ESIO TROT by Roald Dahl, ill. by Quentin Blake
(Cape)

1991

Grand Prize + 5's and under: FARMER DUCK by Martin
Waddell, ill. by Helen Oxenbury *(Walker)*

6's to 8's: JOSIE SMITH by Magdalen Nabb, ill. by Pirkko
Vainio *(HarperCollins)*

9's to 11's: KRINDLEKRAX by Philip Ridley *(Cape)*

W. H. Smith Illustration Awards 🐌

This program continues the Francis Williams Illustration Awards
program designed to "encourage and advance the art of book
illustration." Formerly, the award was given at five-year intervals.

It covered work published in a period between awards, and was given in five categories. Currently, the program is an annual one, with a Premier Prize that may be for either book or magazine work published in the previous year, while two Second Prizes are given for books and magazines. The award submissions form the basis of an annual exhibition at the Victoria and Albert Museum. The award sponsor, W. H. Smith, is a prominent book and magazine retail chain in the UK; the program is administered by Book Trust (Book House, 45 East Hill, London SW18 2QZ, England). In the listing below, winners of the Premier Prize, only, are cited, and then only if the work honored is a children's book. (£3,000 to winner; £1,000 to Second Prize winners)

1968-1972
Michael Foreman, for THE GREAT SLEIGH ROBBERY *(Hamish Hamilton, 1968)* and HORATIO *(Hamish Hamilton, 1969)*

1972-1977
John Laurence, for RABBIT AND PORK *(Hamish Hamilton, 1975)*

1977-1982
Raymond Briggs, for THE SNOWMAN *(Hamish Hamilton, 1978)*

1982-1987
(Premier Prize for adult book)

1988
Charles Keeping, for CHARLES KEEPING'S CLASSIC TALES OF THE MACABRE *(Blackie)*

1989
(Premier Prize for magazine cover)

1990
John Vernon Lord, for AESOP'S FABLES retold by James Michie *(Cape)*

Times Educational Supplement Information Book Awards ❧

Established in 1972 by the *Times Educational Supplement* (Priory House, St. John's Lane, London EC1, England), this award is given for distinction in content and presentation in informational (nonfiction) trade books originated in the United Kingdom or Commonwealth countries. Two panels of three judges each, together with the Editor of the *Times Educational Supplement*, select the winners. Since 1973 awards have been offered for books in both Junior (up to age 9), *J* in the listing below, and

Senior (ages 10-16), *S* in the listing below, categories. (£500 to the winner in each category; £250 to illustrator if appropriate)

1972
INTRODUCING ARCHAEOLOGY by Magnus Magnusson
(Bodley Head)

1973
J: No Award
S: HUMAN POPULATIONS by David Hay *(Penguin)*

1974
J: FROGS, TOADS AND NEWTS by F.D. Ommaney *(Bodley Head)*
S: UNDERSTANDING ART by Betty Churcher *(Holmes McDougall)*

1975
J: SPIDERS by Ralph Whitlock *(Priory)*
S: WINDOW INTO A NEST by Geraldine Lux-Flanagan and Sean Morris *(Kestrel)*

1976
J: WASH AND BRUSH UP by Eleanor Allen *(A. & C. Black)*
S: MACDONALD'S ENCYCLOPEDIA OF AFRICA *(Macdonald Educ.)*

1977
J: STREET FLOWERS by Richard Mabey *(Kestrel)*
S: MEN AND MACHINES. THE MITCHELL BEAZLEY JOY OF KNOWLEDGE LIBRARY *(Mitchell Beazley)*

1978
J: TOURNAMENTS by Richard Barber *(Kestrel)*
S: BUTTERFLIES ON MY MIND by Dulcie Gray *(Angus & Robertson)*

1979
J: THE COMMON FROG by George Bernard *(Oxford Scientific Films/Whizzard/Deutsch)*
S: MAKE IT HAPPY: WHAT SEX IS ALL ABOUT by Jane Cousins *(Virago)*

1980
J: EARTHQUAKES AND VOLCANOES by Imelda and Robert Updegraff *(Methuen)*
S: OXFORD JUNIOR ENCYCLOPEDIA OF MUSIC by Michael Hurd *(Oxford)*

1981
J: No Award
S: SKULLS by Richard Steel *(Heinemann)*

1982
J: A DAY WITH A MINER by Phillippa Aston *(Wayland)*
S: THE EASY WAY TO BIRD RECOGNITION by John Kilbracken *(Kingfisher)*

1983

J: MUM—I FEEL FUNNY by Ann McPherson and Aidan Macfarlane *(Chatto)*

S: DEFENCE by Charles Freeman *(Batsford)*

JUST IMAGINE by Robert Cumming *(Kestrel)*

1984

J: No Award

S: IN DEUTSCHLAND by Rod Nash *(Nelson)*

1985

J: KWAZULU SOUTH AFRICA by Nancy Durrell McKenna *(A. & C. Black)*

S (joint winner): GROWING UP, ADOLESCENCE BODY CHANGES AND SEX by Susan Meredith *(Usborne)*

S (joint winner): THE SUNDAY TIMES COUNTRYSIDE COMPANION by Geoffrey Young *(Country Life)*

1986

J: THE YOUNG GEOGRAPHER INVESTIGATES POLAR REGIONS by Terry Jennings *(Oxford)*

S: THE LEGEND OF ODYSSEUS by Peter Connolly *(Oxford)*

1987

J: BEING BORN by Sheila Kitzinger, ill. with photographs by Lennart Nilsson *(Dorling Kindersley)*

S (joint winner): GALAXIES AND QUASARS by Heather Couper and Nigel Henbest *(Watts)*

S (joint winner): THE ULTIMATE ALPHABET by Mike Wilks *(Pavilion)*

1988

J (joint winner): CONKER by Barrie Watts *(A. & C. Black)*

J (joint winner): MAKING A BOOK by Ruth Thomson *(Watts)*

S: MARTIN LUTHER KING by Pam Brown and Valerie Scheldt *(Exley)*

1989

J: WHY DO PEOPLE SMOKE? by Pete Sanders *(Watts)*

S: THE WAY THINGS WORK by David Macaulay *(Dorling Kindersley)*

1990

J: THE TREE by Judy Hindley, ill. by Alison Wisenfeld *(ABC)*

S: THE NEW OXFORD SCHOOL ATLAS edited by Patrick Wiegand *(Oxford)*

1991

J: IAN AND FRED'S BIG GREEN BOOK by Fred Pearce and Ian Winton *(Kingfisher/Bennett)*

S: AN EGYPTIAN PYRAMID by Jacqueline Morley *(Simon & Schuster)*

Tir na n-Og Awards 🐚

Sponsored by the Welsh National Centre for Children's Literature (Castell Brychan, Heol-y-Bryn, Aberystwyth, Dyfed, Wales SY23 2JB), the "purpose of the Tir na n-Og Awards is to acknowledge the work of authors and illustrators; to raise the standard of writing for children and young people; and to encourage book buying and reading...." Currently, there are awards in three categories: for Fiction (F), original Welsh-language novels, stories, and picture books; for Other (O) outstanding Welsh-language books of the year, but not translations produced overseas; and for the best English-language (E) book with an authentic Welsh background. (A total of £1,000 in prize money is available for the awards, with no more than £500 to a single honoree; prizes donated by Welsh Arts Council and the Welsh Joint Education Committee)

1976
F: TÂN AR Y COMIN by T. Llew Jones (Gomer)
E: THE GREY KING by Susan Cooper (Chatto)

1977
F: TRYSOR BRYNIAU CASPAR by J. Selwyn Lloyd (Gomer)
E: A STRING IN THE HARP by Nancy Bond (McElderry)

1978
F: MIRIAM by Jane Edwards (Gomer)
E: SILVER ON THE TREE by Susan Cooper (Chatto)

1979
F: Y FLWYDDYN HONNO by Dyddgu Owen (Christopher Davies)
E: TIME CIRCLES by Bette Meyrick (Abelard)

1980
F: Y LLONG by Irma Chilton (Gomer)
E: No Award

1981
F: Y DRUDWY DEWR by Gweneth Lilly (Gomer)
E: THE BLINDFOLD TRACK by Frances Thomas (Macmillan)

1982
F: GAEAF Y CERRIG by Gweneth Lilly (Gomer)
E: No Award

1983
F: CROES BREN YN NORWY by J. Selwyn Lloyd (Gomer)
E: BLUESTONES by Mary John (Barn Owl Press)

1984
F (joint winner): Y LLINYN ARIAN by Mair Wynn Hughes (Gomer)
F (joint winner): HERIO'R CERTYLL by Malcolm M. Jones, Cyril Jones, and Gwen Redvers Jones (Gwasg Prifysgol Cymru)

E: THE PRIZE by Irma Chilton *(Barn Owl Press)*

1985

No Awards

1986

F: Y LLIPRYN LLWYD by Angharad Tomos *(Y Lolfa)*
E: THE REGION OF THE SUMMER STARS by Frances Thomas *(Barn Owl Press)*

1987

F: JABAS by Penri Jones *(Dwyfor)*
0: GARDD O GERDDI by Alun Jones and J. Pinion Jones *(Gomer)*
E: THE SNOW SPIDER by Jenny Nimmo *(Methuen)*

1988

F: TYDI BYWYD YN BOEN! by Gwenno Hywyn *(Gwynedd)*
0: YR ATLAS CYMRAEG (no editor/compiler attribution; translates as *The Welsh Atlas*) *(George Philip)*
E: STEEL TOWN CATS by Celia Lucas *(Tabb House)*

1989

F (joint winner): LIW by Irma Chilton *(Gomer)*
F (joint winner, for illustration): BEN Y GARDDWR A STORIAU ERAILL by Jac Jones *(Cymdeithas Lyfrau Ceredigion)*
0: CULHWCH AC OLWEN by Gwyn Thomas and Margaret Thomas *(Gwasg Prifysgol Cymru)*
E: No Award

1990

F: LLYGEDYN O HEULWEN by Mair Wynn Hughes *(Gomer)*
0: LLEUAD YN OLAU by T. Llew Jones, ill. by Jac Jones *(Gomer)*
F: No Award

1991

F: O DDAWNS I DDAWNS by Gareth F. Williams *(Lolfa)*
0: CYMRU, DDOE A HEDDIW by Geraint H. Jenkins *(Prifysgol)*
E: No Award

Whitbread Book of the Year 🦢
CHILDREN'S BOOK CATEGORY

Initiated in 1971, a children's book category became part of this program in 1972. It was the intention of the founders of the award "to acknowledge outstanding books in particular categories of literature not only for the qualities accorded to them by the critics of the day, but for popular qualities which in the opinion of the judges make them readable on a wide scale." Currently, the categoies are Novel, First Novel, Poetry, Biography/ Autobiography, and Children's Novel. Whitbread, sponsor of the award, is a prominent brewery in the UK; the administrator of the program is The Booksellers Association of Great Britain and Ireland (272 Vauxhall Bridge Road, London SW1V 1BA). Panels of knowledgeable judges pick shortlists and winners for each category. Judges representing each of the categories are joined by some others prominent in the arts to select the winning title from the top titles in each catetory. The listing below includes only winners in the children's book category. (£2,000 to winner in each category; Book of the Year receives total of £22,500)

1972
THE DIDDAKOI by Rumer Godden *(Macmillan)*
1973
THE BUTTERFLY BALL AND THE GRASSHOPPER'S FEAST by Alan Aldridge and William Plomer *(Cape)*
1974 (joint winners)
HOW TOM BEAT CAPTAIN NAJORK AND HIS HIRED SPORTSMEN by Russell Hoban, ill. by Quentin Blake *(Cape)*
THE EMPEROR'S WINDING SHEET by Jill Paton Walsh *(Macmillan)*
1975
Category not included in program
1976
A STITCH IN TIME by Penelope Lively *(Heinemann)*
1977
NO END TO YESTERDAY by Shelagh Macdonald *(Deutsch)*
1978
THE BATTLE OF BUBBLE AND SQUEAK by Philippa Pearce, ill. by Alan Baker *(Deutsch)*
1979
TULKU by Peter Dickinson *(Gollancz)*
1980
JOHN DIAMOND by Leon Garfield *(Kestrel)*
1981
THE HOLLOW LAND by Jane Gardam *(Julia MacRae)*
1982
THE SONG OF PENTECOST by W. J. Corbett *(Methuen)*
1983
THE WITCHES by Roald Dahl *(Cape)*
1984
THE QUEEN OF THE PHARISEES' CHILDREN by Barbara Willard *(Julia MacRae)*

1985
THE NATURE OF THE BEAST by Janni Howker *(Julia MacRae)*
1986
THE COAL HOUSE by Andrew Taylor *(Collins)*
1987
A LITTLE LOWER THAN THE ANGELS by Geraldine McCaughrean *(Oxford)*
1988
AWAITING DEVELOPMENTS by Judy Allen *(Julia MacRae)*
1989
WHY WEEPS THE BROGAN? by Hugh Scott *(Walker)*
1990
AK by Peter Dickinson *(Gollancz)*
1991
HARVEY ANGELL by Diana Hendry *(Julia MacRae)*

Young Observer Teenage Fiction Prize 🙰

Sponsored by the newspaper *The Observer*, this awards program was "devised to encourage writers and publishers to provide a wider range of reading material for the teenage market." It was discontinued as of the 1987 award year.

1981
MOSES BEECH by Ian Strachan *(Oxford)*
1982 (joint winners)
AQUARIUS by Jan Mark *(Kestrel)*
THE WATCHER BEE by Mary Melwood *(Deutsch)*
1983
CHILDREN OF THE BOOK by Peter Carter *(Oxford)*
1984
A LITTLE FEAR by Patricia Wrightson *(Hutchinson)*
1985
THE NATURE OF THE BEAST by Janni Howker *(Julia MacRae)*
1986
BURY THE DEAD by Peter Carter *(Oxford)*
1987
MEMORY by Margaret Mahy *(Dent)*

PART IV ❧

Selected International and Multinational Awards

Hans Christian Andersen Awards ❧

Given biennially since 1956 by the International Board on Books for Young People (Nonnenweg 12, Postfach, CH-4003, Basel, Switzerland) to one author and one illustrator (since 1966) in recognition of his or her entire body of work. (Medals)
See also International Board on Books for Young People (IBBY) Honor List

1956
Eleanor Farjeon *(Great Britain)*

1958
Astrid Lindgren *(Sweden)*

1960
Erich Kästner *(Germany: Federal Republic)*

1962
Meindert DeJong *(USA)*

1964
René Guillot *(France)*

1966
Author: Tove Jansson *(Finland)*
Illustrator: Alois Carigiet *(Switzerland)*

1968
Authors: James Krüss *(Germany: Federal Republic)*
José Maria Sanchez-Silva *(Spain)*
Illustrator: Jiří Trnka *(Czechoslovakia)*

1970
Author: Gianni Rodari *(Italy)*
Illustrator: Maurice Sendak *(USA)*

1972
Author: Scott O'Dell *(USA)*
Illustrator: Ib Spang Olsen *(Denmark)*

1974
Author: Maria Gripe *(Sweden)*
Illustrator: Farshid Mesghali *(Iran)*

1976
Author: Cecil Bødker *(Denmark)*
Illustrator: Tatjana Mawrina *(USSR)*

1978
Author: Paula Fox (USA)
Illustrator: Svend Otto S. *(Denmark)*

1980
Author: Bohumil Ríha *(Czechoslovakia)*
Illustrator: Suekichi Akaba *(Japan)*

1982
Author: Lygia Bojunga Nunes *(Brazil)*
Illustrator: Zbigniew Rychlicki *(Poland)*

1984
Author: Christine Nöstlinger *(Austria)*
Illustrator: Mitsumasa Anno *(Japan)*

1986
Author: Patricia Wrightson *(Australia)*
Illustrator: Robert Ingpen *(Australia)*

1988
Author: Annie M. G. Schmidt *(Holland)*
Illustrator: Dûsan Kállay *(Czechoslovakia)*

1990
Author: Tormod Haugen *(Norway)*
Illustrator: Lisbeth Zwerger *(Austria)*

1992
Author: Virginia Hamilton *(USA)*
Illustrator: Kveta Pacovská *(Czechoslovakia)*

Award for Writing Children's Books in German ❧

Sponsored by the Austrian Ministry for Education, Art, and Sports, this biennial awards program honors the most outstanding books for children *(C)* and young adults *(Y/A)* originally written in German. The International Board on Books for Young People (IBBY) National Sections in Austria, Germany, and Switzerland may enter up to five candidates for each award. A jury comprised of experts from the participating IBBY sections selects the winners, and also an Honor List.

1985
C: LIPPELS TRAUM (Lipple's Dream) by Paul Maar *(Oetinger, Germany: Federal Republic)*
Y/A: WIE IN FREMDEN SCHUHEN (Like Being in Someone Else's Shoes) by Renate Welsh *(Jungbrunnen, Austria)*

1987
C: DER HUND KOMMT! (Here Comes the Dog!) by Christine
Nöstlinger (Beltz & Gelberg, Germany: Federal Republic, and
Switzerland; N. B. author is Austrian)
Y/A:
WIE EIN ROSTIGER NAGEL IM BRETT ODER: DIE
ZWEITE FLUCHT (Like a Rusty Nail in a Board or: The
Second Escape) by Hanna Lehnert (Anrich, Germany: Federal
Republic)
1989
C: DRACHENFLÜGEL (Dragon's Wings) by Renate Welsh
(Obelisk, Austria)
Y/A: PLASCHA ODER: VON KLEINEN LEUTEN UND
GROSSEN TRÄUMEN (Plascha or: Of Little People and Big
Dreams) by Inge Meyer-Dietrich (Anrich, Germany: Federal
Republic)

Biennale of Illustrations Bratislava ❧

The Biennale of Illustrations Bratislava (BIB) is an international
competition and exposition of original children's book
illustrations that have been published in book format. It takes
place in September-October of odd-numbered years in the Slovak
city of Bratislava, and typically includes around 3,000
illustrations from over fifty countries worldwide; it is probably
the best single-site source available for studying trends in
children's book illustration internationally. BIB is organized and
administered from Bibiana (Dobsinského nám. 1, 81349
Bratislava, Czechoslovakia), itself a study center and museum
gallery devoted to children's book illustration. Our listing
includes only the recipients of the Grand Prix. (One Grand Prix,
five Golden Apples, ten Plaques, Honorable Mentions, and other
honors; many winners also receive stipends of various amounts)

1967
TARO AND A BAMBOO SHOOT by Masaku Matsuno, ill. by
Yasuo Segawa (Fukuinkan Shoten, Tokyo, Japan)
1969
CHINESISCHE VOLKSMARCHEN by Eva Bednářová (Artia,
Prague, Czechoslovakia)
1971
NARZECOZONY Z MORZA by Robert Stieler, ill. by Ardrezej
Strumitto (Nasza Ksiegarnia, Warsaw, Poland)

1973
DER TRAUMMACHER by Leiselotte Schwarz *(Verlag Heinrich Ellermann, Munich, Germany: Federal Republic)*
1975
ROBINSON CRUSOE by Daniel Defoe, ill. by Nikolaj Popov *(Chudozestvenaja Literatura, Moscow, USSR)*
1977
HARLEKIN by Ulf Löfgren *(Awe/Gebbers, Stockholm, Sweden)*
1979
DER KLEINE DÄUMLING by Klaus Ensikat *(Der Kinderbuchverlag, Berlin, Germany: Democratic Republic)*
TAIPI by Klaus Ensikat *(Verlag Neues Leben, Berlin, Germany: Democratic Republic)*
1981
KRISTOFFERS REJSE by Roald Als *(Borgen, Copenhagen, Denmark)*
1983
ALICA V KRAJINE ZÁZRAKOV by Dušan Kállay *(Mladé leta, Bratislava, Czechoslovakia)*
1985
BESTIARE FABLEUX by C. Meral, ill. by Frédéric Clément *(Editions Magnard, Paris, France)*
1987
HERRA KUNINGAS by Raija Siekkinen, ill. by Hannu Taina *(Otava, Helsinki, Finland)*
1989
KSIEGA BAJEK POLSKICH by Marian Murawski *(Ludowa Spóldzielnia Wydawnicza, Warsaw, Poland)*
1991
DER GESTIEFELTE KATER by Stasys Eidrigevicious *(Nord-Süd, Gossau, Switzerland; N. B. illustrator is Polish)*

Bologna Children's Book Fair Prizes &

Given annually in the spring at the Bologna Children's Book Fair (Piazza Della Constituzione 6, 40128 Bologna, Italy) by the Bologna Fair Organization in three categories: "Fiera di Bologna" Graphic Prize for Children, Graphic Prize for Youth, "Critici in Erba" prize. The first two prizes are decided upon by a committee of adults appointed by the Bologna Fair Organization; the third prize is judged by a committee of children selected by school authorities from schools in Bologna. Participation in the competition is open to all Italian and foreign publishers displaying their books, individually or collectively, at the Bologna Children's Book Fair. As the prizes we list in this edition are actually awarded to the publisher of the winning work, only publishers' names are listed after the titles below. (Golden plate)

C—"Fiera di Bologna" Graphic Prize for Children; Y—Graphic Prize for Youth; C/E—"Critici in Erba"

1966
C: GESU OGGI *(Rizzoli, Italy)*
C/E: L'ALBUM DE BAMBI *(Bias, France)*

1967
C: DREI VÖGEL *(Otto Maier, Germany: Federal Republic)*
Y: DIE ALTE LINDE GONDULA *(Sigbert Mohn, Germany: Federal Republic)*
C/E: ICH SCHENK DIR EINEN PAPAGEI *(Diogenes, Switzerland)*

1968
C: DIE WICHTELMÄNNER *(Atlantis, Switzerland)*
Y: PRIBEHY *(Albatros, Czechoslovakia)*
C/E: ALLA SCOPERTA DELL 'AFRICA *(Vallecchi, Italy)*

1969
C: THE LITTLE BLACK FISH *(Institute for the Intellectual Development of Children and Young Adults, Iran)*
Y: LA CITÉ DE L'AN 2000 *(Casterman, France)*
C/E: POCAHONTAS IN LONDON *(Seymour Lawrence, USA)*

1970
C: 1, 2, 3, EIN ZUG ZUM ZOO *(Stalling, Germany: Federal Republic)*
Y: VERTEL HET UW KINDEREN *(Nederlandsche Zondacs-School Vereniging, Holland)*
C/E: LA STORIA DAI FRANCESCO E CHIARA "RACCONTATA DAI BIMBI DE CROCE" *(Stadiv l'Aquila, Italy)*

1971
C: ARM IN ARM *(Parents, USA)*
Y: TUTTO SU GERUSALEMME BIBLICA *(C.E. Giunti-Bemporad Marzocco, Italy)*
C/E: ALLE MEINE BLÄTTER...*(Gertraud Middlehauve, Germany: Federal Republic)*

1972
C: STADTMAUS UND LANDMAUS *(Atlantis, Switzerland)*
Y: SLAVISCHE MÄRCHEN *(Artia, Czechoslovakia)*
C/E: WALTZING MATILDA *(Collins, Great Britain)*

1973
C: KOPFBLUMEN *(Der Kinderbuchverlag, Germany: Democratic Republic)*

Y: HODINA NACHOVE RUZE *(Albatros, Czechoslovakia)*
C/E: SNOW-WHITE AND THE SEVEN DWARFS *(Farrar, USA)*

1974
C: ROTKÄPPCHEN *(Diogenes, Switzerland)*
Y: THE LAST OF THE MOHICANS *(Felix Gluck, England)*
C/E: A YEAR IN THE WOODS *(Detskaya Literatura, USSR)*

1975
C: TROIS PETITS FLOCONS *(Grasset, France)*
Y: DAS SPRACHBASTELBUCH *(Jugend und Volk Verlagsges, Austria)*
C/E: IL PRINCIPE FELICE *(Paoline, Italy)*

1976
C: MAGIC FOR SALE *(Kaisei-Sha, Japan)*
Y: THE BRONZE HORSEMAN *(Detskaya Literatura, USSR)*
C/E: DAS GELBE HAUS *(Carlsen, Germany: Federal Republic)*

1977
C: SCHORSCHI SCHRUMPFT *(Diogenes, Switzerland)*
Y: TAKERU *(Kaisei-Sha, Japan)*
C/E: DIE GESCHICHTE VON BABAR DEM KLEINEN ELEFANTEN *(Diogenes, Switzerland)*

1978
C: GRABIANSKIS STADTMUSIKANTEN *(Carl Ueberreuter, Austria)*
Y: ANNO'S UNIQUE WORLD *(Kodansha, Japan)*
C/E: NICHOLAS AND THE MOON EGGS *(Collins, Australia)*

1979
C: HISTOIRE DU PETIT STEPHAN GIRARD *(Gallimard, France)*
Y: AURORA *(Dalla Parte delle Bambine, Italy)*
C/E: EIN TAG IM LEBEN DER DOROTHEA WUTZ *(Diogenes, Switzerland)*

1980
C: ANNO'S SONG BOOK *(Kodansha, Japan)*
Y: HIMMELSZELT UND SCHNECKENHAUS *(Sauerländer, Switzerland)*
C/E: DAS BUCH VOM DORF *(Fabula, Germany: Federal Republic)*

1981
C: YOK-YOK *(Gallimard, France)*
Y: L'UNIVERS A DEUX VOIX: INSECTE *(La Noria, France)*
C/E: MR. SQUINT *(World's Work, Great Britain)*

1982
C: LES SECRETS DE L'IMAGE *(Gallimard, France)*
Y: CITY OF GOLD AND OTHER STORIES FROM THE OLD TESTAMENT *(Gollancz, Great Britain)*
C/E: THE PIXIES' INVITATION *(Kaisei-Sha, Japan)*

1983
C: THE FAVERSHAMS *(Gollancz, Great Britain)*
Y: IL ÉTAIT UNE FOIS LES MOTS *(La Farandole/Messidor, France)*
C/E: OUR CHANGING WORLD *(Collins, Great Britain)*

1984
C: LE PETIT CHAPERON ROUGE *(Grasset, France, and Creative, USA)*
Y: ALENKA KRAJI DIVU *(Albatros, Czechoslovakia)*
C/E: MAME'S CATS, 1, 2, 3 *(Kaisei-Sha, Japan)*

1985
C: LEAVES *(Institute for the Intellectual Development of Children and Young Adults, Iran)*
Y: UNTITLED CHILDREN'S STORY (N.B. This is the title of a book by Kit Williams) *(Cape, Great Britain)*
C/E: SOL SOLET *(Edicions de l'Eixample, Spain)*

1986
C: ONE MORNING *(G. C. Press, Japan)*
Y: DER HUT DES KAMINFEGERS *(Basilius, Switzerland)*
C/E: PETER UND DER WOLF *(Sauerlander, Switzerland)*

1987
C: THE GREAT GAMES BOOK *(Black, Great Britain)*
Y: DÉCOUVERTES GALLIMARD *(Gallimard, France)*
C/E: THAT'S MY DAD *(Andersen, Great Britain)*

1988
C: ANIMAL NUMBERS *(Lutterworth, Great Britain)*
Y: LE LIVRE DE LA CRÉATION *(Centurion, France)*
C/E: DIE BLUMENSTADT *(Bohem, Switzerland)*

1989
C: A LONG LONG SONG *(Farrar, USA)*
Y: LES YEUX DE LA DÉCOUVERTE *(Gallimard, France)*
C/E: DEAR MILI *(Farrar, USA)*

1990
C: MIJN HELD *(Querido, Holland)*
Y: DIE GESCHICHTE VON DER KLEINEN GANS, DIE NICHT SCHNELL GENUG WAR *(Nagel & Kimche, Switzerland)*
C/E: A FROG PRINCE *(Holt, USA)*

1991
C: AN ALPHABET OF ANIMALS *(HarperCollins, Great Britain)*
Y: RUE DE LA MÉDITERRANEE *(Hatier/Ragéot, France)*
C/E: KLEINER EISBÄR NIMM MICH MIT! *(Nord-Süd, Switzerland)*

1992
C: OH! *(Rainbow Graphics International/Baronian Books, Belgium)*

Y: "JEDER NACH SEINER ART": KINDERLIEDER VON HOFFMANN VON FALLERSIEBEN *(Beltz & Gelberg, Germany)*
C/E: IRIS *(Aura Comunicación, Spain)*

Premi Catalònia d'Il·lustració 🐚

The Catalonian Prize for Illustration is awarded at a biennial exhibit and competition of original art from published children's books. The event takes place in Barcelona, Spain, and is cosponsored by the Departament de Cultura de la Generalitat de Catalunya, the Consell Català del Libre per a Infants, and by the Fundació de l'Enciclopèdia Catalana, in cooperation with l'Associació d'Editors en Llengua Catalana and l'Associació Professional d'Il·lustradors. The prize is designed to honor "the best illustrations for children's books published anywhere in the world...." In addition to a Grand Prize, the international jury also selects three Plaque and five Diploma recipients. (Sculpture and stipend)

1984
LA LLUNA D'EN JOAN (Joan's Moon) by Carmen Solé i Vendrell *(Spain)*
1986
Z PROWROTEM (The Shelter) by Stasys Eidrigevičius *(Poland)*
1988
THREE CATS by Kvéta Pacovská *(Czechoslovakia)*
1990
EL GUARDIÁN DEL OLVIDO (Olvido's Keeper) by Alfonso Ruano *(Spain)*

European Award of Literature for Children and Young Adults 🐚

Four European publishers—Ediciones B of Spain, Arena Verlag of Germany, Éditions L'Amitié of France, and HarperCollins of the U. K. (c/o HarperCollins Children's Books, 77-85 Fulham Palace Rd., Hammersmith, London W6 8JB, England)—sponsor a projected annual competition "aimed at promoting excellence in writing for young readers between the ages of 8-16 within the EEC." The winning manuscript will be published by the four sponsors. (£10,700 plus publication; a runner-up receives a £2,200 prize)

1991
No first place winner

European Prize for Children's Literature "Pier Paolo Vergerio"

The Premio Europeo di Letteratura Giovanile is designed to honor the best works of European literature that help "to evaluate our culture and civilization...to point out a true humanistic way of development for new generations." In addition to singling out the winner of the European Prize, this program — judged by a European-wide jury — gives prizes for "illustrated albums," poetry, "school literature," and historical fiction, and also includes an Honor List of titles recommended for translation into all European languages. The administrator is Settore Letteratura Giovanil Dipartimento Scienze Educazione, Universita di Padova (via Marsala 59, 35122, Padova, Italia). (3,000,000 lira)

1962
LES ENFANTS DE LA TERRE *(The Children of the Earth)* by Père Castor *(Paul Faucher) (France)*
STORIE MERAVIGLIOSE DEGLI ANIMALI IN PARADISO *(Wonderful Stories of Animals In Paradise)* by Aldo Alberti *(Italy)*

1964
THE PUFFIN BOOK OF NURSERY RHYMES by Iona and Peter Opie *(Great Britain)*
MISTER MASTER by Donatella Ziliotto *(Italy)*

1966
LES CANONS DE VALMY *(The Cannons of Valmy)* by Léonce Bourliaguet *(France)*

1968
CARLA DEGLI SCAVI *(Carla of the Rocks)* by Renée Reggiani *(Italy)*

1973
KRABAT (published in English with same title) by Otfried Preussler *(Germany: Federal Republic)*

1976
LE COEUR SOUS LA CENDRE *(The Heart Under the Ashes)* by Pierre Pelot *(France)*

1978
PIERRE EST VIVANT *(Pierre Is Alive)* by Jean Coué *(France)*

1980
DIE UNENDLICHE GESCHICHTE *(The Neverending Story)* by Michael Ende *(Germany: Federal Republic)*
EL LOCO *(The Fool)* by Alberto Manzi *(Italy)*

1982
VIVA BABYMOON *(Long Live Babymoon)* by G.L. Picciolli
(Italy)
1985
DIE PERLE *(The Pearl)* by Helme Heine *(Germany: Federal Republic)*
1987
HOE SCHILDER, HOE WILDER *(Great Painters, Great Slaughterer)* by Miep Diekmann and Marlleke van Wersch *(Holland)*
1989
LO STRALINCO *(The Crippled Boy)* by Roberto Piumini *(Italy)*

Maxim Gorky International Award for Literature for Children and Youth

The Mez. cena Maxima Gorkého za listeraturu pro děti a mládež awards program has its origins in the International Year of the Child (1979) as a project of some of the National Sections of the International Board on Books for Young People (IBBY) in the socialist countries. The award is named for the renowned Russian writer Aleksei Maksimovich Peshkov (1868-1936), who wrote as Maxim Gorky. Gorky's autobiographical trilogy (1915-1921), and particularly the first volume, *My Childhood*, celebrated the power of storytelling to children. In his later years, and in a position of enormous influence, Gorky insisted that literature and art be informed by social realism. In addition to three equal awards, the program also presents three equal diplomas. The award honors "prose from the contemporary life of children." Recipients are selected by a jury composed of members from each of the participating IBBY sections. It seems likely that 1989 was the last year of the Gorky Award. (Diploma and artifact characteristic of the sponsoring country, which changes regularly)

1980
BEZUMNAJA JEVDOKIJA *(Mad Jevdokija)* by Anatolij Aleksin *(USSR)*
KARAMBOL *(Collision)* by Anna Dániel *(Hungary)*
KILKA MIESIACY CALE ZYCIE? *(How Many Months is a Lifetime?)* by Ewa Nowacka *(Poland)*
1983
BLAGYJE NAMERENIJA *(Good Intentions)* by Albert Lichanov *(USSR)*

CO SLYCHAC ZA TYMI DRZWIAMI? *(What's Behind Those Doors?)* by Ewa Ostrowska *(Poland)*
TÜRHETO LAJOS *(Bearable Louis)* by Katalin Nagy *(Hungary)*
1985
OBJEVENÍ PLANETY MICHOVICE *(The Discovery of the Planet Michovice)* by Bohumil Nohejl *(Czechoslovakia)*
NEŽNI PRIKLŪCENIJA *(Pleasant Adventures)* by Boris Krumov *(Bulgaria)*
SON S PRODOLŽENIJEM *(Continuous Dreams)* by Sergei Mikhalkov *(USSR)*
1987
DAS HERZ DES PIRATEN *(The Heart of the Pirate)* by Benno Pludra *(Germany: Democratic Republic)*
NA TRONIE W BLABONIE *(On the Throne in Blabona)* by Woiciech Zukrowski *(Poland)*
RASSKAZI O LENINE *(Stories about Lenin)* by Sergei Alexseev *(USSR)*
1989
A BOOK ABOUT GRISHKA by Radi Pogodin *(USSR)*
I'VE FALLEN IN LOVE by Kirill Bozhilov *(Bulgaria)*
UMBERTO by Günter Saalman *(Germany: Democratic Republic)*

International Board on Books for Young People (IBBY) Honor List ❧

Every two years since 1956, on the occasion of the Congresses of the International Board on Books for Young People, an IBBY Honor List is announced. In its early days, books selected for the Honor List were identified by the same jury that selects the recipient of the Hans Christian Andersen Awards. At the present time, each National Section of IBBY selects two books (one for the *text* and one for *illustration*), published in a given period before the year in which they are selected, for an IBBY biennial Congress. Those titles are the Honor Books on the List. Important considerations in selecting the Honor List titles are that the books chosen be representative of the best in children's literature from each country, and that the books are recommended as suitable for publication throughout the world, thus furthering the IBBY objective of encouraging world understanding through children's literature. In 1978 a third category was added to the IBBY Honor List, which now includes a *translator*, with at least one notable book of that translator cited as an example of his or her work. The listing below includes only Honor List titles from IBBY National Sections whose main language is English.

New Zealand is not a member of IBBY. In 1986, Nigeria selected
an Honor List title for *Text*: WITHOUT A SILVER SPOON by
Eddie Iroh *(Spectrum)*. (Certificates)
See also Hans Christian Andersen Award.

UNITED STATES
1956
CARRY ON, MR. BOWDITCH by Jean Lee Latham
(Houghton)
MEN, MICROSCOPES AND LIVING THINGS by Katherine
Shippen *(Viking)*
PLAY WITH ME by Marie Hall Ets *(Viking)*
1958
THE HOUSE OF SIXTY FATHERS by Meindert DeJong
(Harper)
1960
ALONG CAME A DOG by Meindert DeJong *(Harper)*
THE WITCH OF BLACKBIRD POND by Elizabeth George
Speare *(Houghton)*
1962
ISLAND OF THE BLUE DOLPHINS by Scott O'Dell
(Houghton)
1964
THE BRONZE BOW by Elizabeth George Speare *(Houghton)*
1966
WHERE THE WILD THINGS ARE by Maurice Sendak
(Harper)
1968
VALLEY OF THE SMALLEST by Aileen Fisher *(Crowell)*
1970
UP A ROAD SLOWLY by Irene Hunt *(Follett)*
1972
THE TRUMPET OF THE SWAN by E. B. White *(Harper)*
1974
Text: THE HEADLESS CUPID by Zilpha Keatley Snyder
(Atheneum)
Illustration: THE FUNNY LITTLE WOMAN retold by Arlene
Mosel, ill. by Blair Lent *(Dutton)*
1976
Text: M. C. HIGGINS, THE GREAT by Virginia Hamilton
(Macmillan)
Illustration: DAWN by Uri Shulevitz *(Farrar)*
1978
Text: TUCK EVERLASTING by Natalie Babbitt *(Farrar)*
Illustration: HUSH LITTLE BABY ill. by Margot Zemach
(Dutton)

Translation: Sheila La Farge, translator of GLASSBLOWER'S CHILDREN by Maria Gripe *(Delacorte/Lawrence)*

1980
Text: RAMONA AND HER FATHER by Beverly Cleary *(Morrow)*
Illustration: NOAH'S ARK by Peter Spier *(Doubleday)*
Translation: Richard and Clara Winston, translators of THE MAGIC STONE by Leonie Kooiker *(Morrow)*

1982
Text: AUTUMN STREET by Lois Lowry *(Houghton)*
Illustration: THE GARDEN OF ABDUL GASAZI by Chris Van Allsburg *(Houghton)*
Translation: Elizabeth Shub for her translations of books by Isaac Bashevis Singer, especially ZLATEH THE GOAT AND OTHER STORIES *(Harper)*

1984
Text: SWEET WHISPERS, BROTHER RUSH by Virginia Hamilton *(Philomel)*
Illustration: DOCTOR DE SOTO by William Steig *(Farrar)*
Translation: George Blecher and Lone Thygesen-Blecher, translators of THE BATTLE HORSE by Harry Kullman *(Bradbury)*

1986
Text: ONE-EYED CAT by Paula Fox *(Bradbury)*
Illustration: THE PEOPLE COULD FLY: AMERICAN BLACK FOLKTALES by Virginia Hamilton, ill. by Leo and Diane Dillon *(Knopf)*
Translation: Edward Fenton for his translations from Greek of books by Alki Zei, such as PETROS' WAR *(Dutton)*

1988
Text: SARAH, PLAIN AND TALL by Patricia MacLachlan *(Harper)*
Illustration: THE PAPER CRANE by Molly Bang *(Greenwillow)*
Translation: Elizabeth D. Crawford, translator of DON'T SAY A WORD by Barbara Gehrts *(McElderry)*

1990
Text: LINCOLN: A PHOTOBIOGRAPHY by Russell Freedman *(Clarion)*
Illustration: OWL MOON by Jane Yolen, ill. by John Schoenherr *(Philomel)*
Translation: Elizabeth D. Crawford, translator of CRUTCHES by Peter Härtling *(Lothrop)*

1992
Text: SHABANU: DAUGHTER OF THE WIND by Suzanne Fisher Staples *(Knopf)*
Illustration: LITTLE TRICKER THE SQUIRREL MEETS BIG TROUBLE THE BEAR by Ken Kesey, ill. by Barry Moser *(Viking)*

Translation: Antonia W. Bouis, translator of WE WERE NOT LIKE OTHER PEOPLE by Ephraim Sevela *(HarperCollins)*

AUSTRALIA
1970
I OWN THE RACECOURSE by Patricia Wrightson *(Hutchinson)*
1972
BLUE FIN by Colin Thiele *(Rigby)*
1974
Text: JOSH by Ivan Southall *(Angus & Robertson)*
Illustration: JOSEPH AND LULU AND THE PRINDIVILLE HOUSE PIGEONS by Ted Greenwood *(Angus & Robertson)*
1976
Text: THE NARGUN AND THE STARS by Patricia Wrightson *(Hutchinson)*
Illustration: MULGA BILL'S BICYCLE by R. A. Pattersonn, ill. by Kilmany and Deborah Niland *(Collins)*
1978
Text: THE OCTOBER CHILD by Eleanor Spence *(Oxford)*
Illustration: THE RUNAWAY PUNT by Robert Ingpen *(Rigby)*
1980
Text: A DREAM OF SEAS by Lilith Norman *(Collins)*
Illustration: THE QUINKINS by Jercy Treazuse *(Collins)*
1982
Text: PLAYING BEATIE BOW by Ruth Park *(Nelson)*
Illustration: THE RAINFOREST CHILDREN by Margaret Pittaway, ill. by Heather Philpott *(Oxford)*
1984
Text: THE WATCHER IN THE GARDEN by Joan Phipson *(Methuen)*
Illustration: WHO SANK THE BOAT? by Pamela Allen *(Nelson)*
1986
Text: DANCING IN THE ANZAC DELI by Nadia Wheatley *(Oxford)*
Illustration: POSSUM MAGIC by Mem Fox, ill. by Julie Vivas *(Omnibus)*
1988
Text: RIVERMAN by Allan Baillie *(Nelson)*
Illustration: FIRST THERE WAS FRANCES by Bob Graham *(Lothian)*
Text: MY PLACE by Nadia Wheatley and Donna Rawlins *(Collins Dove)*
Illustration: WHERE THE FOREST MEETS THE SEA by Jeannie Baker *(Julia MacRae)*

CANADA
1958
LOST IN THE BARRENS by Farley Mowat *(Little, Brown)*

1960
NKWALA by Edith Lambert Sharp *(Little, Brown)*
1962
THE SUNKEN CITY by James McNeill *(Oxford)*
1964
THE INCREDIBLE JOURNEY by Sheila Burnford *(Little, Brown)*
1976
Text: ALLIGATOR PIE by Dennis Lee *(Macmillan)*
Illustration: LES TRAINAUX DE MON ENFANCE by Carlo
Italiano *(Tundra)*
1978
Text (English): THE MOUSE WOMAN AND THE VANISHED
PRINCESSES by Christie Norris *(McClelland & Stewart)*
GARBAGE DELIGHT by Dennis Lee (Macmillan)
Text (French): LES SAISONS DE LA MER by Monique
Corriveau *(Fides)*
Illustration: LA CACHETTE by Ginette Aufousse *(Le Tamanoir)*
1980
Text: HOLD FAST by Kevin Major *(Clarke-Irwin)*
Illustration: LA CHICANE by Ginette Anfousse *(La courte
échelle)*
Translation: Paule Daveluy, translator of LES CHEMINS
SECRETS DE LA LIBERTÉ *(Pierre Tisseyre)*
1982
Text: THE KEEPER OF THE ISIS LIGHT by Monica Hughes
(Hamish Hamilton)
Illustration: PETROUCHKA by Elizabeth Cleaver *(Macmillan)*
Translation: David Toby Homel and Margaret Rose, translator
of THE KING'S DAUGHTER by Suzanne Martel *(Douglas &
McIntyre)*
1984
Text (English): THE ROOT CELLAR by Janet Lunn *(Lester &
Orpen Dennys)*
Text (French): L'HOMME AUX OISEAUX by Robert Soulières
Québec-Amérique)
Illustration: A NORTHERN ALPHABET by Ted Harrison *(Tundra)*
Translation: Claude Aubry, translator of JE T'ATTENDS À
PEGGY'S COVE by Brian Doyle *(Pierre Tisseyre)*
1986
Text (English): SWEETGRASS by Jan Hudson *(Tree Frog Press)*
Text (French): L'ENFANT DE LUMIÈRE by Suzanne Martel
(Méridien)
Illustration: CHIN CHIANG AND THE DRAGON'S DANCE
by Ian Wallace *(Groundwood/Douglas & McIntyre)*
Translation: Paule Daveluy, translator of EMILIE DE LA
NOUVELLE LUNE by Lucy Maud Montgomery *(Pierre
Tisseyre)*

1988

Text (English): SHADOW IN HAWTHORN BAY by Janet Lunn
(Lester & Orpen Dennys)

Text (French): LE DERNIER DES RAISINS by Raymond Plante
(Québec-Amérique)

Illustration: THE EMPEROR'S PANDA by David Day, ill. by
Eric Beddows *(McClelland & Stewart)*

Translation: Marie-Andrée Clermont, translator of JASMINE by
Jan Truss *(Pierre Tisseyre)*

1990

Text (English): BAD BOY by Diana Wieler
(Groundwood/Douglas & McIntyre)

Text (French): LE DON by David Schinkel and Yves Beauchesne
(Pierre Tisseyre)

Illustration: COULD YOU STOP JOSEPHINE? by Stéphane
Poulin *(Tundra)*

Translation: Paule Daveluy, translator of EMILIE DE LA
NOUVELLE LUNE 2 by Lucy Maud Montgomery *(Pierre
Tisseyre)*

UNITED KINGDOM

1956

LAVENDER'S BLUE by Kathleen Lines *(Oxford)*

MINNOW ON THE SAY by Philippa Pearce *(Oxford)*

1958

THE FAIRY DOLL by Rumer Godden *(Macmillan)*

1960

TOM'S MIDNIGHT GARDEN by Philippa Pearce *(Oxford)*

WARRIOR SCARLET by Rosemary Sutcliff *(Oxford)*

1962

TANGARA by Nan Chauncy *(Oxford)*

THE BORROWERS AFLOAT by Mary Norton *(Dent)*

1964

THE TWELVE AND THE GENJI by Pauline Clarke *(Faber)*

1966

THE NAMESAKE by Walter Hodges *(Bell)*

1968

LOUIE'S LOT by E.W. Hildick *(Faber)*

1974

Text: WHAT THE NEIGHBOURS DID by Philippa Pearce
(Longmans)

Illustration: TICH by Pat Hutchins *(Bodley Head)*

1976

Text: THE GHOST OF THOMAS KEMPE by Penelope Lively
(Heinemann)

Illustration: HOW TOM BEAT CAPTAIN NAJORK AND HIS
HIRED SPORTSMEN by Russell Hoban, ill. by Quentin Blake
(Cape)

1978
Text: A YEAR AND A DAY by William Mayne *(Hamish Hamilton)*
Illustration: THORN ROSE by Errol Le Cain *(Faber)*
Translation: Anthea Bell, translator of THE CUCUMBER KING by Christine Nöstlinger *(Andersen)*

1980
Text: THE GODS IN WINTER by Patricia Miles *(Hamish Hamilton)*
Illustration: EACH PEACH PEAR PLUM by Janet and Allan Ahlberg *(Kestrel)*
Translation: Patricia Crampton, translator of THE SEA LORD by Alet Schouten *(Methuen)*

1982
Text: TULKU by Peter Dickinson *(Gollancz)*
Illustration: MISTER MAGNOLIA by Quentin Blake *(Cape)*
Translation: Anthea Bell, translator of THE BIG JANOSCH BOOK OF FUN by Janosch *(Andersen)*

1984
Text: ALL THE KING'S MEN by William Mayne *(Cape)*
Illustration: HANSEL AND GRETEL by the Brothers Grimm, ill. by Anthony Browne *(Julia MacRae)*
Translation: Elizabeth Watson Taylor, translator of THE MAGIC INKSTAND AND OTHER STORIES by Heinrich Seidel *(Cape)*

1986
Text (English): THE CHANGEOVER by Margaret Mahy *(Dent)*
Text (Welsh): Y MABINOGI by Gwyn Thomas *(University of Wales Press)*
Illustration: HIAWATHA'S CHILDHOOD by Henry Wadsworth Longfellow, ill. by Errol Le Cain *(Faber)*
Translation: Patricia Crampton, translator of THE FIFTH CORNER by Kristina Ehrenstråle *(Methuen)*

1988
Text: WOOF! by Allan Ahlberg *(Viking Kestrel)*
Illustration: THE JOLLY POSTMAN OR OTHER PEOPLE'S LETTERS by Janet and Allan Ahlberg *(Heinemann)*

1990
Text (English): SLAMBASH WANGS OF A COMPO GORMER by Robert Leeson *(Collins)*
Text (Welsh): BEN Y GARDDWR by Mary Vaughan Jones *(Cymdeithas Lyfrau Ceredigion)*
Illustration: EASTER by Jan Piénkowski *(Heinemann)*

International Reading Association Children's Book Awards 🕭

This prize program honors new talents in children's literature. Publishers worldwide are invited to submit candidates for the awards, which are designed to single out writers whose early work suggests unusual promise for a successful career in creating books for children. As of the 1987 awards, one prize is for people writing for older readers *(O)*, and a second is for creators of books for younger readers *(Y)*. Administered by the International Reading Association (800 Barksdale Rd., P.O. Box 8139, Newark, DE 19714-8139, USA). ($1,000 to each)

1975
TRANSPORT 7-41-R by T. Degens *(Viking, USA)*
1976
DRAGONWINGS by Laurence Yep *(Harper, USA)*
1977
A STRING IN THE HARP by Nancy Bond *(McElderry, USA)*
1978
A SUMMER TO DIE by Lois Lowry *(Houghton, USA)*
1979
RESERVED FOR MARK ANTHONY CROWDER by Alison Smith *(Dutton, USA)*
1980
WORDS BY HEART by Ouida Sebestyen *(Atlantic-Little, Brown, USA)*
1981
MY OWN PRIVATE SKY by Delores Beckman *(Dutton, USA)*
1982
GOODNIGHT MISTER TOM by Michelle Magorian *(Kestrel, Great Britain)*
1983
THE DARK-ANGEL by Meredith Ann Pierce *(Atlantic-Little, Brown, USA)*
1984
RATHA'S CREATURE by Clare Bell *(McElderry, USA)*
1985
BADGER ON THE BARGE by Janni Howker *(Julia MacRae, Great Britain)*
1986
PRAIRIE SONGS by Pam Conrad *(Harper, USA)*
1987
0: AFTER THE DANCING DAYS by Margaret I. Rostkowski *(Harper, USA)*

Y: THE LINE-UP BOOK by Marisabina Russo *(Greenwillow, USA)*

1988
0: THE RUBY IN THE SMOKE *and* SHADOW IN THE NORTH by Philip Pullman *(Oxford, Great Britain)*

Y: THE THIRD-STORY CAT by Leslie Baker *(Little, Brown, USA)*

1989
0: PROBABLY STILL NICK SWANSEN by Virginia Euwer Wolff *(Holt, USA)*

Y: RECHENKA'S EGGS by Patricia Polacco *(Philomel, USA)*

1990
0: CHILDREN OF THE RIVER by Linda Crew *(Delacorte, USA)*

Y: NO STAR NIGHTS by Anna Egan Smucker, ill. by Steve Johnson *(Knopf, USA)*

1991
0: UNDER THE HAWTHORN TREE by Marita Conlon-McKenna *(O'Brien Press, Ireland)*

Y: IS THIS A HOUSE FOR HERMIT CRAB? by Megan McDonald, ill. by S. D. Schindler *(Orchard, USA)*

1992
0: RESCUE JOSH McGUIRE by Ben Mikaelsen *(Hyperion, USA)*

Y: TEN LITTLE RABBITS by Virginia Grossman, ill. by Sylvia Long *(Chronicle, USA)*

Janusz Korczak Literary Competition 🦢
(ANTI-DEFAMATION LEAGUE OF B'NAI B'RITH)

This awards program is named for the Polish pediatrician, child welfare pioneer and founder and administrator for two Warsaw orphanages, one housing Jewish children and the other Catholic. In 1942 he refused to abandon his wards, an option available to him, and went with them to his death in gas chambers at Treblinka. This competition has been for books exemplifying the principles of selflessness and human dignity characteristic of Janusz Korczak. Prizes have been given in two categories: a book for young readers, fiction or nonfiction, and suitable for use at either the elementary or secondary school level; and a book about the welfare and nurturing of children, directed to parents and educators, as well as to the helping professions. Books published in any language, anywhere in the world, have been eligible. The program continued through 1988, and is currently in abeyance. The administrator has been the International Center for Holocaust Studies (Anti-Defamation League of B'nai B'rith, 823 United Nations Plaza, New York, NY 10017). This listing includes only the winning titles published *for* children. ($1,000 and plaque)

1981
BLACK AS I AM by Zindzi Mandela *(Guild of Tudors Press, South Africa)*

1982
UPON THE HEAD OF THE GOAT: A CHILDHOOD IN HUNGARY 1939-1944 by Aranka Siegal *(Farrar, USA)*

1984
SEAWARD by Susan Cooper *(McElderry, USA)*

1986
DAYS OF HONEY by Irene Awret *(Schocken, USA)*

1988
ELIEZER BEN-YEHUDA by Marla Drucker *(Lodestar, USA)*

Janusz Korczak Literary Prize ❧
(POLISH NATIONAL SECTION OF IBBY)

The Polish National Section of the International Board on Books for Young People (IBBY) (ul Hipoteczna 2, P. O. Box 133, 00-959 Warsaw, Poland) sponsors a literary competition honoring the memory of a renowned Polish physician and Holocaust victim. (See the previous entry for a brief biographical note about Janusz Korczak.) IBBY National Sections worldwide are invited to submit titles that "promote understanding and friendship among children all over the world." There are two winning titles; one is a book *for* children (the titles on our list), and the other a book *about* children. Three additional titles are awarded Janusz Korczak Medals, and three others are designated Honor List titles. (Medal and 200,000 zlotys)

1979
BRÖDERNA LEJONHJÄRTA (The Brothers Lionheart) by Astrid Lindgren *(Sweden)*
NOVÝ GULIWER *(New Gulliver)* by Bohumil Řiuha *(Czechoslovakia)*

1981
DIE UNENDLICHE GESCHICHTE (The Neverending Story) by Michael Ende *(Germany: Federal Republic)*
LAMPAS MALEHO PLAVCIKA (The Ship Boy's Lamp) by Jana Navratila *(Czechoslovakia)*

1983
DZIEŃ, NOC I PORA NICZYJA (Day, Night and Nobody's Time) by Ewa Nowacka *(Poland)*

1985
POGRESZNA STYPKA (The Wrong Step) by Latchesar Stantchev *(Bulgaria)*

1987
DOKAD WRACAJA LATAWCE (Whence Do the Dragons Return?) by Maria Borowa *(Poland)*

1990
HA-I BI-REHOV HA-TSIPORIM (The Island on Bird Street) by Uri Orlev *(Israel)*

Astrid Lindgren Translation Prize ⪼

Sponsored by the International Federation of Translators (Heiveldstraat 245, B-9040 Sint-Amandsberg/Gent, Belgium), this prize is named for the Swedish author and Hans Christian Andersen Medalist whose books have appeared worldwide. Its object is to promote the translation of works written for children and to draw attention to the role of the translator in bringing together people of the world and enriching their cultural and literary lives. The prize is given at three or four year intervals at conventions of the Fédération Internationale des Traducteurs for either a single translation of outstanding quality or for a translator's body of work. (Diploma and/or sum of money)

1981
Åke Holmberg *(Sweden)* for his children's book translations into Swedish

1984
Patricia Crampton *(Great Britain)* for her translations into English of children's books in German, Dutch and the Scandanavian languages

1987
Liselotte Remané *(Germany: Democratic Republic)* for her translations into German of children's books in English and Russian

1990
Anthea Bell *(Great Britain)* for her translations into English of
children's books in German, French, and Danish
Lyudmila Braude *(USSR)* for her translations into Russian of
classic Scandanavian children's literature and of German fairy
tales and legends

Noma Concours for Children's Picture Book Illustrations

Named after its founder, the distinguished Japanese publisher and
recipient of the 1974 International Book Award, Shoichi Noma,
this awards program is sponsored by the Asian Cultural Centre
for UNESCO (No. 6, Fukuromachi, Shinjuku-ku, Tokyo, 162,
Japan). Organized biennially, the program gives prizes for
excellent and original illustrations for picture books by artists in
Asia, the Pacific, Africa, the Arab States, Latin America and the
Caribbean. Entries include both published and unpublished
works. Its purpose is to continue the improvement of the quality
of children's book illustrations in developing countries. The
listing below includes only the recipients of the Grand Prix.
(Grand Prix: $2,000 and a special medal; two second prizes:
$500 and a medal; ten runners up: $100 and a medal; twenty
encouragement prizes: a medal)

1978
THE HERO CHAMPIONS by Ali-Akbar Sadeghi *(Iran)*
IF THE ANIMALS HAD COLORED FACES by Nikzad
Nojoumi *(Iran)*
1980
ANCIENT CHINESE FABLES by Zhang Shi-ming *(China)*
1982
A PLANE AND A VIOLA by Gian Calvi *(Brazil)*
1984
MR. FOX by Gavin Bishop *(New Zealand)*
1986
THE DINOSAUR OF THE DESERT by Kang Woo-hyung
(Republic of Korea)
1988
NAZHA CREATED TREMENDOUS UPROAR IN THE SEA
by Yu Dawu *(China)*
1990
ANIMALS HAVE MANY FACES by Enrique Martinez Blanco
(Cuba)

Nordic Children's Book Prize 🦉

This award is for outstanding achievement in children's literature in Denmark, Finland, Iceland, Norway, and Sweden. It is an activity of the Nordic School Librarians' Association (Nordisk Skolebibliotekarforening, Rønnevej 7, DK 6880 Tarm, Denmark). (Glass vase and certificate)

1985
Maria Gripe *(Sweden)* for AGNES CECILIA, HVEM ER DU? (Agnes Cecilia, Who Are You?) and other books
1986
Tormod Haugen *(Norway)* for DAGEN, DER FORSVANDT (The Lost Day) and VINTERSTEDET (The Winter Residence)
1987
Kaarina Helakisa *(Finland)* for LILLE JONAS (Little Jonas)
1988
Mette Newth *(Norway)* for BORTFØRENSEN (Forced Away)
1989
Svend Otto S. *(Denmark)* for STORMFLODEN (The Flood)
1990
Mats Wahl *(Sweden)* for MAJ DARLIN (May Darlin)
1991
Olavur Michelsen (author, *Faroe Islands*) and Erik Nielsen (ill., *Denmark)* for ROSSINI À SKORADALI (The Horse from Skoradali)

Owl Prize 🦉

For many years original children's book illustrations from around the world were assembled as an annual traveling exhibit that visited five Japanese cities: Tokyo, Nagoya, Kyoto, Sapporo, and Kukuoka. Titled the Exhibition of Original Pictures of International Picture Books, the activity was sponsored by Shiko-sha Co., Ltd., and Maruzen Co., Ltd. As of the 1976 exhibit and tour, and under the supervision of the international children's book specialist Hisako Aoki, people visiting the exhibit were invited to vote for their favorite illustrations. The most popular illustration was awarded the Owl Prize; a listing of other popular illustrations was distributed to cooperating publishers. The activity was discontinued after the 25th exhibit. (Stipend was given to illustrator; illustrator and publisher received diplomas)

1976
KROKODIL, KROKODIL (Crocodile, Crocodile) by Binette Schroeder *(Nord-Süd, Switzerland)*

1977
THE MAGGIE B by Irene Haas *(McElderry, USA)*
1978
DAS SCHÖNSTE GESCHENK (The Most Beautiful Gift) by
Rita Van Bilsen *(Boehm, Switzerland)*
1979
WIE TIERKINDER SCHLAFEN (How Baby Animals Sleep) by
Erika Dietzsch Capelle *(Thienemanns, Germany: Federal
Republic)*
1980
CARRIE HEPPLE'S GARDEN by Irene Haas *(McElderry, USA)*
1981
BRAMBLY HEDGE SPRING STORY by Jill Barklem *(Collins,
Great Britain)*
1982
VIKTOR, DAS FLIEGENDE NILPFERD (Victor, The Flying
Hippopotamus) by Marie-José Sacré *(Boyem, Switzerland)*
1983
FREUNDE (Friends) by Helme Heine *(Middlehauve, Germany:
Federal Republic)*
1984
DIE GESCHICHTE VOM GUTEN WOLF (The Story of the
Good Wolf) by Joséf Wilkon *(Nord-Süd, Switzerland)*
1985
SPATZEN BRAUCHEN KEINEN (A Walk in the Rain) by
Ulises Wensell *(Otto Maier, Germany: Federal Republic)*
1986
DIE KLEINE GÄRTNER (George's Garden) by Bernadette Watts
(Nord-Süd, Switzerland)
1987
DER RABE IM SCHNEE (The Raven in the Snow) by Erwin
Moser *(Belz & Gelberg, Germany: Federal Republic)*
1988
KLEINER EISBAR, WOHIN FAHRST DU? (Little Polar Bear)
by Hans de Beer *(Nord-Süd, Switzerland)*
1989
SIMON AND THE SNOWFLAKES by Gilles Tibo *(Tundra,
Canada)*
1990
GEORGE AND MATILDA MOUSE...AND THE FLOATING
SCHOOL by Heather S. Buchanan *(Methuen, Great Britain)*

UNICEF-*Ezra Jack Keats International Award for Excellence in Children's Book Illustration*

This biennial awards program is designed to encourage illustrators new to children's books (no more than five published books). It is funded by the Ezra Jack Keats Foundation, and named in honor of Mr. Keats (1916-1983), the well-known U. S. illustrator and Caldecott Medal recipient who was also a contributing artist to the UNICEF greeting card program. UNICEF National Committees worldwide select one National Candidate for the award; a jury of international children's book specialists chooses the winner and selects bronze medalists (finalists), as well. Administered by UNICEF (United Nations Children's Fund) Greeting Card Operation (Information: UNICEF House, 3 United Nations Plaza, New York, NY 10017, USA). ($5,000 and silver medal)

1986
Felipe Dávalos for LAS TORTUGAS DE MAR (Turtles of the Sea) *(Consejo Nacional de Fomento Educativo) and* UN ASALTO MAYUSCULO (A Capital Assault) *(Tomas Meyer Brom), Mexico*

1988
Barbara Reid for HAVE YOU SEEN BIRDS? by Joanne Oppenheim *(Scholastic-TAB), Canada*

1990
Jan Thornhill for THE WILDLIFE 1-2-3 *(Greey de Pencier), Canada*

PART V 🙰

Awards Classified

Alphabetical listing of all awards in this volume

Awards that are for, or specifically include, young adult literature

UNITED STATES AWARDS SELECTED BY ADULTS

UNITED STATES AWARDS SELECTED BY YOUNG READERS

Awards that are for, or specifically include, nonfiction

NEW ZEALAND

UNITED KINGDOM (UK)

Awards exclusively for a body of work

UNITED STATES AWARDS SELECTED BY ADULTS

CANADA

UNITED KINGDOM (UK)

INTERNATIONAL AND MULTINATIONAL AWARDS

Awards in which site, e. g., birthplace or residence of author, location of story, etc. is a factor

UNITED STATES AWARDS SELECTED BY ADULTS

CANADA

Awards or competitions for manuscripts or other works that may subsequently be published

UNITED STATES AWARDS SELECTED BY ADULTS

UNITED KINGDOM (UK)

INTERNATIONAL AND MULTINATIONAL AWARDS

PART VI &.

Publications and Lists for Selecting U. S. Children's and Young Adult Books

NOTE: This section is a partial listing of the many publications and (usually) annual lists that evaluate books for young readers, recommending titles considered especially meritorious. Extensive examination of the books in these selection aids would be far more rewarding to a children's literature specialist than an examination of award-winning titles that—by definition—do not represent the variety and scope of books available for young readers. All of the publications and lists appear on the American Library Association-Children's Book Council Joint Committee listing, "Suggested Symbols for Selected Lists and Review Sources for Books for Children and Young Adults in Publishers' Catalogs (1991 revision)."

AMERICAN LIBRARY ASSOCIATION
(50 East Huron St., Chicago, IL 60611)

Booklist. Published twice a month, this periodical reviews children's and young adult books, and prints special-interest lists regularly. It stars especially noteworthy titles. Also runs "Editors' Choices" of the most outstanding books of the year annually.

The Association for Library Service to Children (ALSC) sponsors "Notable Children's Books," an annual list of children's books compiled by a national committee of librarians; available in pamphlet format.

The Young Adult Library Services Association (YALSA) publishes two important lists annually, "Best Books for Young Adults" and "Recommended Books for the Reluctant Young Reader," both available in pamphlet format.

Book Links. Published quarterly, this journal is designed to help teachers make effective use of literature across the curriculum; includes articles and special-interest booklists.

SCHOOL LIBRARY JOURNAL
(249 West 17th St., New York, NY 10011)

Published monthly, this journal reviews nearly all new children's and young adult books, stars those of special merit, and also includes a "Best Books" feature (available in reprint format in bulk) each year in its December issue; the magazine also includes articles and news about the library world, not just school libraries as its name might suggest.

THE HORN BOOK MAGAZINE
(14 Beacon St., Boston, MA 02108)

This venerable publication is published six times a year; includes reviews of (mainly) recommended children's and young adult titles, and stars some of them; also publishes "Fanfare," a highly selective annual list of highly recommended books that appears in an issue of the magazine.

The Horn Book Guide is a semi-annual work that evaluates as many current books as possible, both those the reviewers like and do not like.

BULLETIN OF THE CENTER FOR CHILDREN'S BOOKS
(1512 North Fremont, Chicago, IL 60622)

This monthly (except for summer) book review publication was affiliated with the University of Chicago for many years, and is now published by the Graduate School of Library and Information Science, University of Illinois at Urbana-Champaign. It uses a symbols rating scheme — "R" for recommended through "NR" for not recommended — in addition to providing critical reviews; some of the "R" books are asterisked to indicate that titles are highly recommended; curriculum and developmental uses are indicated at the end of each review. The journal also includes interesting editorials from time to time — when there is something one of its editors feels is worth writing about.

KIRKUS REVIEWS
(200 Park Ave. So., New York, NY 10003)

This pre-publication review service uses "pointers" to single out children's and young adult titles of special merit.

NEW YORK TIMES BOOK REVIEW
(229 West 43rd St., New York, NY 10036)

The "national newspaper of record" reviews children's books weekly, and also publishes special Spring and Fall children's book issues. In addition, it makes selective semi-annual choices of outstanding children's books.

NEW YORK PUBLIC LIBRARY
(455 Fifth Ave., New York, NY 10016)

Children's Books: 100 Titles for Reading and Sharing and *Books for the Teen Age* appear in booklet formats annually. They are listed here as they are well-established and prestigious; many fine library systems throughout the U. S. publish similar listings.

CHILDREN'S LITERATURE CENTER, LIBRARY OF CONGRESS
(Library of Congress, Washington, DC 20540)

"Children's Books of the Year" is an annual booklet listing recommended titles evaluated by a committee of Washington,

D.C.-area children's literature specialists under the chairmanship of the Library's Children's Literature Specialist.

PUBLISHERS WEEKLY
(249 West 17th St., New York, NY 10011)

This magazine reviews forthcoming titles weekly. It also carries a "Children's Book Scene" feature weekly, and publishes an interesting "Children's Booksellers" list each month, based on reports from stores and other vendors.

AMERICAN BOOKSELLERS ASSOCIATION
(560 White Plains Rd., Tarrytown, NY 10591)

The monthly magazine *American Bookseller* includes semi-annual "Pick of the Lists" of forthcoming children's books, titles booksellers predict will have a vigorous sales life in bookstores.

VOICE OF YOUTH ADVOCATES (VOYA)
(Scarecrow Press, Dept. VOYA,
52 Liberty St., P. O. Box 4167, Metuchen, NJ 08840)

This publication reviews books intended for a young adult readership; it uses a dual rating code in evaluating titles, one relating to the quality of the writing and presentation, and the second relating to the likely appeal of a book to adolescents. VOYA also reviews other media and publishes articles, as well as lively editorials.

WILSON LIBRARY BULLETIN
(950 University Ave., Bronx, NY 10452)

A monthly publication that includes reviews of children's, middle-grade, and young adult books on a selective basis; the children's book reviews are frequently idiosyncratic, in a positive way, with thought-provoking ideas about ethnicity and cultural biases.

INTERNATIONAL READING ASSOCIATION (IRA)
(800 Barksdale Rd., P. O. Box 8139, Newark, DE 19714)

The journals *Reading Teacher* (elementary-middle school) and *Journal of Reading* (middle-high school, and advanced) review books in each school-year issue.

"Children's Choices," a project of the IRA-CBC Joint Committee, is an annual listing of about 100 titles that 10,000 young readers on five teams across the country have voted their "best reads." It is published in October issues of *Reading Teacher*; reprints (s-3 oz.-s/a/e-6 x 9 min.) are available free from IRA, which sells the list in bulk as well.

"Young Adult Choices" and "Teachers Choices" first appear in IRA journals and are offered on the same terms as "Children's Choices."

NATIONAL COUNCIL OF TEACHERS OF ENGLISH (NCTE)
(1111 Kenyon Rd., Urbana, IL 61801)

The journals *Language Arts* (elementary-middle school) and *English Journal* (secondary) review books in each school-year issue.

NCTE'S publications program includes booklists for children's through young adult books, including "Adventuring with Books," "Your Reading," and "High Interest-Easy Reading for Junior and Senior High School Students."

THE BOOK REPORT
(Linworth Publishing, Inc., 480 East Wilson Bridge Rd., Suite L, Worthington, OH 43085-2372)

Regularly reviews children's and young adult books; emphasis is on curriculum uses, though not exclusively.

CHILD STUDY ASSOCIATION
(Bank Street College of Education, 610 West 112th St., New York, NY 10025)

"Books of the Year" is a booklet listing a generous sampling of outstanding titles that reinforce the Child Study Children's Book Committee's conviction that good books deal honestly and courageously with the great and small problems of the world.

THE FIVE OWLS
(2004 Sheridan Ave. So., Minneapolis, MN 55405)

An attractive newsletter-format publication with accessible articles, occasional booklists-in-depth, and reviews that are longer than most.

PARENTS' CHOICE
(P. O. Box 185, Waban, MA 02168)

This newspaper-format publication deals with all media that interest parents who wish to expose children to high-quality materials—film, video, games, toys and books. The publication gives "Parents' Choice Awards" to books and other products. CBC has considered including the awards in Part I of this volume, but so many excellent titles are now honored, the awards seem to us more a booklisting activity than an awards program.

Special-Interest Lists, Publications, Etc.

AMERICAN INSTITUTE OF GRAPHIC ARTS (AIGA)
(1059 Third Ave., New York, NY 10021)

Sponsors The Book Show annually, a big selection of titles—including many children's books—chosen for excellence in design and manufacturing. Criteria for inclusion have varied from year to year. The annual *AIGA Graphic Design USA* (Watson-Guptil) includes The Book Show.

THE KOBRIN LETTER
(732 No. Greer Rd., Palo Alto, CA 94303)

Nonfiction for young readers.

APPRAISAL
(605 Commonwealth Ave., Boston, MA 02215)

Science books evaluated by subject specialists and librarians.

"OUTSTANDING SCIENCE TRADE BOOKS FOR CHILDREN"
[Reprint available free from CBC, 568 Broadway, Suite 404, New York, NY 10012 for a s-3 oz.-s/a/e (6 x 9 min.)]

An annual listing sponsored by The National Science Teachers Association (NSTA)-CBC Joint Committee that first appears in NSTA's journal *Scie.... and Children.*

"NOTABLE CHILDREN'S TRADE BOOKS IN THE FIELD OF SOCIAL STUDIES"
[Reprint available free from CBC, 568 Broadway, Suite 404, New York, NY 10012 for a s-3 oz.-s/a/e (6 x 9 min.)]

An annual listing sponsored by The National Council for the Social Studies (NCSS)- CBC Joint Committee that first appears in NCSS's journal *Social Studies*.

KLIATT YOUNG ADULT PAPERBACK BOOK GUIDE
(425 Watertown St., Newton, MA 02158)

Major issues in winter, spring and fall, and five newsletter issues.

Academic Journals Reviewing Children's Books

CHILDREN'S LITERATURE
(University of Connecticut, Dept. of English, U-25, 337 Mansfield Rd., Room 442, Storrs, CT 06269-1025)

THE LION AND THE UNICORN
(The Johns Hopkins University Press, Journals Division, 701 West 40th St., Suite 275, Baltimore, MD 21211)

THE NEW ADVOCATE
(Christopher-Gordon Publishers, Inc., 480 Washington St., Norwood, MA 02062)

Title Index 🙢

Person Index 🌰

Please note that our Person Index does not include authors who were not a party to the creation of the particular edition of a book that has been cited for honors in this volume. Thus, while their names appear in the awards listings themselves, Andersen, the Brothers Grimm, Charles Perrault, and others are not included in this index.